STILL SMALL VOICE

New Edition

New Library of Pastoral Care

BEING THERE
Care in Time of Illness
Peter Speck

CRISIS COUNSELLING
Caring for People in Emotional
Shock
Howard Stone

GOING SOMEWHERE
People with Mental Handicaps and
their Pastoral Care
Sheila Hollins and Margaret Grimer

HOLDING IN TRUST
The Appraisal of Ministry
Michael Jacobs

INTEGRITY OF
PASTORAL CARE
David Lyall

LETTING GO
Caring for the Dying and Bereaved
Peter Speck and Ian Ainsworth-Smith

LOVE THE STRANGER
Ministry in Multi-Faith Areas
Roger Hooker and Christopher Lamb

MADE IN HEAVEN?
Ministry with Those Intending
Marriage
Peter Chambers

MAKE OR BREAK
An Introduction to Marriage
Counselling
Jack Dominian

SIN, GUILT AND FORGIVENESS
The Hidden Dimensions of
a Pastoral Process
Mary Anne Coate

SOCIOLOGY FOR PASTORAL
CARE
George Furniss

STILL SMALL VOICE
An Introduction to Counselling
Michael Jacobs

SWIFT TO HEAR
Facilitating Skills in Listening
and Responding
Michael Jacobs

A DICTIONARY OF
PASTORAL STUDIES
edited by Wesley Carr

STILL SMALL VOICE

*A Practical Introduction to Counselling
in Pastoral and Other Settings*

New Edition

Michael Jacobs

Published in Great Britain in 1982
First edition reprinted eight times
New edition 1993
Revised 1997 and 2001
Society for Promoting Christian Knowledge
Holy Trinity Church
Marylebone Road
London NW1 4DU

British Library Cataloguing-in-Publication Data

A catalogue record for this book is available
from the British Library

ISBN 0-281-04697-2

5 7 9 10 8 6

Typeset by Pioneer Associates, Perthshire
Printed in Great Britain by
The Cromwell Press, Trowbridge, Wiltshire

Contents

Foreword   vii

Preface to the New Edition   ix

Preface to the First Edition   xi

Part One: Counselling in Context   1

  1 A Different Perspective   3

  2 Some Definitions and Distinctions 14

Part Two: Counselling in Practice   41

  3 First Principles   43

  4 Starting with Yourself   56

  5 Some Early Difficulties   81

  6 Boundaries of Time and Space   106

  7 Levels of Intervention   130

  8 Meeting Resistance   151

  9 The Counselling Relationship   178

 10 Beliefs and Values   205

 11 Endings   230

Bibliography   250

Index   256

Foreword

The *New Library of Pastoral Care* has been planned to meet the needs of those people concerned with pastoral care, whether clergy or lay, who seek to improve their knowledge and skills in this field. Equally, it is hoped that it may prove useful to those secular helpers who may wish to understand the role of the pastor.

Pastoral care in every age has drawn from contemporary secular knowledge to inform its understanding of men and women and their various needs and of the ways in which these needs might be met. Today it is perhaps the secular helping professions of social work, counselling and psychotherapy, and community development which have particular contributions to make to pastors in their work. Such knowledge does not stand still, and pastors would have a struggle to keep up with the endless tide of new developments which pour out from these and other disciplines, and to sort out which ideas and practices might be relevant to their particular pastoral needs. Among present-day ideas, for instance, of particular value might be an understanding of the social context of the pastoral task, the dynamics of the helping relationship, the attitudes and skills as well as factual knowledge which might make for effective pastoral intervention and, perhaps most significant of all, the study of particular cases, whether through verbatim reports of interviews or general case presentation. The discovery of ways of learning from what one is doing is becoming increasingly important.

There is always a danger that a pastor who drinks deeply at the well of a secular discipline may risk losing a distinct pastoral identity and become 'just another' social worker or counsellor. It in no way detracts from the value of these professions to assert that the role and task of the pastor are quite unique among the helping professions and deserve to be clarified and strengthened rather than weakened. The theological commitment of the pastors and the appropriate use of their role are recurrent themes of the series. At the same time pastors cannot afford to work in a vacuum. They need to be able to communicate and co-operate with those helpers in other disciplines whose work may overlap, without loss of their own unique status. This in turn will mean being able to communicate with them through some understanding of their concepts and language.

Finally, there is a rich variety of styles and approaches in pastoral work within the various religious traditions. No attempt is made to secure a uniform approach. The Library will contain the variety, and even perhaps occasional eccentricity, which such a title suggests. Some books will be more specifically theological and others more concerned with particular areas of need or practice. It is hoped that all of them will have a usefulness that will reach right across the boundaries of religious denomination.

Preface to the New Edition

I had not realized, until I began to re-read the First Edition of this book, how much had changed in the field of counselling since I put down my pen in 1981. First of all, the original Preface reminded me of a number of significant changes in my personal circumstances. My colleagues are now different ones. My former typist, a dear elderly lady who loved typing, has died; and in any case I now type straight on to a word processor. My job has shifted in its emphasis (twice). I have moved house (three times). And, like a number of others, I am now in a different marriage. It is probably this sheer number of changes that many people make (or have to make) that partly accounts for the huge demand for personal counselling.

It is scarcely surprising then that counselling itself (which, after all, was still quite young when I first wrote) has changed too. In re-reading the first chapter of the First Edition, I hardly recognized my picture of counselling in Britain and the churches. As I read on, I realized that in some respects my thinking and my style has changed and developed. This was my first book, and I have since written others that have superseded some of the sketchy material I included in the First Edition. For example, my second volume in this series, *Swift to Hear*, is about basic counselling skills. It should in a sense have been the first book, but I learned more about the need for teaching basic skills after the publication of *Still Small Voice*. I was able to build upon the Appendix A that appeared in the First Edition. The publication of my *Insight and Experience*, together with *Swift to Hear*, makes the section on practical exercises redundant, and it is therefore omitted from this edition. Similarly, there is now much more published in Britain, and by British authors, on the different schools of psychotherapy and counselling. I have therefore incorporated some of the former Appendix B into the main text, and referred the interested reader to the most accessible and readable literature. I have omitted the original Appendix C (Further Reading) and instead have included all the books I wish to recommend in the main text and notes. These are listed in the Bibliography.

There is one other major revision. I have in this edition identified nearly all the examples as being from my own practice. We are now sufficiently distant from the 1970s for it to be unlikely that anyone would recognize the clients, or even for the clients to recognize themselves. I have also added a few examples to illustrate new points. That they nearly all came from working within one context does not, I believe, detract from their value to pastoral counsellors or those who work in other settings.

What I have remained aware of throughout is that part of the success of *Still Small Voice* in its First Edition (and it sold nearly 20,000 copies) might have been that it was my first book. It reflected a particular stage of my own professional development as counsellor and therapist. As such, I think the book communicated more easily to readers who were similarly at an early stage of their own development as counsellors. In revising the text for this edition (and it is a radical change of style, as well as a substantial revision of content), I have tried to stay at the same level – although taking account of the increased sophistication of those learning counselling in the 1990s. I have therefore added to the detail of some of the concepts. Although some concepts covered are difficult ones, I have endeavoured not to overload the reader (whom I still assume to be a beginner in this field) with too many complications. At the same time, I have given indications of some of the complexities. I trust this remains a good book with which to make a start.

Michael Jacobs
Leicester 1992

Preface to the First Edition

When SPCK approached me to write a book on pastoral counselling, it was a happy coincidence that mention was made of building upon R. S. Lee's *Principles of Pastoral Counselling* for an introductory volume for the New Library of Pastoral Care. It was Roy Lee whom I was advised to meet in 1967 when I was considering a psychological study of an English mystic. He promptly advised me to read Freud, and not Jung, who up to that point had fascinated me. Although we met only once, he started me on a personal and professional pilgrimage through Freud and post-Freud, which led from reading to practice under supervision, more formal training and personal therapy, and to a full-time post in counselling and psychotherapy. In recent years this work has expanded into the training of professional and voluntary 'care-givers' in counselling methods and theory. The work on the mystic got no further, and I have moved a long way since then. But I am glad to be able to continue that lead given to me (and others) by Roy Lee.

Since this book is itself an introduction, it needs little introducing. I should say that many of my references to both counsellors and clients appear to confine them to the masculine gender. It scarcely needs saying that this is a convenient literary device, and that as far as I am concerned I do not confine the ministry (priestly or otherwise) to men. I should also point out that I have disguised the details of every example I have used, because I would have no wish that those who have helped me to learn should identify themselves. There is one exception, which though disguised could have led to recognition, and I am grateful to that person for her permission to use her counselling as an example of what can be achieved.

There are so many people who have taught, guided, influenced and sustained me that to list them would bore the reader, and would probably lead to someone being missed. Those who know me can rest assured of my thanks. Fellow-members of the Association for Pastoral Care and Counselling, the British Association for Counselling, and the Student Health Service in Leicester have been foremost in my personal and professional development over the last ten years. Three people in particular I do wish to single out for my thanks and to crave their indulgence: Jimmy Crighton, who trusted me as an inexperienced counsellor with a post in his team, and who will now sometimes wonder whether he has gained a counsellor who spends too much time teaching and writing; Isobel Hunter-Brown, who has taught me so much in supervision, and who will I hope forgive the errors in analytic technique which have crept into this book; and Doreen Schofield, who has a way of helping me cut through jargon and verbiage, but who will have to forgive my constant use of terms like 'exploration'. They have been valued colleagues.

I am also grateful to Mrs Florence Townsend for typing this and other manuscripts for me. Above all, it is difficult to thank enough my wife Valerie, and our three children Mary, Andrew and Susanna, both for their tolerance of a frequently absent husband and father on counselling business, and latterly at the typewriter, and for the secure and loving environment they create at home. Without their support I doubt whether I would have survived intact the early, painful years of learning, and I would be the poorer now both as a person and as a counsellor.

Michael Jacobs
Leicester 1981

PART ONE

Counselling in Context

CHAPTER ONE

A Different Perspective

The counselling perspective has come so much to the fore that it is less likely today that a young man such as Alan would have approached me, as he did in the early 1970s, with the request for information about receiving communion. I was a university chaplain at the time, and his reason for posing such a question was perhaps because it was a 'door' through which he could come, in order to meet and talk. Even at the time, though, Alan's request revealed that he had a certain rigidity to his thinking, and that he was one of those students (rare in what was then a new university) for whom what was proper was right.

I arranged to meet Alan at a different time: I was already aware that behind some questions lie other, more difficult, requests. I knew that providing space – both privacy and time – would be important. When we met, Alan rather hesitantly asked if he was permitted to take communion, because he did not believe in the resurrection of the body.

My own views (working at the time in a fairly radical environment) included considerable doubts about literal inter-pretations of Scripture, and (working in an ecumenical setting) an impatience with legalistic rules about who can and cannot receive communion. Others in a similar position in a different setting might have adopted a more orthodox viewpoint. But my response to Alan was still what I hope might have been my response had I thought differently. I asked him what *he* thought about the resurrection. His views were more important than mine for the purposes of our meeting.

'I can't believe his actual physical body rose from the dead. When the Gospels were written people thought differently – not as we do today. I don't know what to believe, but I guess it stands for something. But the Bible says it's true, and I mustn't contradict the Gospels.'

I commented that what Alan thought was not very different from the thinking of some of the theologians writing at the time. But I added, 'Do you think you have to take the Bible literally?'

'I don't like to question things like the Bible – it's got God's authority behind it.'

'And you don't like to question authority?'

'I guess I don't. My father always knows what he wants for me, and I find it difficult to disagree with him . . .'

And so our conversation went on, taking a different direction from the original question. Or was it? Because the issue of authority, which was Alan's difficulty (and also one of my own concerns), led us in the end to Alan making his own decision: that he would take communion, even though he was not confirmed. But, to my view even more importantly, we arranged to meet regularly, because Alan began talking about his anxiety in this year of his final examinations; and also about a severe psychotic breakdown he had had when at school. He was terrified he would 'crack up' again. He was also anxious that counselling might reactivate his paranoid feelings. So I met him twice a week, for half an hour each time, partly supporting him, partly looking at past difficulties, and partly helping him through the year.

Had we met today, in similar roles, I suspect it might have been different. I doubt whether Alan would have been so bothered by an essentially ecclesiastical question. I imagine that he might have asked to see me to talk about things that were worrying him. He could well have told me straightaway that he was feeling anxious about his finals, and asked if he could see me for counselling. Many people – not just students in universities who now have their own counselling services – are aware of the value of talking about their worries, and also that there are often reasons for feeling the way they do. They may not immediately open up about aspects of their experience that make them feel ashamed, guilty or embarrassed, but they find some way of hinting at deeper issues than the ones that are overt.

This is a remarkable change, one which took place with great rapidity over the course of less than thirty years. In the

1970s those who held positions of authority (teachers, clergy, doctors, social workers, etc.) might, had they begun to discover the value of counselling or counselling skills, offer more than was obviously being asked of them. Now those who approach teachers, clergy, voluntary agencies and others who are in the 'business' of caring might well expect to be heard at a deeper and more intimate level. It is little wonder, then, that training in counselling has become so popular. Many of those who seek training do so because of their own interest in the various perspectives of understanding, in alternative ways of relating, and in the many ways of offering help. But they also seek training because such responses are demanded of them by a public that has, for the time being at least, faith in the counselling process.

Many professional or voluntary helpers know that simply answering questions, or solely offering advice, is seldom enough. They have sufficient sensitivity to recognize that people frequently want more than information, and that there is much to be learned about alternative ways of responding. If anything, there is the danger in going too far in the other direction: of not recognizing a genuine question when it is asked. In Alan's case it certainly was appropriate to be able to discuss religious ideas, and the relative weight to be attached to history and myth. In other situations too information remains important, in order for people to make decisions about what they think and do. But such information (whether about ideas or about practicalities) can seldom be given in the way it once was, with an authoritative command that applies in every case. The answers to questions that people ask often need to be tailored to suit the particular request; and, in any case, they are generally more satisfactorily addressed through dialogue than through standard replies. The age of information technology can provide us with more data than we shall ever need. What we miss, and which counsellors are often able to provide, is the opportunity to process information, to set it in context, and to reflect upon its relevance to our lives.

This book provides information about counselling, although I do not suggest that counselling is the answer to all difficulties. For a long time, the case had to be argued that counselling could help, but there is a danger in any 'newly discovered' approach (I question this phrase below) that it will be seen as the universal and ultimate means of salvation. In its secular form as well as its pastoral expression, there is a danger that counselling can be seen as just such a salvific movement. There are other approaches to helping that remain valid: teaching, educating (not necessarily the same approach as teaching), advising, managing, and sometimes (in cases of extreme danger) even taking control of a person's welfare and safety. These approaches remain part of the resources of any helper, including counsellors. But in this book I concentrate upon the particular perspective that informs the counselling approach.

I am aware that this book has become a standard text for students of both pastoral and secular counselling, used on training courses in churches and elsewhere. I have therefore had in mind throughout the different perspectives of the book's readers: those who work from a spiritual or religious perspective; those who would not wish their own convictions to impinge upon their work with clients; as well as those who may doubt the value of a spiritual approach, but who will inevitably work with some clients for whom a religious upbringing or a present commitment is relevant.

Since readers themselves approach counselling from these different positions, it is important to acknowledge that the alternative methods of offering help vary from setting to setting: those in the social work field can sometimes offer a degree of material help; those in the medical field have physical treatments that complement counselling; those who work in the churches may offer spiritual direction or, in some traditions, the sacrament of reconciliation (what used to be known as penance or confession) – these approaches make more use of counselling skills, and sometimes there may be a didactic element in such help. Since those who work in a caring capacity, whether salaried, self-employed or in a voluntary setting, are likely to meet many different presenting difficulties, it is valuable to have a repertoire of other helping skills available, as well as to be able to understand what those in other professions and settings might be able to offer.

None the less, counselling itself has very particular skills and techniques, which form the substance of the following chapters. Counselling is characterized not by active intervention, as in the approaches outlined above, but by the 'still small voice' of my title. Stated briefly (since later chapters will spell out the approach in more detail), it is a way of helping others that stresses the gentle stillness of the helper in listening, absorbing, containing, understanding and reflecting back. It is also based upon the premise that counselling tries to help the person who is seeking help to find their own 'still small voice' within. The psychologically minded might call this 'the unconscious', the spiritually minded might refer to it as 'the spirit': whatever term we use, the phrase encapsulates the subtle dialogue that takes place between client and counsellor, and the often even more subtle dialogue that takes place between the different 'parts' of the same personality.

A counsellor needs to convey calmness in the face of, and sometimes in the active presence of, the distress and turbulence that the client experiences and shows. There is, or there has probably recently been (as in the passage from which my title is taken) an 'earthquake, wind and fire'[1] disturbing the person who has come for help. The temptation is often to meet force with force, but the counsellor must set this aside and encourage the 'still small voice' within both the counsellor and the client. However, it may take quite a long time for a person in distress to pass through the storms inside and for that voice to begin to be heard. It is in the stillness, the unhurried calm, the quietness (but not the quiescence), that a person who is in distress can be helped to listen more fully, whether it is to herself or himself, or (when using counselling skills in the course of other caring situations) to the advice of the normally more active helper.

Many ways of helping those in distress concentrate upon the most immediate and pressing difficulties. Counselling does not ignore the obvious, but it does seek to reach behind the presenting issues. This is why it nearly always involves offering more time than is usual in other forms of help. It often means arranging a series of meetings to enable the person in distress to uncover and reach some of the less obvious and less acceptable feelings and thoughts that contribute to their unhappiness, discomfort and dis-ease. The object is, in what has become a rather trite phrase, to help people to help themselves: a much more difficult task than is recognized by many of those who frequently use the expression. Counselling is seen at its most effective when the client begins to come to her or his own conclusions, and is able to identify ways in which he or she might begin to change. It is above all an approach that tries to understand what goes on inside people, and how internal difficulties can stand in the way of change, rather than looking solely at external factors or external solutions. Again, good counsellors do not ignore external realities, but they believe that frequently people are enabled to cope better with, or even to change, such realities when they can identify and cope with what is going on within themselves.

Although counselling provides the paid and the voluntary helper, whether in a pastoral or other setting, with an identifiable set of skills that can be used in caring, there is nothing new in the skills themselves. Fashionable though it has become (with the dangers that attend popularization), there is nothing particularly novel about a way of helping that relies more upon listening, upon people arriving at their own decisions and insights, and even upon the use of paradox and metaphor. Wise men and women, oracles, gurus, prophets, witches, alchemists, priests, philosophers and fools (particularly the Shakespearean) have all in their own ways demonstrated similar skills and techniques, which Freud and his followers, psychotherapists and counsellors have adopted. The Fool talks in riddles; Zen masters frequently answer questions with questions; Jesus often responded by telling parables capable (as many a commentator or preacher knows) of different interpretations; and when King Solomon refused to judge which of the two women was the real mother of the disputed baby, he showed the type of psychological insight that is typical of a counsellor or therapist. He might have appeared uncaring when he ordered the child to be cut in two, but his response to the situation provoked a threat that identified the true mother of the child.

'Counsel' is a word with a fine tradition, both in theology and in political life. Counselling is not an activity that can be confined to professional or voluntary counsellors as we now know them. Early in its development, the British Association for Counselling and Psychotherapy rightly stated in the preamble to its definition of counselling that it 'has no proprietary rights to the use of the word'.[2] A particular development that has taken place with the increasing use of counselling is the distinction between formal counselling and 'counselling skills'. Counsellors have identified and stressed certain therapeutic factors in caring relationships, while at the same time they have suggested playing down other aspects such as giving answers, expressing sympathy, or actively trying to change the circumstances that appear to contribute to the distress. Many of these skills that counsellors have developed can be also used in teaching and in giving guidance and direction.

The approach that I describe in this book is based on the practice of what might be called *formal* counselling. What I explain is the practice of many of those who offer counselling on a regular basis, at a set time, week by week. Some of those who use this book will wish to practise as counsellors in this way. Others (particularly clergy and others whose role is more diverse than the specialist's) will wish to adapt the practice of formal counselling to their own situations. It is not only basic skills that are capable of use in other settings: there is much to be learned about time boundaries, the counselling setting, the therapeutic relationship, and working with (rather than against) natural psychological defences that can be applied outside the formal counselling session. It is my experience that it is of great value, even to the busy generic helper, to offer formal counselling to one or two people. By working (under supervision) in more depth, and over a longer period of time with a few people, we develop ways of listening, understanding and responding that can be applied more extensively in more informal and brief contacts with greater numbers. By offering counselling to a few, a pastor, health visitor, teacher, social worker, or any other professional upon whom there are many varied demands, will acquire knowledge capable of being effectively used in the other aspects of their caring for the many.

In some chapters I give particular attention to *pastoral* counselling where it differs from a secular approach, but most of what I write in this book is relevant to a variety of situations and contexts. It may help the reader to know that I see no technical distinctions between counselling in what might be styled a 'secular' setting and counselling in a pastoral or religious setting. The issues that are brought to the counsellor are sometimes different, though, and the values implicit in the setting may influence the client's attitude to the counsellor. The examples I use nearly all come from my own practice, and where I allude to religious issues they nearly all arose in the context of 'secular' counselling. Religious readers need not fear that I seek to undermine their faith, but likewise readers who are suspicious of religion need have no fear that I seek to peddle pastoral counselling in a subversive approach to convert them to a religious faith. In my view, counselling is essentially non-partisan, although there are important questions concerning every counsellor's value system and beliefs that I raise in Chapter 10. It will become clear that the counsellor, whether pastoral or otherwise, is in one sense a neutral figure in the helping relationship. But neutral does not mean being uncaring, uninvolved or impotent. Those who care for others, wherever they work and whatever their beliefs, will find some guidance here to enrich all that they offer.

It is a sign of how rapid the change was in the last quarter of the twentieth century that whereas in the 1970s there were very few professional counsellors, they are now employed in much greater numbers in primary care trusts, in psychological services, by industry and commercial institutions through employee assistance programmes and as professional directors of local counselling centres. There are also a large number in independent practice. This is not the place to comment upon such developments, which raise issues about the professionalization of care, about standards, commercialism, lack of statutory services, etc. The churches, if anything, lag behind in what they offer, although there are a large number of lay members of the churches doing fine work in counselling centres, usually in a voluntary capacity. There is indeed still a large voluntary sector – Relate (formerly Marriage Guidance but now offering a more general service), centres affiliated to the WPF Counselling, and other groups which specialize in caring for those suffering from particular disabilities or difficulties. There are many training courses in counselling; some of these unfortunately appear to want to cash in on the counselling bonanza, although the British Association for Counselling and Psychotherapy accredits courses which reach the right standards. The training of clergy in all denominations usually includes counselling skills, and such training is also seen in preparation for other professions, which have recognized the importance of the personal relationship in the interaction between the professional helper and the patient or client.

The widespread availability of counselling training enables me to emphasize that the right place to learn counselling is with others, and preferably on a reputable course. A book can only help the reader learn *about* counselling. This text is essentially for reference in the context of learning through seminar and practical training. I may help the reader to become more attuned to their own 'still small voice', but in acquiring and sharpening the skills of listening and responding to the 'still small voice' of another person, an interpersonal setting for learning is essential. What we expect of those who come to us for help – that is, a capacity to talk about themselves – we must also expect of ourselves. While this book will, I hope, continue to serve its purpose as a theoretical text for counselling courses, the practice of counselling and the fine tuning of skills rightly comes from experiential learning in small groups and in supervision. Practical exercises for use in such contexts form the substance of another volume in this series – *Swift to Hear*.[3] A training course including counselling skills exercises for use with parish groups training lay visitors is also available.[4]

Whether the decline of institutionalized religion (at least among the majority in the Judaeo-Christian tradition in Europe) is one of the contributing factors to the phenomenal interest in counselling is a matter for debate. In some respects counselling has become an alternative to religion, as Paul Halmos in Britain and Philip Rieff in the United States were quick to recognize in the title and subject of their respective books: *The Faith of the Counsellors* and *The Triumph of the Therapeutic*.[5] Over-simplified though it may be, there is more popular understanding of Freud than there is of theology. Many of those who ask for help come with a vocabulary that has been informed by populist psychological writing in the press, magazines, and by the jargon of counselling, therapy and psychological understanding. This has often been percolated through soap operas and sit-coms as well as through more serious productions. Counsellors, whether in the pastoral or any other setting, cannot play the amateur psychoanalyst now that their clients have become more aware of what goes on inside them and in their relationships with others.

Although there is a danger of generalizing, many more people today are not only prepared to acknowledge their feelings, but also know that there are dangers in suppressing them. There is a backlash against the over-use of prescriptions. The stress that can be caused by life events is now more recognized: there

is far less shame about owning up to distress or anxieties at the
birth of a baby, problems with children, choices about education and careers, teenager/parent conflicts, marriage, moving,
unemployment and redundancy, illness, retirement, old age,
dying or bereavement.

Many people want good relationships, and even if there is a
tendency to expect the ideal, there is also no reason why they
should put up with bad, violent or stultifying partnerships. The
significance of the past, the influence of upbringing and the
importance of childhood experiences – all these are becoming
common knowledge. Clients often look for explanations as to
what makes them feel and react the way they do. Psychological
terms and conditions may sometimes be misappropriated or
even used pejoratively, but many words have none the less
become part of a common vocabulary: introvert, extrovert,
neurotic, identity crisis, male menopause, PMT, dependent,
obsessional, hysterical, and adolescent angst are just a few of
them. Although of itself this phenomenon does not necessarily
indicate deeper psychological or personal awareness, popular
culture has provided a base from which the counsellor, or
counselling-minded professional or voluntary helper, can work.

Particularly in the non-fee paying or low-cost counselling
sector there is no need to compete for clients. Voluntary agencies almost always offer high professional standards and are
hard-pressed to keep up with the demands for counselling
made upon them. There is plenty of room both for pastoral
counselling and for counselling in other settings. What makes
it difficult for the churches to offer a pastoral counselling
ministry is that they are often tainted with an image (not always
outdated) of censoriousness and moralizing, with a language
about sin and guilt, and with a heritage of authoritarian
injunctions. Other professionals may have similar problems of
image: doctors, for instance, even if they wish to offer more
counselling help, not only have the problem of pressure of
time, but also the stereotype of 'reaching for the prescription
pad'; some patients feel cheated if they do not leave the surgery
with a piece of paper. Perhaps that is why, in both medical and
religious settings, the 'lay' person seems to be rather better at
counselling than the person identified as the professional.

Counselling and religion, psychology and spirituality,
theology and psychoanalysis, all have more in common than

divides them – despite the wish of various protagonists to set them at odds with one another. At the heart of all the arguments and theories is the attempt to understand, to live with, to experience and, in some sense, to control, what it is to be a human being. Counselling and spirituality, East and West, share the same view that out of crisis comes opportunity and new possibilities; that experiences of loss and death, appallingly painful though they may be, can give rise to new life; both seek a sense of 'meaning' even if there is a danger of that becoming an over-used word. Indeed, it is scarcely surprising that Becker's definition of religion in his book *The Birth and Death of Meaning* could serve just as much as a satisfactory description of counselling and therapy: 'an ideal of strength and of potentiality for growth, of what man might become by assuming the burden of his life, as well as being partly relieved of it'.[6]

NOTES

1. 1 Kings 19.11–12. Other readers will be more familiar with the phrase from Whittier's popular hymn, 'Dear Lord and Father of Mankind'.
2. *Counselling – a Definition*. British Association for Counselling 1979.
3. M. Jacobs, *Swift to Hear*. SPCK 2000 (2nd edn).
4. S. Cumming, R. File and M. Worthington, *I Didn't Seem to Say Very Much*. Details of this six-week course (available as a tutor's handbook, and with student handouts) can be obtained from Vaughan College, St Nicholas Circle, Leicester LE1 4LB.
5. P. Halmos, *The Faith of the Counsellors*. Constable 1978 (2nd rev. edn); P. Rieff, *The Triumph of the Therapeutic*. Penguin Books 1973.
6. E. Becker, *The Birth and Death of Meaning*. Penguin Books 1972, p. 196.

CHAPTER TWO

Some Definitions and Distinctions

The rapid expansion of counselling, both in its practice and in training courses, and also in the large amount of literature that has informed and accompanied these developments, means that while many people now know and use the term 'counselling', it may in fact stand for a variety of ways of helping. Like the allied and parent field of psychotherapy, counselling has developed through a number of different approaches. There is a bewildering number of alternative counselling groups, reflecting a similar sectarianism in the history of the churches. As in the relationships between churches, the relationships between the various 'schools' of therapy and counselling has not always been as understanding as one might expect. It is indeed curious that those who profess to understand other people are sometimes unable to recognize their own hostility towards those who practise within a different orientation or use what they consider to be unacceptable techniques. The situation is improving, though, and there is now much more acknowledgement of the common ground between approaches, as well as the differences. There is also research that seems to show that when it comes to actual practice, the most experienced therapists and counsellors of various persuasions approximate more closely to one another than either their teaching, their writing or their theoretical positions would suggest.[1]

The practice of counselling does not require detailed knowledge of the history of psychotherapy, but there are some important differences that not only appear in the literature, and in the underlying orientation of training courses, but that reflect what may in the end be useful and complementary (if different) emphases in the various traditions. In this chapter I want to distinguish psychotherapy and counselling from some of the other similar-sounding approaches; to examine the difficult question of the relationship between psychotherapy and counselling; to summarize some of the main approaches that apply both to psychotherapy and counselling; and finally, to see what is distinctive about pastoral counselling. The reader who is impatient with such matters may wish for the time being to move straight on to practice (Chapter 3). There comes a time, though, when all practising counsellors need to see the distinctions I examine here as being relevant to felt and perceived levels of competency.

THE PSYCHOLOGICAL PROFESSIONS

Counselling has developed from psychotherapy, but psycho-therapy itself initially emerged within the medical context, leaving some confusion over the various terms that are used for those who in one way or other treat the mind. The Greek word 'psyche', which is at the root of many of the terms I examine here, in fact means 'soul', and Freud himself certainly used 'psyche' more in that sense than as an expression for the 'mind'. Bettelheim re-works the inaccurate translation into English of one of Freud's essays to demonstrate Freud's use of the term: 'Psychical treatment hence means "treatment of the soul" . . . by measures which influence above all and immediately the soul of man.' He notes that the translators rendered the same passage misleadingly as: 'Psychical treatment means "mental treatment" . . . by measures which operate in the first instance and immediately upon the human mind'.[2]

Psychoanalysis thus literally means 'analysis of the soul'. There are, of course, questions about the relationship of body, mind and soul or spirit that have taxed the greatest philosophers and theologians, and to which I do not here propose a solution. What is valuable is to acknowledge that counselling is seldom concerned with the 'brain' as such, and that terms like 'mind', 'heart' and 'soul' are essentially metaphors for what takes place within a person: a complex interaction between thoughts and feelings, and between brain and body, which gives rise to other factors that are not easily described, which are certainly not to be located physically, but which also cannot be reduced to the biological or the chemical.

Interest in the mind and the brain as a physical organ of the body, and the study of the way in which genes, chemicals and other phenomena affect the brain, with resultant changes to thought patterns, behaviour and emotions, is very much the professional province of psychologists and psychiatrists. Psychiatrists have trained as medical doctors and have specialized in the diagnosis and treatment of mental disorders. Some of them view mental illness as principally organic, caused by genetic inheritance, or through some other dysfunction of the brain – such as that caused by chemical imbalance. Psychiatrists who lean towards such explanations of human difficulties tend to favour the use of psychotropic drugs to change the biochemical balance of the body. They may even advocate, where necessary, neuro-surgery or electroconvulsive therapy (ECT). Other psychiatrists see mental disorder as being the result of developmental factors, and of disturbances in relationships within the family, etc.; they tend to prefer the 'talking' therapies: behavioural or analytic psychotherapy, group therapy or therapeutic communities. Their workload is such that they will often refer patients to clinical, counselling or educational psychologists, occupational therapists and other ancillary medical services, or to counsellors or psychotherapists. Some psychiatrists have themselves specialized in psychotherapy, and spend some or even all of their time functioning in that role.

The division I make here between two types of psychiatrists is somewhat artificial, and sharply defined for convenience only. There are some mental disturbances that clearly fall into one category or the other, and that *most* psychiatrists and psychologists would acknowledge as purely the result of organic disease, or, conversely, the outcome of relationship problems. While counsellors sometimes find they are able to provide effective help for very disturbed people, and therefore do not need to refer all such clients to a psychiatrist (who would probably be able to give the person less time than the counsellor), counsellors and therapists none the less need to have access to the type of expertise that will help them to identify those clients who need to be referred for drug and other physical treatments. Just as psychiatrists differ in their view of the principal cause of emotional, behavioural and cognitive (thinking) difficulties, general practitioners also fall into such camps – although many more are recognizing the value of referrals to counsellors, either attached to their practice or outside of it.

Psychologists are not normally doctors of medicine. Following a degree in psychology, they train in specialized areas, such as clinical or educational psychology, or counselling psychology. While some of their work involves psychological testing (IQ, personality, aptitude and projective tests), they also provide therapy – a term that means 'healing' and that refers to many types of treatment, including the physical. Historically the principal therapy used by clinical psychologists has been behavioural psychotherapy, now extended to cognitive-behavioural therapy, which I explain more fully below. While there have always been some clinical psychologists who have trained as psychoanalysts and psychodynamic psychotherapists (which again I explain below), there is an increasing and more widespread interest in other forms of psychotherapy, and in what has become known as counselling psychology. This academic and practical discipline seeks to bring together the most valuable knowledge from psychological research on the one hand and counselling practice on the other.

The term 'psychoanalyst' (or 'psychoanalysing') is sometimes mistakenly used of psychotherapists or psychiatrists. In fact, psychoanalysts are relatively few in number. They are usually medical doctors, psychiatrists or clinical psychologists who have taken a particular training that is lengthy and expensive, and as a result somewhat elitist. The title 'psychoanalyst' is usually reserved for those who are members of their own particular professional society, which normally signifies a training in the tradition of Freud or Klein (see below). The equivalent term for those trained in the tradition of Jung is 'analytical psychologist'. Others, who have similar but rather less lengthy training, often call themselves 'psychoanalytic psychotherapists', although the term 'psychotherapist' is also used much more widely of a variety of helpers.

Psychoanalysis is a confusing term because it is used in a number of senses: first, it refers to a particular professional training and practice, such as that outlined above, that is rather exclusive. It refers similarly to a therapeutic method that may consist of hourly sessions four or five days a week, often going on for a number of years. In this sense, psychoanalysis is confined to the few. But it also refers to a method of practice that is less intensive; and to a theory of personality structure, of human development and of the cause of emotional and cognitive difficulties that forms the basis for a broader and often somewhat briefer method of treatment – often known as psychodynamic psychotherapy or psychodynamic counselling. This is the approach that informs my own work and therefore much of this book. I explain it more fully below, and illustrate it in the chapters that follow.

PSYCHOTHERAPY AND COUNSELLING

The British Association for Counselling and Psychotherapy was wise to accept that the word 'counselling' can be used in a variety of ways, although it has also tried to distinguish between the different skills and competencies required in counselling, in advice, in guidance and in the use of counselling skills. Similarly, the term 'psychotherapist' covers a multitude of approaches, although the United Kingdom Council for Psychotherapy represents the attempt on the part of many of the principal therapy associations to place some order upon its use and upon standards of practice. Counselling and psychotherapy are by and large derivatives of psychoanalysis, although counselling was perhaps at one time regarded as the poor relation (offering less time and apparently less expertise than the 'parent' groups of analysis and psychotherapy). My impression now is that counselling has all but come of age, and hard and fast distinctions between the two expressions of similar practice are much less easy to make.

For example, there are some forms of therapy that are used by counsellors, but that are never given the title 'counselling': transactional analysis (TA), for instance, is a quite popular method of trying to help people look at the games they play, and the styles of relating they adopt. But it is never called transactional *counselling*. Cognitive-behavioural therapy is not usually styled 'counselling', even though this approach is used by some counsellors as well as by many clinical psychologists. Gestalt therapy similarly may be a method used by psychotherapists and counsellors alike, with no real distinction between its use by either group. Even when both terms are used by a particular orientation, as in person-centred therapy and person-centred counselling, the distinction in this case is largely between an American usage (therapy) and a British usage (counselling). Exactly the same principles are used, and there are no implied differences in experience or expertise.

Yet undeniably there are those who practise as psychotherapists and those who practise as counsellors who see their respective areas of work as somewhat different; at the same time, there are others who call themselves both psychotherapist *and* counsellor. This latter group regard their work with some clients as being psychotherapy; and with others they feel that the term 'counselling' better describes the type of activity in which they are involved. Most of those who call themselves both titles acknowledge clear differences between the two ends of the spectrum, but they are also aware of a continuum where it is not always possible to draw hard and fast lines. Furthermore, it is possible to draw a distinction between role and function. It may be in time that only those who are registered as such can call themselves psychotherapists or counsellors: this is, as it were, their title and role. Yet each may function slightly differently from time to time with particular clients: so that with one client a psychotherapist engages in psychotherapy and with another he or she offers counselling; similarly, a counsellor may normally practise counselling, but occasionally finds that he or she is engaged in psychotherapy.

The dilemma is one that is similarly present in this book, which aims to explain counselling and to describe how counsellors might work. Yet the main method that I describe (although not exclusively) is the psychodynamic tradition, which comes initially from psychoanalytic and psychotherapeutic practice. Although I do not intend this book as a manual for trainee psychotherapists, I do draw upon the principles of psychotherapy. In what might the difference between that parent body and counselling consist?

Sometimes the distinction that is drawn is that of the length of the therapeutic contract, or the number of sessions offered to the client. I would expect a person who sees clients twice a week to be a psychotherapist rather than a counsellor, partly because seeing clients two or more times a week creates a particular dependency which requires extra-special experience. Yet there are occasions (especially when someone is clearly in a crisis that is predicted to be a short-term one) when it can be appropriate for a counsellor to offer a second appointment for a week or for a few weeks. There are also many clients who see psychotherapists just once a week, and who in terms of frequency itself are indistinguishable from counselling clients.

Even the ongoing length of help offered or received is no real measure of the difference, although again it is a contributing factor to the difference. Some people whom I have seen in what I experience as a counselling style I have seen supportively (see Chapter 7) for a year or more. I have also experienced what I understand as a more psychotherapeutic style with clients whom I have arranged to see for only a few weeks.

Although psychoanalysis has tended to become a very lengthy method of therapy, it has not always been universally so. Freud describes at least one case in which he met his patient just once, informally, on a mountain top![3] And his first biographer records how Freud apparently cured the composer Mahler of impotence during a lengthy walk one afternoon in the park![4] Freud also saw patients six times a week, and in some cases for many years, and psychoanalysis tended towards great length both because he and others used it as a research method (to learn more about the workings of the unconscious) and because it was felt that a long training in analysis was a prerequisite of all who wish to practise as therapists. Lengthy treatment does not, however, necessarily mean more effective results, and many counsellors can be proud of what the much shorter contracts they offer can achieve.

The search for more efficient use of a therapist's time and skills, so that more people could be offered help, has resulted in the development of brief psychotherapy. Franz Alexander[5] experimented with such methods in the 1930s in Chicago, although he was criticized at the time for watering down the 'pure gold of analysis'. Although there is a continuing debate about the efficacy of many psychotherapeutic approaches, the work in the 1960s and 1970s at the Tavistock Clinic appears to demonstrate the possibilities of effective treatment over a period of about thirty weekly sessions. Careful selection of patients is clearly one reason for success, but Malan[6] also isolates the use of transference (see Chapter 9), working with the ending of the contract (see Chapter 11), and focusing on particular issues as being essential for change. Important claims for the efficacy of its short-term therapy are also made by those who have developed cognitive-analytic therapy, an interesting combination of the psychoanalytic and the cognitive approaches.[7]

Similarly, counselling is sometimes described as either 'long-term' or 'short-term'. It is probable that long-term counselling or therapy provides more opportunities for sustained insight; it may also be the treatment of choice where a person has been suffering for many years. The huge demand for counselling help has forced many agencies to look at ways of offering early assessment interviews and, through them, deciding who can best be helped through short-term work and who may require longer-term help. Assessment is also useful in allocating clients to the most appropriate counsellors, as well as in sorting out who needs priority and who might be able to go on to a waiting list. Counselling tends in any case to be shorter than psychotherapy. This does not mean that counselling need be any the less intense in the expression of deep feelings. Even the briefest period of counselling can on occasion reach very rapidly and deeply into memory, as well as enabling real pain to be expressed and shared. Length of time does not always equal depth, as many a psychotherapist knows from trying to work with highly defensive clients. I examine the different levels of intervention made in counselling and therapy in Chapter 7.

While many therapists from the various key orientations might define the difference between counselling and psychotherapy in a variety of ways (or sometimes see no difference at all), my own background, the psychodynamic one, suggests to me that some of the difference lies in a less intense use of the actual relationship between a counsellor and a client, than would be the case in the relationship between psychotherapist and client. Here I have to anticipate some of the definitions of different schools that belong more appropriately below, as well as in later chapters, but it may be that the orientation known as 'psychodynamic' makes the greatest distinction between psychotherapy and counselling. One difference between the two forms of help that psychodynamic writers sometimes make, is the more explicit use in psychotherapy than in counselling of a way of relating in therapy that is known as 'transference' (which I explain more fully in Chapter 9). In fact, this particular form of relating occurs whenever two or more people meet each other, and it is just as present in counselling as it is in any other kind of healing relationship. But counsellors generally make less use of it. Counsellors who adopt a psychodynamic orientation may use their understanding of the relationship

with the client implicitly, reserving its more open use to times
when there are particular difficulties in their work together. In
no way do I suggest that the counselling relationship is less
significant: but I believe it may be expressed differently.

.The words used to describe differences between psychotherapy and counselling (such as 'depth') are best understood
as metaphorical and should not be taken as expressing 'better'
or 'worse'. The 'depth' of psychotherapeutic work as compared
to counselling may be distinguished by the 'layers' of the
human 'mind' (another multiple metaphor) into which a psychotherapist tries to reach. It is possible (as Freud initially did)
to think of three 'layers' in the mind: conscious thoughts and
feelings; memories that are accessible at will to consciousness
(which Freud called the pre-conscious); and repressed and
largely forgotten memories, phantasies, feelings and ideas
(which Freud called the unconscious). While these 'layers' are
present in everyone, counsellors are generally less concerned
with purposively trying to uncover the unconscious.

A further difference can be seen in the practical use made
of a psychodynamic term called the 'triangle of insight'. The
three 'points' of the triangle are: (a) past relationships, feelings
and events; (b) present relationships, feelings and events in the
everyday life of the client; and (c) the relationship between the
therapist and the client. Psychotherapists prefer to make interpretations about the client that link the possible connections
between all three points of the triangle. In contrast, counsellors,
where they make such connections, tend to concentrate on
linking similar examples of present situations, or past and
present events and relationships, but seldom the complex
network of past and present, and conscious and unconscious.
Although it appears that counselling is generally therefore less
conceptually complex than psychotherapy, in practice much
depends on what the client brings to the session, and how
far the client shows an inclination to disentangle the web of
interrelated events and their associated fears, phantasies and
feelings. Bearing in mind the continuum between the two
forms of help, many counsellors can find themselves in effect
engaged in psychotherapy, and psychotherapists are from
time to time limited to counselling by the particular client.

It is clear that the lines between psychotherapy and counselling cannot be too finely drawn. It is both professionally
territorial and academically pedantic to make too hard and fast

a distinction. Yet there are valid reasons for posing these questions. Active use of transference interpretation, as well as willingness to explore unconscious thoughts, memories and emotions, inevitably intensifies the relationship between the therapist and client and makes it more complex. It is the responsibility of every helper to ensure that they know the limits of their skills and the dangers of attempting more than their training and supervision has prepared them for. Although in this book I draw upon psychotherapeutic techniques and insights, and illustrate how they apply to counselling, I do this to enable those who are training to recognize their limitations as well as the opportunities that come with this particular way of offering help.

THE PRINCIPAL ORIENTATIONS

I have already described the main (although not the sole) approach of this book as psychodynamic. This is one of the major models of theory and practice in counselling and psychotherapy, but there are other orientations that are also significant, and that are widely taught and written about. Most of these have developed from the highly original techniques pioneered by Freud, sometimes as extensions of his own thinking and practice, but sometimes because fresh insights have not been sufficiently acknowledged or accepted by the 'parent' body. Although I would not wish to disguise the bitterness and acrimony that has sometimes accompanied the divisions of therapy and counselling, there are many positive features to these diverse movements that highlight the many aspects involved in understanding people and their problems. There is currently a large body of literature that admirably explains these different approaches, and my references point the reader to these works. My purpose here is to indicate the richness of this wealth of practice, without piling too much upon the reader's plate!

The development of therapy and counselling spans decades as well as continents, each with its distinctive cultural bias. To simplify the picture, there are three main divisions: the psychodynamic therapies, the humanistic therapies, and the cognitive and behavioural therapies. There is sometimes a fourth force added to these three, known as transpersonal psychology, because it includes concern for the transcendent and the spiritual. In practice it is closely allied to the humanistic schools, which are not necessarily as humanist (in the sense of being sceptical about the spiritual) as one might think. The cultural bias I have referred to is found through all the different schools. In the United States, for example, the optimism of that culture, which sometimes appears to believe it can conquer everything, is reflected in a much more positive approach to therapy, whether it is psychoanalytic or humanistic, and an interest in the workings and strengthening of the conscious ego. In Europe, on the other hand, particularly in psychoanalytic thought, there is less confidence in being able to change or alter the deep-seated problems of the human condition, and a far greater interest in therapy in trying to understand and come to terms with the mysteries of the unconscious.

Common to these broad divisions is the fact that therapists and counsellors mostly work with individuals (often known as 'one-to-one'), sometimes with couples or families, and sometimes with groups. Thus both a psychodynamic and a person-centred counsellor may specialize in individual work or groupwork, there being particular skills for each situation, but the same basic principles underlie both, according to the emphasis of either orientation. Some counselling methods (e.g. psychodrama) necessitate groupwork, but most are adaptable to both contexts.

1. THE PSYCHODYNAMIC THERAPIES

Freud is probably the most important figure in the development of psychotherapy and counselling. There is a sense in which all counselling methods other than the behavioural have flowed from his initiatives. He recognized the importance of listening to his patients, and from them he learned a method of therapy and a way of investigating the causes of both psychological health and disturbance. It was Freud who first identified many of the techniques that are still central to therapy and counselling: encouraging people to speak whatever they think and feel without imposing judgements upon themselves; free-floating attention on the part of the therapist; recognition and careful handling of resistance and defensiveness; the problems as well as the opportunities provided by the relationship between the therapist and the client; the repetition of the past, etc.[8] He also began to map out the significance of childhood in personal formation and development, and proposed a model of personality structure, which was initially partly mechanistic and partly biological, with strong emphasis on drives and impulses. Various aspects of these theories have inevitably been challenged, although it is generally disputes about theory more than about the basic techniques Freud practised that have caused the various splits in the original psychoanalytic movement.

Alfred Adler[9] was the first to be forced to break away, and although his system of Individual Psychology is one of the least well known of the analytic schools, Adler's concern for the part which the family, the social structures, and education play in individual problems was taken up by the next generation, particularly by a group now known as the Neo-Freudians – Karen Horney[10] and Erich Fromm[11] perhaps being the best known among them. They too recognized cultural influences, and Fromm in particular had wide-ranging interests, bridging psychoanalysis and politics and religion.

Carl Jung is probably as well known as Freud, and his ideas have had particular influence, both on those interested in psychology and religion, as well as on those who find symbolism and imagery powerful and evocative.[12] Whereas Adler stressed inferiority and superiority, and the significance of the wish for power, Jung has given us terms like introvert and extrovert, which have entered common language. His emphasis was on the search for some kind of faith – although not necessarily a formal Christian faith. His particular interest in the importance of the second half of life distinguishes him from Freud, who concentrated his attention on the first five years of life, and who had little patience with religious solutions and spiritual questions.

I would not wish to give the impression that either the Neo-Freudians, following Adler, or the various wings of Jungian psychology, are insignificant, but it is not appropriate to list or explain further the key figures in either group. Similarly it is a forbidding task to try and single out the key figures who worked from within the psychoanalytic movement, even though in some cases their ideas were radically different from Freud's. It would be inappropriate not to mention the work of Erikson[13] in particular in the United States, and Melanie Klein[14] and Anna Freud[15] in Britain. Anna Freud was one of the pioneers of child therapy and contributed much to the theory of child development. Melanie Klein similarly practised child analysis, and also deepened the study of the first few months of life. Particular British psychoanalysts, such as Fairbairn,[16] Winnicott[17] and Bowlby,[18] have represented a more independent and challenging movement within the psycho-analytic tradition, and have made sufficient impact upon the theory and therapeutic attitudes of many of those who teach and practise psychodynamic counselling to deserve a reference. British psychoanalytic thought in particular has developed away from the instinctual model that Freud first proposed to a far greater emphasis on personal relations, which technically is known as object relations theory, or the object relations school.

This variety of approaches – Freudian, Kleinian, Jungian, Object Relations, Neo-Freudian, etc. – can be given the generic title 'psychodynamic therapies'. I have defined 'psychodynamic' elsewhere as:

the way in which the psyche (as mind/emotions/spirit/self) is seen as active, and not static . . . The activity of the psyche is not confined to relating to people, or to objects outside the self . . . Activity also takes place within the psyche, in relation to itself . . . These internal aspects (or 'objects', as they are sometimes called in psychodynamic literature) of the psyche are formed over the long years of a child's development, as counterparts of external relationships which predominate in early childhood, principally those with mother and father.[19]

Counsellors who call themselves psychodynamic in their orientation adopt a similar approach to practice whether they are of one wing or another. There will of course be differences of style, and some personalities are attracted to one approach more than another. Although there are clearly differences between the different theories underlying practice, many who practise as psychodynamic counsellors and therapists, who were not trained by a particular training society, adopt what might be called an 'eclectic' approach, which in their case means drawing from different psychoanalytic schools. The student beginning in counselling need not be troubled by such distinctions, although I do wish to point to the treasure house of important thinking about therapy, and about people, that accompanies the various psychodynamic therapies. It is this that singles out this set of therapies from other approaches, which by and large concentrate far more upon the practice of therapy and give less attention to a detailed psychology of human personality and development. The richness of this thought leads some counsellors, trained in humanistic therapies, to turn eventually to psychodynamic literature, to 'flesh out' the issues that are arising for them from their practice.

2. THE HUMANISTIC THERAPIES

While all the humanistic therapies have in common a greater concern for the conscious and for the here-and-now than interest in the past, transference and the unconscious (as seen in the psychodynamic therapies above), the differences in technique within the humanistic therapies are great. This is illustrated by the fact that the series 'Counselling in Action' has one volume that covers the psychodynamic therapies, but different volumes to examine the techniques used by person-centred counselling, Gestalt therapy, transactional analysis and, to include one of the transpersonal approaches, psychosynthesis.[20] Each emphasizes a different dimension.

One of the most popular schools of counselling is the person-centred, which has developed from the work of Carl Rogers.[21] Originally known as non-directive, and then as client-centred counselling, it is particularly attractive (and useful) because its central principle is giving full attention to the client. Although this requires considerable skill and training, the approach encourages meeting each client as a unique individual. It appears to be relatively free of a body of theoretical and technical knowledge which, once learned, can all too easily be pushed upon the client. The danger of some approaches to counselling is that they teach a technique and a theory that encourages the anxious therapist or counsellor to stay in control, and 'do something'. It may be significant that Carl Rogers developed his particular style of therapy against the background of psychoanalytically-inspired quackery (at worst) and psychoanalytic confidence (at best) of the 1920s in the United States. It sometimes appears as if by contrast that Rogers discovered what it meant to listen to clients. In fact, Freud had already discovered the value of much that Rogers later reiterated about the practice of therapy, although Freud's emphasis on the neutrality of the therapist is different from Rogers's identification of the core conditions of therapy or counselling that he believed enabled clients to change and grow: genuineness, empathy, congruence and non-possessive love.

That what amounts to personal qualities in the counsellor are just as important as counselling skills is an important point to have in mind throughout the technical aspects of counselling that I introduce in this book. Carl Rogers's writing provides a very sound foundation for all counselling, whatever its orientation. There are also common features to basic counselling skills, most of which are shared by person-centred and other humanistic counsellors as well as by psychodynamic counsellors. The way to listening and responding effectively that I outline in Chapter 3 is not very different from the basic counselling skills learned in other orientations. My own reservation about person-centred counselling is that it does not go far enough, and although it may provide sufficient understanding of the therapeutic process when a counsellor works with highly-motivated, thoughtful and expressive clients, counselling can be a lot more complex than portrayed in the literature.[22] While I do not doubt that person-centred counsellors might work equally effectively with more difficult clients, I do not find in their writing sufficiently deep an analysis either of the complexity of technique in more difficult cases, or of the dynamic relationship between counsellor and client (together) and within the counsellor and client (as separate persons), to inform the thoughts and the emotions that I experience as a therapist, or the strategies (I use the word deliberately) that I might need to consider as a helper.

Person-centred counselling is practised widely in a large number of different settings, but particularly by school and college counsellors. Like Carl Rogers, some other therapists became dissatisfied with their psychoanalytic training, and developed alternative approaches; these are often more immediate, more accessible to a number of clients, and frequently (unlike Rogers) suggest a more active and directive technique. Gestalt therapy owes its origins to the former psychoanalyst Fritz Perls;[23] transactional analysis arose from Eric Berne's wish to make psychotherapeutic jargon more down-to-earth, with its language of parent–adult–child and games that people play.[24] Other therapies emphasize the body (bio-energetic,[25] massage, and dance therapy), or provide opportunities for participants to act through their situations (psychodrama[26]), or to re-enact their birth trauma (primal therapy[27]). Therapists who use these methods actively intervene to propose exercises or other ways of working that will draw the clients out. Counsellors of a humanistic eclectic persuasion may draw upon a variety of these different therapies with different clients or even with the same client, and sometimes describe such a multi-dimensional approach as 'integrative counselling'.

Such a list is not exhaustive. Counselling and psychotherapy also take place through hypnotherapy, co-counselling, astrology and other activities that it is tempting to identify as 'fringe' movements. To do so is perhaps an injustice to those who sincerely and responsibly practise forms of healing that have their own appeal, unorthodox though they may seem to mainstream counsellors. There are frauds, charlatans and counsellors and therapists of all orientations who abuse the powerful position they have over clients.[28] Nevertheless, when counselling becomes fashionable, all manner of people are ready to jump on the bandwagon. Potential clients, and those who are in a position to make referrals or suggestions of counselling, should do all they can to check the credentials of the counsellor and the status of the parent organization behind anyone who offers counselling or therapy. Britain is not quite like the west coast of America in the 1960s and 1970s, but where there is need there is always the risk of exploitation, and it is sadly on the fringe of this group of therapies that excessive claims can be found.

3. THE COGNITIVE AND BEHAVIOURAL THERAPIES

The one orientation that does not owe its origins to Freud, although some of the examples of it do spring from his erstwhile followers, is behaviourism. Behavioural psychology comes partly from the pioneering work of the Russian psychologist Pavlov, whose salivating dogs are perhaps as well known as any of Freud's patients; and partly from the research of two American psychologists, Watson and Skinner. Its main hypothesis is that all behaviour is learned (in other words, we are conditioned to behave in particular ways) and that, through a process of re-education, inappropriate behaviour

and responses can be unlearned and replaced by more appropriate behaviours. Extended to the area of cognition or thought
processes, it is similarly believed that irrational ideas can be
challenged and altered, and people's ways of responding
emotionally to situations reviewed and revised. Behaviour therapy is a structured form of help, which involves identifying
the client's difficulties and then developing a programme of
alternative behaviours; this programme is often graded in
difficulty, so that a person starts with small changes and pro-
gresses to a position where they can face their greatest fears.
While behaviour therapy has often been held up as the treatment of choice for phobias and ritualistic behaviours, varia-
tions of this form of therapy are applied to other presenting
difficulties, through, for example, rational-emotive therapy,[29]
cognitive-behavioural counselling[30] or reality therapy.[31] Relax-
ation, desensitization, operant conditioning, social skills training, etc. are some of the ways in which behavioural therapy is
used. In the past it has been claimed by research psychologists
that the shorter, more focused methods of these therapies yield
more obvious results than the psychodynamic or person-centred
approaches. Now more and more research is showing clearly
positive results across the board: 'there is now general agreement within counselling that different approaches are equally
effective'.[32] Those who use a particular orientation have their
own views on their effectiveness, which are no doubt biased
towards their own preferences.

Arguments between behavioural therapists and psychodynamic and humanistic counsellors about their results and
about their methods will no doubt go on, even though in
recent years there has been greater mutual recognition of the
overlap between these different schools.[33] It is not unusual to
hear person-centred and behavioural therapists employing
the concept of transference; psychodynamic and cognitive
counsellors acknowledging the value of self-disclosure; or of
non-behavioural counsellors suggesting a plan of action that
clearly involves a form of desensitization! One example is sex
therapists who work for Relate (an organization once geared
around Rogerian principles). They may use a behavioural
approach to help change the partners' physical actions and
responses, but may also use a psychodynamic approach to try
to analyse attitudes and to understand a couple's resistance to
experimenting with alternative sexual behaviours.[34]

Although there are indications of greater openness to the techniques and understanding offered by different schools of therapy and counselling, the beginner is faced with a bewildering range of possibilities. The basic orientations of the range of courses on offer are more limited than the number of therapies outlined here suggests. The British Association for Counselling and Psychotherapy, in its recognition of training courses, insists on a core orientation which may be one of those described in this chapter, or on an integrative model. The British Psychological Society Diploma in Counselling Psychology insists on experience of at least two different approaches. Integrative counselling, which draws upon different models of counselling, has a solid foundation in basic skills, and aims at a unified theory and practice. Eclecticism is not necessarily the same as integrative, although it similarly draws upon different ideas as they are deemed useful with a particular client. There is much to be said for being rooted in one approach before drawing upon alternative theories in the search for fresh insights or different strategies. Even then apparently opposing systems sometimes discover that their description of a client, although expressed in different jargon, reveals a similar picture.

PASTORAL COUNSELLING

Counselling takes place in a variety of settings, but psychotherapy less so – since it tends to be confined to private practice or to medical settings and in a few cases is available in student counselling services. Counsellors, like other helpers, can specialize in particular areas of concern, or they may work with specific groups of people. University and college counsellors, school counsellors or youth counsellors all work predominantly with one age group. Others, such as Relate, pregnancy counsellors or careers counsellors, specialize in working with areas of particular concern, but across a wider age span. The prefix describing a counsellor or a counselling service provides a way in for clients, who often initially experience their discomfort as especially connected with a relationship, their work, or perhaps their faith. Of course, once initiated, counselling need not confine itself to the problem presented. Work or religious problems, for instance, sometimes exist in isolation, but it is far more likely that they are symptomatic of other difficulties – including intimate relationships.

Pastoral counselling describes the practice of counselling within a spiritual setting, although some would want to insist that pastoral counselling concerns not the context alone, but also the specialist issues with which the counsellor is especially equipped to deal. One possible confusion must be clarified. The term 'pastoral care' is also used of care, welfare and counselling work by teachers (and perhaps by school counsellors in the educational context). Although this is in common use in educational circles, it is not the sense in which I use it in this book. Reference to pastoral counselling or pastoral care here is to either the context or the work of counsellors (or those who use counselling skills) for whom religious faith is a major or important concern, and who probably work in the context of a religious setting. Pastoral psychotherapy is not a term that is used in Britain; it is confined to the United States where it refers to specialist therapists working in church contexts, where the distinction from pastoral counsellors is that of depth as described earlier.

The remit of pastoral counselling might best be described through examples of different situations. Pastoral counselling might include:

- a member of the clergy approached for counselling about a domestic dispute
- a member of the clergy approached over a difficulty of belief, which is then discussed in a series of counselling sessions
- a lay counsellor asked to provide help with a family problem, because she is known to attend church, and therefore a safe person for a Christian client who is worried that his faith may not otherwise be understood
- a lay counsellor who works in a counselling centre sponsored by the local council of churches, and advertising itself as a 'pastoral counselling centre'
- a secular therapist who is working with a non-churchgoing client whose faith becomes a central part of their discussions together, and where matters of ultimate concern are a legitimate part of their agenda

Pastoral counselling is not necessarily confined to religious matters, and even when these are raised as a central issue they often act as pointers to other concerns. And although pastoral counselling usually takes place within the context of a place, person or institution identified with religion or spirituality, it may be the right term to use for matters of religious or spiritual concern in an otherwise ordinary counselling context. Although counsellors in other settings, in addition to pastoral counsellors, are often presented with immediate, down-to-earth issues, some clients move beyond initial presenting problems to an exploration of self and their relationship to others and their world, which involves deep and puzzling questions about life and death. Existentialist counselling (one of the humanistic therapies) also describes working with such concerns.[35]

Although these are some of the contexts and some of the concerns that are relevant to pastoral counselling, the question remains whether pastoral counselling also involves a particular type of work – for instance, the use of religious practices such as prayer, or theological explanations such as biblical answers to difficulties. The only fair way of describing the situation is to delineate the different approaches to pastoral counselling. There are some whose practice and understanding is no different from any other counsellor of their particular orientation: the only difference therefore is that they work within a setting where pastoral concerns are likely to be a 'way in' for the client. Others make it clear, but only if a client asks, that they too have their own faith, and may use the client's religious language and ideas as part of the therapy. They may, for example, pray with the client if the client requests this, or encourage the client to pray; but they might also, with other clients, keep well clear of anything remotely religious. Yet others, who tend to call themselves Christian counsellors, are explicit about their own faith, and may clearly include Christian belief and practice as part of the therapy they offer.

These alternative approaches to pastoral counselling can be clarified by a brief description of two separate organizations that are specifically concerned with pastoral counselling. The Association for Pastoral and Spiritual Care and Counselling (APSCC),[36] a founder division of the British Association for Counselling and Psychotherapy, includes in its membership Jews as well as Christians, and people who do not have any particular faith. It has links with the International Council for

Pastoral Care and Counselling. It began in 1970 as an informal association of groups that had pioneered pastoral counselling in Britain: the Westminster Pastoral Foundation, the Richmond Fellowship, Clinical Theology, the Salvation Army Counselling Service, the Dympna Centre (RC), the Raphael Centre (Jewish), etc. It now mainly consists of individual members as well as representatives of the founding associations. Both the groups and membership it represents vary greatly in their formal religious faith and commitment, and it describes itself as of value to different caring professionals and volunteers, 'Christians, Jews, other religions and non-committed'. The Association's objectives include a concern 'to raise standards in the teaching and exercise of pastoral care and counselling, and to draw upon the developing traditions and insights of theology and the social behavioural sciences wherever they lead to a greater understanding of human beings and offer resources to meet their needs'.[37]

It is an indication of the place counselling occupies in society that evangelical Christians (having at first had little to do with it except through those more liberal evangelicals who trained with Clinical Theology) have now formally adopted the counselling approach too. They have formed an Association of Christian Counsellors (ACC).[38] Like APSCC, ACC is concerned with training, standards, supervision and accreditation of counsellors. Also like APSCC, it sees itself working in the community without necessarily explicitly referring to the Christian faith. In the pastoral setting, however, 'Christian assumptions and aims will usually be *explicit*'.[39] It defines counselling that is distinctively Christian as 'that activity which seeks to help people towards constructive change and growth in any or every aspect of their lives through a caring relationship and within agreed relational boundaries according to Biblical assumptions, aims and methods practised within a framework of Christian commitment, insight and values'. In its Statement of Faith and Practice, ACC 'affirms the central truths of the Christian faith, as expressed in the Bible and in the historic creeds. In particular it affirms God as Triune, Father, Son and Holy Spirit, and it is committed to expressing the Lordship of Jesus Christ and the authority of Scripture in all areas of belief and practice'.

These two associations represent very different expressions of pastoral counselling. I need to state clearly at this point that

I find myself unable to agree with the tenor of the practice advocated by the ACC. While in its Statement of Faith and Practice it says that it is not the purpose of the Association to create a unified theory and practice of counselling by Christians, it is its purpose to 'seek specifically Christian perspectives on the assumptions, aims and methods of counselling'. This wish to impose a Christian interpretation upon counselling, and also to require of members a reference regarding their Christian faith, is foreign both to my theological and my counselling convictions, even though I accept that an association for *Christian* counsellors can expect such commitment of its members. The problem is not so much that there are counsellors who are Christian who might wish to join together in their own association, but that this gives support to a type of counselling called Christian counselling. This is not what I mean by pastoral counselling. While I hope therefore that this book may be of value to such Christian counsellors who are concerned with competence and accountability (aims of the ACC with which I concur), I need also to assure readers who find that expression of faith alien that I do not make these assumptions about pastoral counselling. I examine these matters further, in a way that I trust is also useful to counsellors who do not have a specific religious faith, but who are interested in how matters of faith can be a legitimate part of the counselling process.

Functioning as a pastoral counsellor, or in a pastoral setting, has certain difficulties, which are illustrated by my concerns in the last paragraph. Some clients approach the pastoral counsellor for support and confirmation of a faith that the pastoral counsellor does not share, and indeed may even deeply question. Other people might go out of their way to avoid a counsellor or a centre described as 'pastoral' because it appears to them to represent an approach that will involve 'preaching' or 'moralizing', or the imposition of religious answers. Identification with the Church or with a religious faith is a help for some clients, but a handicap for others. A pastoral counsellor has to be aware of what this particular 'label' could mean to those who come for help.

There is one final distinction to be made, that between pastoral counselling and pastoral care (again here referring to the religious or spiritual context rather than the educational setting). As in so much else in this chapter, I cannot avoid pointing to yet another overlap between these two areas of help, especially since the practice of counselling has given rise to the identification of counselling skills that can be used in visiting on behalf of the local church, etc. I use the term counselling or pastoral counselling in this book to describe both a specific task (what might be called formal counselling, within certain boundaries of time, frequency of meeting, and most probably in the counsellor's office) and a less structured approach to listening and responding to people (which I call counselling skills or informal counselling).

The ministry of pastoral care provides many opportunities for this informal approach, using counselling skills and knowledge of human development. The boundaries are frequently less clear-cut, but this need not prevent people talking and expressing themselves more fully. Knowledge of counselling techniques and of personality development (both normal and abnormal), which is essential in formal counselling, is no less valuable in pastoral care. Recognition of the way in which people use defences against seeing themselves as they really are, the way in which the helper can be regarded as a transference figure, and other topics that are introduced in later chapters, can enhance the provision of pastoral care as much as more formal counselling. Pastoral care involves other aspects than counselling alone, but within the context of a visit to a home, the preparation of a couple for marriage, in the few words that can be exchanged with mourners when on crematorium duty, or in the casual encounter in the street, the conversation can provide opportunities to go deeper than pleasantries or empty phrases – even on occasions leading to a more regular and formalized counselling contract.

Pastoral care is not, however, a watered-down version of counselling, any more than counselling is an inferior form of psychotherapy. The helper who meets a client for a greater length of time, in the relative privacy of his or her own office and in a situation where a person has clearly asked for help, can engage more easily in counselling than the same helper using counselling skills in an informal interaction, where there is less time to reflect and where distractions from other people are more likely to make concentration difficult. It is also sometimes harder for those who know or are known to the pastor, and who meet him or her in other settings, to be as frank and open about their emotions as they can be with a relative stranger.

Some pastors (ordained and lay) are involved in pastoral counselling as well as in pastoral care. Each aspect of their work enhances the other. Pastoral care will involve meeting people in their homes, and understanding issues face-to-face that are talked about in counselling. Similarly, the practice of more formal counselling enables the skills acquired to be more naturally applied in pastoral care. Many pastors (and indeed, other helpers) have no wish to become full-time counsellors, but there are always opportunities for seeing some people in a more defined counselling contract; and in turn, to apply that experience and learning to the other aspects of their ministry.

As Bernard Mobbs observes, the role of the counsellor does not always lie easily alongside the role of the ordained minister or parish priest.[40] He or she is probably in a more difficult situation than the social worker or psychiatrist who chooses to see some people for more formal counselling. Like the general practitioner (for whom it can be difficult to combine a necessary physical examination with formal counselling of the same patient), a member of the clergy (or a lay minister) meets parishioners in a variety of settings; and he or she has other roles, as preacher or teacher, in chairing committees, and even sometimes in friendship. Clergy often also have informal social contact with members of their congregation. This puts limitations on the formal counselling that they can offer to these particular people, although the solution is to make better use of shared or co-operative ministry. There is no reason why a pastor, aware of the value of counselling for a parishioner, might not suggest the parishioner sees a colleague who is trained in counselling from another parish or another town; and similarly, if a minister wishes to develop a counselling ministry of her or his own, there is considerable advantage in being able to offer such a valuable service to the clergy of neighbouring churches and parishes, who are also looking for people to whom they can refer their own pastoral contacts.

In our present society, counselling has achieved a high profile, and its practitioners and its professional bodies have become even more concerned about offering the public the highest standards of help. Some of the distinctions in this chapter clarify the respective roles that psychotherapists, counsellors and other helpers may have in their work. We have come considerably far along the path that Freud once envisaged as being desirable: the development of a professional way of offering care and therapy that belongs neither to medicine nor to the Church. It is still the case, however, that counselling in particular has a place as part of, as well as alongside, other professional disciplines, and in the care that people give voluntarily to people in a variety of needs. Just as other helpers, both salaried and volunteers, begin to learn how best to make use of counselling, so members of religious groups (ordained and lay) also have these opportunities to incorporate the creative and valuable insights of the counselling discipline into their own ministry.

NOTES

1. See, for example, the study by F. E. Fiedler, 'A comparison of therapeutic relationships, in psychoanalytic, non-directive and Adlerian therapy', *Journal of Consulting Psychology* (1950), 14, pp. 436–45. The question of comparative techniques and their efficacy is an exceedingly complex but fascinating one: see W. B. Stiles, D. A. Shapiro and R. Elliott, 'Are all psychotherapies equivalent?', *American Psychologist* (1986), 41, 2, pp. 165–80.
2. B. Bettelheim, *Freud and Man's Soul*. Penguin Books 1989, pp. 73–4.
3. S. Freud and J. Breuer, *Studies on Hysteria*. Penguin Freud Library 1974, volume 3, pp. 190–201.
4. E. Jones, *The Life and Work of Sigmund Freud*. Penguin Books 1964, pp. 358–9.
5. F. Alexander and T. M. French, *Psychoanalytic Therapy: Principles and Application*. New York: Ronald Press 1946.
6. D. H. Malan, *A Study of Brief Psychotherapy*. Tavistock Publications 1963; D. H. Malan, *The Frontier of Brief Psychotherapy*. Plenum Medical Books 1976.
7. A. Ryle, *Cognitive-Analytic Therapy: Active Participation in Change*. John Wiley 1990.
8. M. Jacobs, *Sigmund Freud*. Sage Publications 1992.
9. A. Adler, *The Practice and Theory of Individual Psychology*. Routledge & Kegan Paul 1929.
10. K. Horney, *New Ways in Psychoanalysis*. Routledge & Kegan Paul 1947.
11. E. Fromm, *Psychoanalysis and Religion*. Yale University Press 1950.
12. C. G. Jung, *Memories, Dreams and Reflections*. Fontana 1967; F. Fordham, *An Introduction to Jung's Psychology*. Penguin Books 1953.
13. E. Erikson, *Childhood and Society*. Penguin Books 1965.
14. J. Segal, *Melanie Klein*. Sage Publications 1992.
15. A. Freud, *Normality and Pathology in Childhood*. Penguin Books 1973.

16. W. R. D. Fairbairn is best approached through the writing of H. Guntrip, such as in *Personality Structure and Human Interaction*. Hogarth Press 1961.
17. M. Jacobs, *D. W. Winnicott*. Sage Publications 1995.
18. J. Bowlby, *Child Care and the Growth of Love*. Penguin Books 1972.
19. M. Jacobs, *Psychodynamic Counselling in Action*. Sage Publications 1999 (2nd edn), pp. 6–8 (*passim*).
20. D. Whitmore, *Psychosynthesis Counselling in Action*. Sage Publications 1991.
21. B. Thorne, *Carl Rogers*. Sage Publications 1992.
22. D. Mearns and B. Thorne, *Person-Centred Counselling in Action*. Sage Publications 1999 (2nd edn).
23. P. Clarkson, *Gestalt Counselling in Action*. Sage Publications 1989.
24. I. Stewart, *Transactional Analysis Counselling in Action*. Sage Publications 1989; I. Stewart, *Eric Berne*. Sage Publications 1992; E. Berne, *Games People Play*. Penguin Books 1964.
25. A. Lowen, *Bio-energetics*. Coventure 1977.
26. I. A. Greenberg, *Psychodrama: Theory and Therapy*. New York: Behavioral Publications 1974.
27. A. Janov, *The Primal Scream*. New York: Putnams 1970.
28. A. Guggenbuhl-Craig, *Power in the Helping Professions*. Dallas: Spring 1971.
29. W. Dryden, *Rational-Emotive Counselling in Action*. Sage Publications 1989.
30. P. Trower, A. Casey and W. Dryden, *Cognitive-Behavioural Counselling in Action*. Sage Publications 1988.
31. W. Glasser, *Reality Therapy*. New York: Harper & Row 1965.
32. J. McLeod, *An Introduction to Counselling*. Open University Press 1998 (2nd edn), p. 331.
33. P. Wachtel, *Psychoanalysis and Behavior Therapy*. New York: Basic Books 1977.
34. Also see, for example, in H. Kaplan, *The New Sex Therapy*. Penguin Books 1978.
35. E. van Deurzen-Smith, *Existential Counselling in Practice*. Sage Publications 1987.
36. Details of the Association of Pastoral and Spiritual Care and Counselling are available from The Secretary, APSCC, British Association for Counselling and Psychotherapy, 1 Regent Place, Rugby, Warks CV21 2PJ.
37. Quotations are taken from APSCC publicity literature.
38. For further details, contact the Association of Christian Counsellors, King's House, 175 Wokingham Road, Reading RG6 1LU.
39. This and other quotations are taken from the Policy Document of the Association of Christian Counsellors, 12 May 1992.
40. M. Jacobs and B. Mobbs, 'Therapy, counselling and pastoral care', *Contact – Interdisciplinary Journal of Pastoral Studies* (1965), 85, pp. 2–8.

PART TWO

Counselling in Practice

CHAPTER THREE

First Principles

It is clear from much of the research that has been undertaken on the effectiveness of therapists and counsellors that, despite there being differences of method, of theoretical understanding, and also various levels of experience, a consistent and key factor in the felt success of therapy is the relationship between the helper and the client. Counsellors may in one sense be born, not made. Their natural disposition, and also their character, formed through their family experiences and adult relationships, is as important as their knowledge and technical skills. It is heartening when counsellors who are starting out (or at least some of them) achieve so much when they are accidentally allocated a client who turns out to have severe difficulties (such that normally only an experienced therapist would tackle). The strong wish to help in such counsellors, their tenacity, and sometimes even their innocence, can sometimes work miracles.

It is important to have this in mind at the start. But bear in mind also that I have qualified these remarks about the effectiveness of counsellors who are starting out by suggesting that this applies to 'some of them'. Good counselling is not just a question of being the right type of person. What comes naturally to those with innate abilities can be developed in training so that in time such people become very fine therapists indeed. Others, who at the beginning of their training are either too active or too anxious, over-helpful or lost for words, can be taught skills and encouraged to look at the way they relate to their clients so that eventually they become dependable counsellors, able to provide valuable help to the majority of their clients. Some will already have, and others may develop, what might be called a flair for counselling which distinguishes their work. But some people, however much training they have, will never become good counsellors. Their abilities lie in other directions.

There are particular skills involved in counselling and therapy that need to be learned. Those who have natural ability already use them, and need to become aware of the even greater use they can make of them. These are often known as 'micro-skills' because they are small, often apparently obvious, ways of listening and responding that together form a therapeutic attitude. Many of these micro-skills are common to the various counselling approaches outlined in the last chapter. What a counsellor primarily seeks to create is a setting and an ambience in which clients (a technical term that I continue to use for its convenience) can express themselves – both what they think and what they feel – as fully as possible. These skills are more than social skills, because counsellors develop a different way of relating – one that provides a place for the 'still small voice' to be heard. A fly on the wall of a counselling session might take some time getting used to the relative silence of the counsellor: the calm, apparently relaxed, manner; the lack of a definite agenda; and the careful timing of her or his interventions. Much of this has been built upon natural ability, but it also requires training and the learning of definite skills.

Such developed natural abilities are often sufficient when working with well-motivated clients who have a clear idea of what it is that is troubling them, and who need space and support through a time of crisis. There are other clients, as well as occasions in the course of straightforward counselling, where even greater skill is called for on the part of the counsellor. Although in this chapter I concentrate upon the basic skills that a counsellor uses to facilitate the conversation, and to help a client to express herself or himself more fully, it is often by returning to this underlying way of relating that even the most difficult situations are eased, and a way found through the defensiveness, the panic, or the complex conflict of feelings, of the clients who are hardest to work with.

Some of those who start training as counsellors find these skills too obvious for words and are impatient to move on, but there is no substitute for this solid foundation of technique. Others are worried that in using the term 'technique', counsellors are being artificial. Yet it is not enough to assume that personal qualities are sufficient, or that helpers, by virtue of their wish to care, automatically possess the right manner. 'Tender loving care' is a good prescription for any doctor to give a patient, but it is only recently that medical schools have woken up to the fact that this does not necessarily form part of brilliant academic results.

'Techniques' are not the same as 'tricks', nor are they a substitute for sincere human relationships. The analogy that best describes what I want to set out is that of learning to drive. To be able to drive a car opens up many horizons, provides opportunities to meet people, enlarges the number of places to visit, and helps manage more easily many of the necessities of daily life. Small wonder that learning to drive has become a virtual necessity for every young person. It is an inescapable aspect of preparation for adult life. Learning to drive means mastering a large number of micro-skills; these micro-skills are not ends in themselves, but contribute in sum to the ability to drive and, as a result of this ability, to appreciate all that such increased mobility brings with it.

Learning the basic skills of counselling widens the horizons of the helper, provides opportunities to 'meet' more people at a different level, enlarges the opportunities to help, and facilitates any necessary management aspects in a caring or helping relationship. Counselling training enhances the capacity to listen, and develops the art of gently exploring what is said.

The basic skills are as numerous as those involved in learning to drive a car: steering, footbrake, handbrake, clutch, accelerator, gear lever, rear mirror, side mirror, indicators, lights and, when it is wet, pressing the windscreen wiper lever rather than the horn! It is all very confusing at first, but soon becomes second nature – and we eventually travel from A to B without needing to think about driving skills at all. The basic skills of counselling are as straightforward to describe as learning to drive, although perhaps a little more difficult to put into practice. Old ways of relating, or ways that are fine in other settings, die hard. Ultimately the new skills become so well integrated that counsellors cease to be aware that they are using them; in the beginning, though, it can be difficult to hold them all together at the same time, and we fear learnt skills must be artificial ones.

When listening to people who are able to express what they are thinking and feeling, it is often enough to use just the basic counselling skills, just as when learning to drive it does not take long to master steering, changing gear and braking – particularly when there is little traffic about. Unfortunately, to pass a driving test you are not permitted to take it in such ideal conditions. The real difficulties for the learner driver come from the inescapable presence of other road-users, and from having to use the car on roads that have sharp corners, steep hills, traffic lights and pedestrian crossings. The learner driver also has to learn how to reverse round corners, make three-point turns, park in small places, and execute other necessary manoeuvres. There are similar complications in counselling. Some clients are not self-aware, find it difficult to put what they feel into words, or even come for help from motives that are not always on the side of the counsellor – for example, some clients are 'sent', or see everything as everyone else's fault. That is why, in addition to the basic skills, counsellors have to learn more advanced skills and approaches.

Nearly every counselling method emphasizes the value of listening, of remembering, of not being critical, of trying to understand, as well as the necessity of a good working relationship. Because none of this is enough in some of the more awkward situations that a counsellor or client may face, different counselling methods have developed various responses to be used with difficult clients, or with clients who have particular difficulties. For example, what should a counsellor do when a client who appears to be talking freely is in fact going round in circles and avoiding the issues that the helper thinks are important? These situations require the refinement of basic skills and a deeper understanding of what might be happening to the client and in the relationship between the counsellor and the client. I examine some of these aspects, as well as the creation of a good working environment for the use of counselling skills, in subsequent chapters. It is with regard to some of these points that different counselling approaches vary.

For the time being I stay with the essential foundations for counselling, and those counselling skills that can also be used in informal counselling situations. These are not skills that can be learnt simply by reading a book. The value of training courses is that they provide opportunities to practise these skills in a relatively safe environment; and at some point every counsellor starting out has to try them out 'live' and 'for real', because this (and supervision) is where the greatest learning will take place. In another book in this series called *Swift to Hear*,[1] I have at greater length set out guidelines for listening to people and for responding to them, together with exercises that can be used in training groups. These guidelines are not rules – although rules do exist in counselling and are often summarized in a counsellor's or an agency's code of ethics. The guidelines that I have developed, and summarize below, are not hard and fast laws that can never be broken, but they are sound principles that should nearly always be followed. Sometimes they are framed as 'avoid ... where possible'. These are the 'do's' and 'don't's' of good counselling practice, and which in the end will become second nature.

1. LISTEN

There are three aspects to listening, which are not always easy to combine. The first is to listen to the client with undivided attention. We rarely listen to people so carefully that we put out of mind our own concerns, our own constructions or interpretations of what they are saying, and we often colour our hearing with our prejudices. We often hear what we want to hear, not what is being said. We listen to some details and we ignore others. We take to be important what we find interesting, and not necessarily what the other person regards as most significant to them. Above all, it is not easy to learn to listen without interrupting, or without feeling you have to make an intelligent response. What I am stressing here as the first guideline is just to listen, simply concentrating on what the client is saying.

However, such plain listening is complicated because a counsellor also listens to what else the client is 'saying', that is, the meaning under the words being spoken. This is listening at another level, to the less obvious feelings and thoughts that are not being expressed verbally, but that may be just beneath the surface. It is what I call the 'bass line' as in a piece of music, although the similar sounding 'base line' also points to the same hidden meanings. One way of listening in this way is to catch the tone of a person's voice, which may differ from the content of the phrases they use – for example, a person's voice may catch with a hint of choked-back tears. It is helpful too to watch for other signs of hidden feelings: a clenched fist perhaps showing anger, or eyes watering showing a person feels upset, even if their words convey a different message. Listening in this way is like deliberately listening out for the bass line in a piece of music, while still concentrating, as in the first type of listening, upon the obvious melody. Sometimes the client is unaware of hidden feelings, so the counsellor is very careful to choose the right moment and the right words to point them out to the client. A tentative suggestion is often necessary to test out whether the counsellor's perception is indeed correct.

The third aspect to listening is to listen to yourself, and to what might be called your own 'still small voice'. This further dimension to listening is sometimes called 'the third ear'. It is by imagining yourself in a client's situation that you can some-times spot other reactions that the client is hinting at but not saying. Listening to yourself helps you to listen beneath the obvious. But the first aspect to listening still applies: we can mistake our own interpretations and be influenced by our own prejudices by hearing – as I indicated above – what we want to hear, not what we are being told. For this reason a counsellor has to be even more careful about giving expression to this type of inner listening. Nevertheless, this type of listening is sometimes the most helpful listening of all, since we all have the ability to identify with other people, which at times can be almost uncanny in its accuracy. These are abilities that coun-sellors need to develop, but that also need to be used with the greatest care. Certainly there is one way of identifying that should nearly always be avoided, and that is relating your own experiences directly to the client. It is not helpful to say 'I was in that situation once – I remember how dreadful it was', or 'I would have done this'. Only on rare occasions does a coun-sellor's own experience actually help the client. Counsellors are not there to tell their own stories; this risks turning the focus on to the counsellors and perhaps even eliciting sympathy for them.

Nevertheless, the counsellor's experience, which may be remembered at these times of listening to yourself, or the counsellor's feelings as he or she hears the client's story, can be used indirectly, again tentatively and carefully: 'I wonder whether you felt . . .', or 'What you are saying makes me feel angry on your behalf, but you do not seem to be concerned.' This type of listening, to yourself, and to what is not quite so obvious, is close to what counsellors call 'empathy' – the ability to put yourself in the shoes of the person speaking, or get under the skin of your client, and from that angle to reflect some of the feelings and thoughts that the client is not expressing directly. Empathy is not a skill that can easily be taught or learned: it is a quality that some people have more than others. But it can be encouraged and developed by attending to what we are thinking and monitoring what we are feeling, and discriminating between what belongs to us and what may be triggered off in us by what the client is saying.

2. REMEMBER

It is a rare experience to be carefully listened to. But what is even better, because it shows just how well you have been heard, is when someone remembers you and recalls what you have said:

> As we were drawing to the end of our last hour, I asked Brenda how she felt about our sessions. I had experienced our early meetings as tense, although I was aware how the atmosphere had changed, and I shared my perception with her, inviting her own opinion. 'Yes, it was difficult to begin with,' Brenda replied, 'but I began to trust you when I realized that you actually remembered what I was saying; and sometimes you remembered what I had told you from a while back.' It was only then that I also remembered that in one of our first sessions Brenda had asked somewhat aggressively whether I kept notes. I had replied (which was true in her case) that I didn't, and she had responded more gently that she thought I might need some way of remembering what people said.

It is surprising just how much we are all capable of remembering. Counselling has convinced me of the amount we are able to store away, which bubbles back to the surface when it is relevant. Remembering is so much easier when we listen carefully (with undivided attention), but also when the amount we say ourselves is kept in check. It is much more difficult to remember 'chatty' sessions, much easier to recall those that were allowed to flow, with the client really taking the initiative. It is obviously important to remember names, dates, events and other details (which a counsellor can record as an *aide-mémoire* after the session). Referring to people by name or recognizing that a particular date or time of the year has come round again is important to the client, and may even impress the client with the care that the counsellor takes; but especially valuable to the more experienced counsellor are the times when he or she remembers apparently trivial details, or when little phrases and words seem to have some significance.

Counsellors sometimes have a large number of clients, and those who use counselling skills in the caring professions meet many more people in the course of their work. It is not easy to remember all the details in such circumstances. Careful listening at the time, however, enables the helper to make notes after the counselling session. Unless needing to note specific information that the client knows is of practical use (such as the client's address for emergency contact), it is unwise to make a record of the session at the time: there is a risk of creating too clinical an atmosphere, and note-taking prevents a counsellor from listening attentively as well as from observing facial and other non-verbal expressions.

There are other ways of recording, and therefore remembering, such as taping sessions. Although there is some value in this for supervision purposes when a counsellor is in training, it is not a method I recommend for most counselling situations. Clients can be put off by the presence of a machine, and listening to tapes afterwards is a time-consuming process. Remembering counselling sessions for supervision is of course very important, and taping is the only reliable means of ensuring perfect recall: but there are other ways of reporting one's work in supervision, such as verbatim accounts (for relative precision), and the free associations of the counsellor's memory of the session (for getting in touch with the less obvious aspects of the work). These matters are related more to supervision than to basic counselling skills, and should be discussed by a counsellor with a supervisor or trainer.[2]

3. RELAX AND STAY CALM

There are a number of reasons why the setting in which coun-selling takes place needs to be a relaxing and calming one. Freud at first used hypnosis, then later abandoned it in favour of straightforward listening. However, he did not abandon the couch, because he wanted his clients to be relaxed, and to talk from an almost dream-like state. Today a couch would make most people anxious rather than relaxed (at least at first), but it is still important that a counsellor provides comfort, peace and low levels of sensory stimulation. The helper wishes to free the client to express whatever comes to mind without being over-self-conscious: no jarring noises; privacy and freedom from interruption (especially where possible from the telephone ringing); no falsely bright colours; occasional furnishings and pictures that do not distract; comfortable seating arranged at an angle to avoid the embarrassment and tension that can come from 'eyeball-to-eyeball confrontation'.

Above all, and this is difficult when there is so much else for a helper to think about, a counsellor needs to convey in her or his own manner and mannerisms a sense of calm, a clear indication of being receptive, of listening without judging, and without being shocked or surprised. This is not so much a counsel of perfection as it first seems, because it is not possible for a counsellor to avoid involuntary reactions: there are obviously times when the counsellor feels very anxious, panicky, shocked and critical. (I will examine some of the occasions for responses in later chapters.) What is important is *not* to show this to the client, which sometimes does happen by responding without thinking, or by giving away unhelpful reactions through facial expressions or body movements.

The child psychotherapist Donald Winnicott wrote about the need for a *facilitating environment*, both in child-rearing and in the provision of therapy.[3] It is this that this guideline seeks to encourage, first in the counsellor and the counselling setting, and then in the client as well.

4. AVOID SPEAKING TOO SOON, TOO OFTEN AND TOO MUCH

Part of the art of counselling is learning to listen. Another part of the art is learning to contain, and holding on to what the client expresses without needing to reply immediately, and without responding inappropriately. A further part of the art lies in knowing how to reply to the many different ways in which the client relates to the counsellor: I mean here both how the client relates his or her story, and the actual relationship which is then built (or fails to be built) between them.

I have set out the different types of responses that are helpful at greater length in *Swift to Hear*, together with practice exercises.[4] A counsellor helps clients to relate: both what they want to say, as well as to make relationships. Responses that are particularly helpful include:

- paraphrasing and summing up from time to time what the client appears to be saying
- reflecting what the client appears to be feeling or saying beneath the surface, including the counsellor's empathic understanding of the client
- picking up a phrase and simply repeating it, as an invitation to the client to develop what they are saying
- asking questions (although it is good practice to keep questions to a minimum, using them when something is unclear or when more definite information is needed that might help fill in missing facts)

Except where precise information is needed, it is helpful to phrase questions as openly as possible, so that the client is given a range of options in answering them. Again, all this is fully discussed in *Swift to Hear*.[5] All helpers find it very tempting to ask questions. Counsellors in training discover just how many questions they ask, many of which are irrelevant or change the subject. Questions are often used as an immediate 'silence-filler', because the counsellor is too anxious to pause and think of a more relevant response.

5. AVOID LOADED REMARKS

Perhaps for most people the most worrying aspect of talking to anyone is that they will not like us, or not approve of us, or be critical of us. This particularly applies when what we need to say is about intimate matters, and times when we have indeed had feelings or experiences that are strange and unfamiliar, or socially unacceptable and forbidden. When people approach others for help, especially those who are perceived as experts like doctors, lawyers, clergy and counsellors, they usually have good expectations of them. They are in one way safe people in whom to confide, because they are seen as knowledgeable in handling people's problems. But these experts are also authority figures, and as such are invested with a lot of power. Their disapproval is worse than anyone else's; they carry images of being judgemental as well as caring. In terms of what I shall later call transference, professional people and people in caring positions are invested with both good parent images (they will make it better) but also bad parent images (they will be angry).

Not surprisingly, phrases such as 'Why on earth did you do that?' or 'That was a silly thing to do' carry messages reminiscent of parental anger. But even more gently worded responses, like 'I wonder if that was wise', may put some people off being open in case they show themselves up or, at worst, drive a client away. It is so easy to be critical, or to be perceived as judgemental, even when not intending it. It is preferable to work towards helping people make their own assessment of themselves or of their actions – e.g. 'Did you feel that was a good thing to do?', 'You sound a bit uneasy about what you felt', and 'What else might you have said, given the difficult circumstances?' There are many ways in which a counsellor can inadvertently wound a client without intending to, so it is vital to develop appropriate responses and learn how to avoid inappropriate responses to the various thoughts and feelings that clients express.[6]

The various types of loaded remark that should be avoided include exclamations of surprise or shock, expressions of over-concern, being condescending or patronizing, hints of ridicule or blame, appearing rejecting and intolerant, and also using flattery or excessive praise and offering unnecessary reassurance. And it is not just her or his words that a counsellor needs to watch: all these inappropriate responses can be seen in facial expressions, emphasizing the earlier guideline of remaining calm and relaxed, although not impassive. While avoiding these inappropriate reactions, counsellors also need to know when it is right to offer reassurance and sympathy, and how to convey open-mindedness, even when a client is being irrational or holds quite alien values.

This summary of the basic guidelines for counselling includes ways of listening and responding that are valuable in situations other than formal counselling, but where counselling skills are applicable. Teachers, general practitioners, the police, as well as lay visitors for local churches, can all adopt these ways of communicating with others in their work, even though they obviously have to carry out other duties as well as listening, and have at times to adopt quite different ways of relating to the people they meet. Many of these micro-skills may seem like common sense, and just natural forms of expression. This is quite true, although it appears that some people have either forgotten how to be natural, or that their professional role has got in the way of ordinary human ways of responding. These basic elements in the helping relationship are not so elementary that they always come naturally. Simple though it sounds to be told to listen, to be calm, or to avoid speaking too much, these are not in fact simple skills. These few pages may not hold the fascination of the more complex situations and advanced guidelines that the following chapters explore, but I cannot stress too much that these basic skills must support and indeed shine through every aspect of counselling practice. No one, especially counsellors who begin to feel more confident as they gain experience and want to take short cuts, can afford to lose touch with these very first lessons of all.

NOTES

1. M. Jacobs, *Swift to Hear*. SPCK 2000 (2nd edn).
2. See also my 'answer' in *Questions and Answers on Counselling in Action* (ed. W. Dryden), Sage Publications 1993; and, if still available, two articles in *Counselling* (April 1981), 36, obtainable from the British Association for Counselling and Psychotherapy, 1 Regent Place, Rugby, Warks CV21 2PJ: M. Jacobs, 'Setting the record straight', and Windy Dryden's 'Some uses of audio-tape procedures in counselling: a personal view'.
3. D. W. Winnicott, *The Maturational Processes and the Facilitating Environment*. Hogarth Press 1965. See also Jacobs, *Swift to Hear*, pp. 41–4.

4. Jacobs, *Swift to Hear*, ch. 3.
5. ibid., pp. 51-4.
6. A useful summary of these and similar points can be found in L. R. Wolberg, *The Technique of Psychotherapy*. Heinemann 1967, pp. 584-90.

CHAPTER FOUR

Starting with Yourself

If part of listening is that counsellors should listen to the 'still small voice' within themselves, their ability to do this is obviously linked to their self-knowledge. They need to know what they are listening for in themselves. Yet, at the risk of being circular, counsellors will not know themselves unless they start to listen to themselves. It is because it is so hard to break into this circularity that one of the best ways for counsellors to learn about themselves is to go for counselling, or to make sure that the training course that they attend includes plenty of opportunity for personal exploration and feedback from one's peers.

I make no apologies for delaying the reader from learning about the practice of counselling, first (as in the last chapter) by discussing basic listening, and then (in this chapter) by looking at basic motives. Helping people is not just about caring for others, or putting others first at some personal cost. We have our own reasons for wanting to help others, and there are many elements of personal satisfaction in counselling that need to be recognized if the counsellor's own needs are not to get in the way of the client's welfare. Counsellors, as well as clients, can be diminished when the less obvious motives for helping go unacknowledged; and at worst, these hidden factors can lead to emotional damage to either party in the counselling relationship.

These are strong words, and with good reason. There is a growing number of counsellors, and more of them than ever before are offering a service to the public. There are also, inevitably, more opportunities for exploitation and abuse of the public. Counselling and therapy are open to the criticism that it can be dangerous to interfere and intrude upon another person's suffering, however well-meaning the counsellor and however willing the client. Some of those who hold out the promise of relief cause more suffering than they relieve.

The increased recognition of the importance of counselling has perhaps inevitably, but still unfortunately, led to the opportunity for some people who are not as sensitive as might be hoped to practise as counsellors. Occasions of inappropriate responses, ineffective promises, or even abusive practice are reported by clients who have suffered at the hands of counsellors, who in many cases have not even realized what damage they might have caused. Such bad practice (it is not necessarily deliberate malpractice) makes it essential that counsellors in training and in practice should give the highest priority not simply to the development of good practice (which is largely a matter of conscious effort), but also to their unconscious reasons for counselling, which might just as much trip their clients up. There is little more precious that people can share with us than their most intimate thoughts and feelings. Counsellors therefore have just as much at stake in responsibility for their clients as surgeons have for their patients or engineers have for an aircraft's safety. There are life-and-death issues at stake, and I do not simply mean by this suicidal risks. The risk of suicide exists in a counsellor's work with some clients, but not with most. A client's self-harm may be the most obvious fear that a counsellor has, but it is the more subtle ways in which counsellors can hurt their clients that matter as much. Counselling not only involves helping people with important life decisions or emotional difficulties: it also frequently consists of working with people who are already emotionally damaged when they ask for help, and for whom further harm through careless counselling could well be a crushing blow.

This responsibility is all the more difficult to exercise because, unlike the surgeon or the engineer, for whom the potential dangers are fairly obvious and who can depend upon sophisticated equipment, counsellors have only themselves to offer, with little back-up except their supervisor; and supervisors are not present in the counselling session. In offering themselves, counsellors cannot help but offer all of themselves, including their unconscious wishes and fears. Like the teacher, a counsellor's effectiveness depends to some extent (some might say to a very large extent) upon personal factors.

We know that it helps recovery if a patient trusts a surgeon, and that a pre-operation visit can help create this trust; but the surgeon's ability to heal lies in medical knowledge and surgical skills. An engineer's effectiveness depends upon technical skills, but does not depend overmuch upon personal emotions, unless personal pressures lead to slapdash work. In different jobs the relationship between technical skills and personal factors varies.

Counsellors need the technical skills and practical knowledge described in this book, but none of this is sufficient. They also need to be aware of the obvious and the more hidden factors in themselves, which will one way or the other influence their work and therefore their clients. It is therefore essential for counsellors to cultivate continuous self-awareness, since this will underpin all other learning. Such self-knowledge is indeed one of the aims of counselling offered to clients, so counsellors cannot expect less of themselves. 'Physician, heal thyself' is an apt phrase. What Hugh Eadie writes of the clergy is just as true of other helpers: 'Considering his potential influence on the lives of those to whom he ministers, the clergyman's health has pragmatic, psychological and theological repercussions which cannot be treated casually.'[1]

If it is difficult to teach practical skills through a book, it is impossible to teach self-knowledge to the reader: that is an essentially personal task, which can perhaps only be effectively done with the help of others. Indeed, it is this principle, that it takes the presence of another to help me see myself, that lies at the heart of the therapeutic relationship. I can only write generally, hoping that I may touch upon a number of personal factors that are sure to be present in most of those who read this chapter. Perhaps what I write will trigger off awareness of aspects in my readers of which they had previously been unaware. I run the risk of causing some anxiety, because it is difficult to read books on psychology or therapy without discovering all the worst aspects in oneself! While I do not wish to cause unhelpful anxiety (I too have to choose my words carefully), it is my intention to encourage a measure of self-awareness and self-understanding.

Some of the ideas I consider are based upon research. There are inevitably arguments about the amount of weight that can validly be attached to statistics, and to the opinions based upon them. Since it is claimed, for example, that up to two-thirds of clergy (and therefore it is implied other caring professionals too) show some of the characteristics I examine in this chapter, we need to be careful about what this figure means. Statistics produce a generalized statement from the particular. I do not imply that every motivation or personal characteristic I describe applies to every reader. This is only a guide to thinking about oneself.

Apart from the help that another or others give in self-awareness, a responsible counselling practice or ministry includes regular supervision. This may be 'one-to-one', or in a pair, or in a small group. It may be with an experienced counsellor or with peers of equal standing. Supervision, like personal awareness, often enables features of practice to be seen which are not obvious to the counsellor. Being at one remove clarifies vision in the same way as standing back from a painting provides a different perspective. It is encouraging that so many people ask for supervision, not just because it is required of them, but because they have come to appreciate the learning and the support that comes from it.[2] Counsellors should also seriously consider experiencing the counselling process as a client. It is still a characteristic of many helpers that they find it difficult to ask for help for themselves, although some may find it more palatable by calling it 'training'.

Those who do not recognize themselves at all, in any of the descriptions in this chapter, might need to take a closer look. But those who are unable to find anything good about themselves, after reading this chapter, may also become aware of how critical they are of themselves. Since one of the basic guidelines is to learn how to accept clients, whatever they say, without obvious horror, without damning judgement and without rejecting them, counsellors need to learn to be as kind to themselves. Accepting is not the same as condoning, and it is essential to accept either oneself or others before going on to examine what particular behaviour, thoughts and feelings might be about. It is difficult for those who work in the helping professions, particularly when they are in training, especially when self-assessment is closely bound up with assessment for professional qualification. In this chapter I do not intend to accuse, or to condemn, or to sort the sheep from the goats. I do condemn lack of awareness when it damages clients, but here

I want to encourage the reader to go deeper than any initial shame or guilt towards a level of insight that will not only bear upon counselling practice, but that will also lead eventually to greater fulfilment for the helper.

In essence I view the characteristics of the helping personality as 'neutral' in themselves. They are personal features that can either be used constructively or destructively in counselling and other helping. Recognizing our true motives for helping, and accepting them rather than projecting them, can release us to work more effectively. Where we discover motives that could be to the detriment of others, understanding them may help temper their influence, and so minimize the risks of manipulating and damaging clients.

I worked once with a client who was a social worker. She was afraid to confront some of her most difficult clients with their manipulative behaviour. They were often out when she called or, if they were in, she found herself coming away from interviews with them full of resentment. At the same time she found herself being persuaded to take their side against other agencies, and she felt that she generally went along too readily with what these clients expected of her. She complained that she found it difficult to show them any of the anger she felt.

Knowing how to handle one's own anger is a common difficulty for a helper. If this social worker had been more at ease with her angry feelings, she might have been able to confront her clients more easily. That is not to say that there was no value in her being 'slow to anger'. Others might have vented their feelings impulsively and destructively, which of course is what this person feared doing. We worked together to get in touch with her anxieties about being angry, and to see just how very angry she in fact was with being pushed around. She was then able to confront these particular clients, in a way that was considered but firm. She drew upon using her natural disposition towards a gentle approach, so that while she expressed herself forcefully enough to make her point, she was not so blunt as to destroy the confidence her clients had in her. Indeed, perhaps it was only then that she was more able to cultivate and keep their trust, which she had rightly felt to be so important. Being soft had done nothing to help her clients feel they could trust her: they must have sensed that pushed too far, she could blow up, as she herself feared.

Rayner observes in his book *Human Development* that many types of work entail mastery of skills, and also of anxieties. The dustman has to master disgust, the pilot the fear of heights, or a nurse the fear of death.[3] The particular anxieties that many counsellors have are about handling feelings of love, aggression, sexuality and power. Training for counselling and therapy requires firstly mastery of the *anxiety* about such feelings, rather than, as most starting-out helpers assume, mastery of the *feelings themselves*. When we can accept the presence of such feelings in ourselves, and learn how to use them appropriately in counselling, we will also be much less afraid of them in our clients.

THE DESIRE TO BE LOVING

One of the most common motivations for helping is the need to see oneself, or be seen by others, as caring, compassionate and loving. Such a motivation clearly has positive features to it: it contributes to the gentleness, patience and tolerance necessary in a counsellor. The problem with such an ideal is that there is a danger of it turning into an over-idealized concept, with an antithetical opposite that must at all times be avoided. One antithesis is that helpers strive too hard to be caring and good, sometimes taking away their clients' ability to help themselves and decide for themselves. Another antithesis is that helpers tend to feel they should not be concerned for themselves; that they must not allow themselves to have 'negative' emotions of their own such as impatience and anger with clients, or dependence upon others and the need to be needed. They believe their care, for instance, must stem from pure non-possessive and non-sexual love.

This can be a recipe for repression of the helper's own feelings, including their feelings about clients, which are reckoned to be taboo. Such repression of negative or selfish feelings (as they are thought to be) can impose considerable stress on the helper. Helpers seem to find it more difficult to tolerate such negative feelings in themselves, even when they readily accept them in those they help. Such helpers fight the situation by redoubling their care for others, and absorbing clients' feelings and their own feelings until they can contain them no longer.

It is then that these feelings burst out, perhaps by the helper threatening the client. Or the feelings can be turned inwards against the counsellor, manifesting perhaps in depression, anxiety or burn-out. Alternatively, counsellors who deny their own feelings may find themselves employing more subtle ways of expressing them: anger that is bottled up may turn into resentment of all or some of those who want help, and may be converted into missing or forgetting appointments, changing times around, starting late, or expressing interventions in a rather vindictive manner. Helpers begin to take their frustrations out on others outside the therapeutic setting – partners, colleagues and families can easily become the recipients of exaggerated and unjustified reactions that belong in fact to the work with clients. Anger and other negative feelings can also be turned inwards on the self, so that the helper experiences less and less self-esteem.

Those who would help others are not always so careful about looking after themselves. Counsellors could do well to look again at that far from outdated injunction to 'love your neighbour, as *yourself*'. In effect, those who devote their lives to caring for others often need to be loved and cared for themselves, but feel that they have to disown that need or are frightened of that need. This does not prevent such a need coming out in other ways, so that although they do not deliberately seek it, their *work* can bring helpers the admiration and approval they would like for *themselves*. Helpers may receive praise, at least face to face, for the sacrifices they have made and the valuable work they do. Behind their backs it can be another matter, because those who give too much can be taken for 'suckers' or be seen as 'gluttons for punishment'.

The wish to care, to give love, and to find pleasure in helping, are all of course natural expressions of the nurturing relationship of parent and child, and in adult life of the co-operative spirit of a community. The problem in counselling, even more so than with other expressions of care, is that it is difficult to know exactly what is the best way of caring. It can take a long time before there are any results, and in the meantime the client may see the counsellor as far from helpful. 'You don't do anything: I don't know why I come' is not an isolated complaint rarely heard in counselling. Because it is normal for a person to have their work valued, counsellors can look too hard for affirmation from their clients; or, more likely, they find it hard to take up the hints the client drops of disillusion and frustration with the counsellor, who is not turning out to be the 'saviour' they had hoped for. Helpers may therefore find it difficult to accept the criticism or anger that would otherwise be expressed towards them by their clients. As far as the clients are concerned, the opportunity to vent these negative feelings, and to know that they do not damage the counsellor in doing so, is often a turning point in their ability to express their negative feelings appropriately in other relationships. However, if a helper is too desperate to preserve a 'good' and 'nice' image, this may well result in opportunities being lost for clients to express themselves more fully.

One way in which helpers care more for themselves, especially when their upbringing has stressed the importance of being 'unselfish', is by projecting their hidden wish for love on to the client, and surrounding the client with the care and attention that the helper really wishes he or she could have. Although this may work powerfully for some of those clients who need care and value care, and they may grow as a result of it (unaware that their helper is depleting), there are some clients who are very demanding and who make their demands felt. If the helper neglects her or his own needs, and at the same time is afraid of accepting such clients' negative feelings at being let down, and not getting enough, the helper can be in real difficulty.

There are counsellors, just as there are people in the Church, who have an over-optimistic view of human nature. They do not spot those people who will take advantage of their help, and who will constantly test out a counsellor's patience, pushing harder and harder until they are rejected. If he or she is desperate to be useful, a helper may give too long a time in one session; or too frequent appointments to those in distress; or may drop everything to respond to a cry of distress, without first assessing the seriousness of the situation or the wisdom of an instant solution. Responding blindly to others' needs is not just bad practice. Some people, who are particularly hungry for love, also feel guilty about having their demands met, and may break off from the counsellor who responds too readily. They are frightened of the power they have over others. If such people do not break off contact, the counsellor may begin to feel drained and increasingly tired, and may even consider breaking off the contract and referring them elsewhere, rejecting the client who 'always felt this would happen anyway'. (It may, of course, be necessary to make a referral to people with more appropriate skills or expertise when a client's state is too much for the skills of a particular counsellor. What I am describing here is referring a person on too late, out of sheer desperation, and not as a result of careful thought and planning in the initial stages of counselling.)

It is very sad when all this happens, but some people do not seem to change however much love is showered upon them. They destroy loving gestures, they ignore the positive affirmation given to them; they soak up love and concern, but it makes little difference. They are not necessarily angry – indeed, they may appear gentle, although very needy. They can express anger in a passive way, making everyone else angry around them. They can sometimes also explode, and leave the helper for good, with the helper wondering what he or she has done wrong and what more they could have done. Some of these people too may be helped at the point when they can recognize how angry they are and can express their negative feelings in a safe situation. The counsellor (or indeed any other helper) who gives and gives, and fails to face the passive-aggressive behaviour, and who may well deny her or his own anger and frustration, may unwittingly be doing a disservice. It is like giving to an alcoholic begging for money, who then abuses the helper's generosity by spending it on more drink, and so puts off facing the desperation of his or her condition.

The converse of this picture is that counsellors who need admiration are prone to hang on to those clients who tell them how valuable they are, and who flatter them in other ways. The counsellor may favour working with people who are attractive and co-operative clients, who say all the right things and who 'get better'. The counsellor who looks for results may be unaware that some of these people are themselves anxious to convey a good impression because, like the counsellor, they are afraid of being rejected if they show a less flattering side.

THE DESIRE TO BE USEFUL

All this may seem an ominous picture, although it is one that helpers will find rings true of some of their more difficult clients. When counsellors depend upon clients to affirm their ideal self-image, there will always be some people who will play along with this, while there will be others who seem to go out of their way to destroy that good image. Justification by works has been appropriately criticized at various points in the history of the Church, and workaholics are recognized as a modern version of the same. There is no shame in helpers needing to be loved, but it is much better for their clients when counsellors can love themselves for who they are, and not for what they are and what they do. To rely upon work alone to prove yourself is dangerous for the counsellor and might not always help the client.

I am the last person to want to denigrate doing a job well, and taking pride in it. Just as there is nothing wrong with wanting love, there is nothing wrong with taking pride in one's abilities as a caring professional, as a voluntary helper, and as a counsellor. Counselling consists of very much more than being loving and caring. It may include being able to accept compliments, but it also involves being able to take criticism with equanimity, even when some of it is unjustified. A counsellor has to be open to receive a wide range of responses, not just positive ones. He or she also needs to learn to look at the remarks a client makes about the counsellor and counselling as not necessarily being statements about himself or herself, but indications of the way in which the client reacts and responds to other people.

High ideals are often accompanied by severe self-criticism and self-denigration, especially when those ideals are not met. Those whose idealism and energy are devoted to the good of others, and who appear very enthusiastic and contented, frequently have a more private side of themselves which can all too easily feel depressed by shortcomings or failure. Indeed the higher our ideals, the more risk there is of an inevitable gap between what we desire and what we can achieve. When the gap is not in some way bridged, there can be anxious feelings of guilt. Eadie writes of a condition that clergy can develop called 'the hardening of the oughteries'. I suspect it is not confined to clergy; and although it is obvious in some clients, it can also be a curse for counsellors in other settings too. A particularly vicious spiral is to work harder, perhaps by taking on more and more clients, and more frantically trying to lessen the gap between the ideal and actual achievement in order to alleviate guilt. Such hard work imposes its own stresses, impairs effectiveness, leads to even greater frustration, and so widens even more the gap between the critical and the idealistic parts of the helper's personality. Helpers of all kinds can become over-conscientious, and neglect to recognize that in their busy-ness they are as much concerned for their own needs (which are crying out to be recognized and met) as they are for the needs of those whom they help.

In counselling, such ambition and zeal takes different forms. Some helpers immediately concentrate upon the client's initial presenting problems and do not take time to look at the whole person. This is less likely in counselling, where there can be an opposite difficulty, that of going on for so long in order to achieve success that the value of short-term work can be forgotten. Short-term counselling, and indeed some long-term work, benefits from the counsellor focusing her or his interventions on particular issues, while still encouraging clients to talk about the issues and feelings that are uppermost for them. The focus is not always on initial presenting problems, since these are often only pointers to more central issues.

A helper who needs to be useful sometimes tries to solve clients' problems for them, not allowing them to take their own initiative and make their own mistakes as well as enjoy their own successes. To provide or to arrange for material help, to give advice or information, to answer questions that clients validly ask – none of this need be foreign to a counsellor's practice, even though it is not strictly counselling. But decisions to give advice or manage an aspect of a person's life are steps that should be taken only after due consideration of the necessity and the effect of such action. What I draw attention to here is the unthinking response, which arises out of concern for one's image as a helper rather than out of genuine concern for the welfare of the client. These are temporary strategies in counselling, with one of the greatest satisfactions for the counsellor being the client finding her or his own way through practical difficulties as well as through emotional distress. It is like the satisfaction of a parent whose child has grown strong enough and confident enough to take on previously parental responsibilities for herself or himself.

Another way of trying to achieve results and to feel useful is to change counselling techniques before considering first why a particular method, suggestion or intervention may not be working. I have only briefly discussed some of the different counselling techniques in Chapter 2, where I urged a foundation in one method before extending the range of one's expertise through learning other approaches. Certain Gestalt techniques, for instance, enable held-back emotions to be expressed more readily, but I would be cautious about using them just because a client feels stuck. There may be reasons why a client cannot allow himself to express a feeling, which need looking at before proposing, for example, pounding a cushion to release pent-up anger. In Chapter 8 I examine respect for a person's defences: exploring such resistance is as much part of a psychodynamic approach to counselling as encouraging the expression of feelings. I would not expect counsellors who believe that catharsis of emotions is valuable to adopt a different model if their client is reluctant to 'let it out'; similarly, I would hesitate as a psychodynamic counsellor from changing my approach of gradually helping clients to discover their less acceptable thoughts and feelings, of helping them to understand some of their reasons for holding them back, and helping them to find appropriate ways of expressing them in their relationships.

Freud once wrote to a friend, 'I would advise you to set aside your therapeutic ambition and try and understand what is happening. When you have done that, therapeutics will take care of itself.'[4] He alluded to the motto of an early surgeon, commending it to analysts: 'I dressed his wounds, God cured him.'[5] A person-centred counsellor might express it differently, but would endorse the sentiment that it is not the counsellor who achieves the healing, but the client, through the provision of those core conditions that enable people to discover their capacity for what person-centred counsellors call self-actualization. There are a number of different indicators for suitable clients for counselling, including the client's wish to change, and sufficient discomfort at her or his condition to want to change. Given suitable clients, counselling is building up a good record of effecting change, although every counsellor needs to accept that counselling will be only one of the circumstances that enables this to happen. Where motivation to change is less strong, or where there are conflicts that make change more difficult, a counsellor's effectiveness lies not in finding rapid solutions, but in patiently helping clients examine their doubts and hesitations. Short-term measures, although they sometimes have a temporary effect, are more often than not placebos for client and counsellor, which in an equally short time afford neither any lasting satisfaction.

THE DESIRE FOR REPARATION AND REVENGE

A different way of defining the wish to be useful might be to call it the wish to make better. Those who are in helping work clearly do so because they want to ease distress, to alleviate pain, and to heal the hurt and damage that their clients have experienced. They wish to do this because of a variety of personal experiences. Some helpers have suffered themselves, and may even know what it is like to have to suffer alone, without anyone to help them. They are determined that others should not suffer the same fate. Some have grown up in families where they have been put into a major caring role, even as children, looking after a parent in distress, or even having to grow up too quickly because a parent is more dependent on the child than the child on the parent. Some people have had experiences, in their childhood in particular, where they feel (or were made to feel) that they caused pain and harm to others. Whether they in fact did so is often questionable, because parents can sometimes exaggerate how much their children have hurt them, or children can themselves draw false conclusions about what damage they may have caused:

> Carol was very ill as a little girl and had to spend a long time in hospital. About the time she came home, her father began to develop symptoms which were later diagnosed as the first stages of a terminal illness. Within two years he was dead. Carol was convinced that because as she had got better and her father had got worse, it must have been her that had taken the life out of him. When I met her, Carol was training for one of the caring professions.

What is undeniable is that all of us have in some way caused (and indeed still cause) pain and hurt in other people in the course of our lives, although what we have done or said will not on the whole have been irreparable. Yet as children we may not have realized that, and one of the motives for caring for others may be in some way to repair the damage we feel we caused to others at earlier times. Furthermore, counsellors may be people who are anxious in the face of suffering. Indeed, their anxiety is a powerful and positive force which leads them to want to make things better for those who are in some kind of pain. It is important nevertheless to recognize that the wish to alleviate distress may be partly to ease the counsellor's own pain, as much as being about wanting the client to feel better. One of the difficulties for the counsellor is that this particular way of helping often means sitting by while the client experiences great distress, without being able to do more than provide the calming presence of someone who cares. At other times, counselling involves taking up feelings and issues that the client has hinted at, but apparently can take no further. The counsellor is aware of touching raw nerves when he or she says, 'Can you tell me more about that?'; or of causing more distress when he or she observes a client's eyes watering, and says, 'You look as if you might be upset' – a remark that could open the floodgates of long pent-up tears.

The necessity of causing pain in the process of healing is not peculiar to counselling. Before the advent of anaesthetics, surgeons must have felt something of the same dilemma, knowing that in order to bring about healing they had to inflict severe pain. Even with pain-killing drugs, doctors and nurses often have to cause discomfort or severe pain in order to diagnose, mend or heal. Similarly, counselling has no anaesthetic to offer other than the quiet compassion of the counsellor. And even that concern does not take away pain, though it may make it more bearable.

It is one thing to acknowledge such wishes to make reparation. But counsellors are human, and they need to come to terms with all that makes them human, warts and all; or, as Jungian therapists express it, they have to recognize the shadow side of their personalities. Like most people, counsellors are compassionate; like everyone else, they have caused pain to other people; and, also like other people, they have their own sadistic wishes. If that seems over-strong as a motive for helping, it might be necessary to think of those moments when a helper has to sit helplessly by a client who is pouring out the most horrific story, and feels just like a voyeuristic ghoul; or those occasions, that are even more frequent, when a counsellor knows that it is right to 'twist the knife', and draw out the deep pain of the client. It is also not unusual, at the end of a particularly painful hour with a client, for a counsellor to say something like: 'Phew! That was a really painful session, but what a lot we achieved.' There is a curious satisfaction that comes partly from knowing the long-term value of the client's present pain, but I am sure it has other less reasonable aspects to it at times.

It is necessary to use as strong a term as sadism, because on the one hand counsellors must learn to overcome their distaste at digging deeper; and, perhaps even more important, they need to be aware of their unconscious capacity to cause pain, to avoid pressing a client when they should be comforting, and to avoid cutting open when they should be healing. Unless counsellors come to terms with their aggression, they may find it difficult to disagree with their clients, or to be assertive and firm over boundaries, or to face people with sensitive and painful aspects of themselves that they would prefer to avoid. But if they do not recognize the sadistic aspects of helping relationships, they may find themselves caught on one end or another of a sado-masochistic partnership. It can be the client who is the sadistic one, in one way or another being punitive towards the helper, and the helper taking it all without achieving anything other than personal exhaustion; or it can be the counsellor, unaware of her or his own sadistic power, who bombards the client with inappropriate and damaging responses, while the client masochistically comes back for more and more.

One reason for such inappropriate behaviour is the principle of 'an eye for an eye': we do to others what has been done to us. Clients who have been badly treated in the past will perhaps treat the counsellor badly. This, of course, is what a counsellor comes to expect when working with damaged people. It is an example of the repetition of the past in the helping relationship, which a counsellor uses to help clients look at what has happened to them and what they in turn do to others. In a counsellor, the type of 'eye for an eye' behaviour that damages the client might similarly have come from bad experiences in the past or from poor models seen when they themselves received help. Unfortunately there are always some members of every profession who use the opportunity to care for others as a means of exacting revenge: sadistic teachers, abusive residential care workers, paedophile clergy, harsh judges, authoritarian doctors, nagging nurses. They let down the majority of their much finer colleagues, but they also demonstrate how the motives for entering a helping profession can include the wish for revenge.

'An eye for an eye' is one way in which what is called the law of talion can be expressed. There are, however, alternative and positive ways of expressing the law of talion: 'do to others what you wish them to do to you' contains the possibility of initiating a cycle of care and concern, rather than simply repeating the common cycle of deprivation. This is essentially what a counsellor can model for a damaged client. It may also be what partly motivates counsellors, that they wish to share with others some of the good experiences they have themselves received, although I have suggested at greater length elsewhere that helpers may also be partly motivated by the wish to show up those who did not care adequately for them, as a type of revenge.[6]

THE DESIRE FOR SAFE INTIMACY

If I am to remain true to the purpose of this chapter, in this context intimacy means closeness, but also includes the erotic and the sexual feelings in the helper. In his commentary on his research into the caring personality, Eadie observes how curious it is that those who are motivated by the 'appeal of loving', and who find it appropriate to be affectionate, gentle and concerned, find it unacceptable to admit sexual and erotic wishes. He cites some evidence, mainly from his study of clergy, which suggests that they and caring professionals generally may be more inhibited and less sexually active than those in other professional groups.[7]

The counselling relationship is a strange one. Guntrip describes the therapist/patient relationship as 'midway between the parent/child relation and the husband/wife relation. It is not a relation between an actual parent, and an actual child, nor is it a relation between two adults on terms of equality. It is a relation between the unhappy and undermined child in the adult patient and a therapist whose own "internal child" ought to have been taken care of by his own training analysis'.[8] Guntrip does not qualify what he means by the husband/wife relationship in this analogy. It is clear from what he says about the parent/child relationship that the term 'husband/wife' needs to be treated with caution, although it is possible to make sense of what Guntrip means. There is in counselling and therapy the greatest intimacy imaginable: the client may share with the counsellor experiences, thoughts and feelings that he or she has never breathed to anyone else. Occasionally a counsellor or psychotherapist knows more about a client than anyone else: that is, more than anyone else knows about the client, but also more than the counsellor knows about anyone else. At the same time, it has to be said that this intimacy is very one-sided: the client knows little about the counsellor's private life. However, to complicate this further, a client often knows a counsellor very well, because they meet so regularly and so often that the relationship has its own history. The client also gets to read the counsellor like a book, such as one of my clients who told me that she always knew when I was about to disagree with her, because I invariably shifted in my chair.

The closeness of the counselling relationship is one of the factors that gives it therapeutic potential. There are other sides to it. Counselling (for client and for counsellor) can be a way of seeking intimacy with another person, while at the same time avoiding it. Eadie draws attention to this feature in some helpers: they engage in a wide range of caring relationships that are distant and safe, but they avoid genuine intimacy. He writes of the clergyman (and the 'man' might here be relevant): 'the pulpit, study and vocational image in particular make him a man "set apart", though he overcomes his basic sense of isolation by numerous pastoral relationships'.[9] Counsellors are no less prone to finding their intimacy through seeing a large number of clients, with whom they of course share little of their innermost experiences, and with whom they can indulge in phantasies of what relationships should really be.

Intimate phantasies might include sex. There is enough evidence of sexual exploitation of clients by counsellors to make my assertion of the desire for sex an accurate one as a motive for some helpers. Although the majority do not act it out, counsellors can indulge in rich phantasies involving some of their more attractive clients, and engage (without always realizing it) in subtle (and judging by some reports, not so subtle) sexually stimulating talk. Both male and female counsellors are capable of exploiting their clients, although it is male counsellors and helpers who have the worst record for active sexual behaviour with clients.

I do not suggest that counsellors should be embarrassed by their sexual thoughts. Searles has argued that at some points in psychotherapy these phantasies are important pointers to a client's recovery, although it has to be said that Searles writes about the appropriateness of such phantasies with great care.[10] Clients are able to be more open about sexual and other intimate physical matters than they were when Freud first started writing, and some people are more at ease with their sexual feelings than they are with their hate, envy or jealousy. It is important that counsellors are not worried about discussing any type of feeling. Too inhibited an attitude towards sexuality can lead to the counsellor avoiding the sexual difficulties that a client is also hesitant to share.

On the other hand, too keen an interest in sexual matters on the part of the counsellor may result in intrusive probing into the intimate details of a client's life. The counsellor may even get vicarious and voyeuristic pleasure, while making the client feel a type of mental rape. It is especially important in all instances where a helper suspects there may have been sexual abuse or sexual violence that the client is allowed to reveal intimate experiences at her or his own pace. It is also important not to be seduced by some clients into thinking that sexuality is their only problem, neglecting the many other emotions that are involved in interpersonal relationships.

Both partners in a counselling relationship may invest a great deal in their work together; indeed, the ideal is that each should be totally involved. But for neither partner is a counselling session the same as the total give and take that is typical of close families and real friendships. For clients the therapeutic relationship is one that is ultimately, however long it takes, a step towards making better relationships with the people for whom the client feels most. If counsellors look to those they help to achieve an intimacy that they cannot find elsewhere, they risk teasing their clients and deluding themselves. Person-centred counsellors describe the relationship as 'non-possessive love'; Freud talked about 'aim-inhibited love'. Either term expresses a special kind of love. Likewise, counsellors who are frightened of this type of love, and avoid the intimacy that legitimately exists in the therapeutic partnership, might need to ask themselves if they avoid intimacy outside as well. These and other feelings for and about the client are examples of what psychodynamic counselling calls 'counter-transference' reactions, which I explain further in Chapter 9.

THE DESIRE FOR POWER

It is apparent from the way in which clients can apparently allow themselves to be abused, sexually or aggressively, by some helpers, just how powerful a position every helper is in. It is not sufficient to explain these incidents, as they have some-times been, as the client seducing the counsellor, or as asking for punishment. In this chapter I have stressed the counsellor's responsibility not only to understand her or his own motives, but to protect the counselling process.

There is no clear evidence as to whether helpers are more prone to being authoritarian or submissive, although I have already suggested that they can suffer from quite authoritarian consciences. I suspect that many helpers tend to be passive in direct relations with authority figures, but in turn they may exert considerable authority over those they care for – at the same time seeing themselves as much more egalitarian than they actually are. But the picture is not clear: some counsellors are too dominant and tell their clients what to do, others are submissive and allow themselves to be pushed around.

By the same token, clients differ. Some (though less obvious in most counselling practices) are aggressive. There are many more who are apparently passive people, but who succeed in mobilizing so much concern and panic around them that they soon discover how powerful their distress can be. Others hand over all their strength to their helpers, endowing their counsellor with qualities of knowledge and wisdom and the ability to perform miracles, and hanging on to their every word. This can be gratifying to the person who, as early sections in this chapter have shown, needs to be needed and wants to feel helpful; but other counsellors soon become aware of the way in which their words and actions are taken out of context and misunderstood. They realize how carefully they need to weigh what they want to say, not only to be clear and accurate as I suggested in the last chapter, but also to be as free as possible from the politics of power that can bedevil helping relationships.

It is less the case than it once was that clients come for help knowing little about counselling. Nevertheless, with their smattering of knowledge about counselling, they may mistakenly believe that counsellors do know answers, but that they have to discover them for themselves. They may still endow a counsellor with the power of mind-reading, with penetrating insight, and with superhuman personal qualities. Anyone who becomes a counsellor to bolster their self-esteem can misuse this phantasy: some using their flattering position to give too much, others playing with the client by giving too little. In fact, when a counsellor first meets a client, he or she has at best only general knowledge, and it takes a long time before clearer understanding of the individual client becomes possible. Even then, such understanding is only tentative:

> I had been seeing a highly intelligent, and generally confident, professional man for a number of weeks. On one occasion I suggested an idea that had occurred to me, but about which I was not particularly sure. I started to check out what I had thought. 'I'm not sure,' I said, 'and I haven't got a complete picture yet, but in my own mind I felt...' and I expressed my idea. To my surprise, when we met the next week, my client started by saying, 'I must tell you how relieved I was last week when you talked about... It wasn't just what you said, but the way you said it. I know rationally that you don't know everything, but I've been finding it so difficult not to see you as someone who knows everything about me. The fact that you said you weren't sure has made me feel a lot more secure.'

I do not suggest that counsellors, any more than people in other occupations, do not in the end acquire considerable knowledge and expertise. Competent counsellors often know a lot, without knowing just how much they know. I am more suspicious of the counsellor who 'knows it all'. The experience of working with people gradually builds up an understanding that is worth any number of books on psychology. At the same time every client is unique, each with a particular set of circumstances that have led to their present life position. The type of knowledge that counsellors acquire, and indeed demonstrate to their clients, is not erudite theory, nor is it a knowledge of psychopathology, which can sometimes be used to label people indiscriminately. A largely self-taught naturalist I knew once described to me his concept of what he called '*sweet* power'. By this he meant the ability to stand in the countryside and to understand the relationship between the different forms of natural life, and the relationship to himself as the observer. This he felt was quite unlike the power gained from learning the scientific names of the flora and fauna, and then showing off this knowledge to others. His idea of 'sweet power' is a useful concept for the type of power a counsellor has, and which he or she shares with each client.[11] There is a similar sense of the right power balance in the terms used in one training manual, where the client is described as 'the worker' and the therapist as 'the assistant'.[12] To apportion authority in the therapeutic relationship in that way seems right, stressing as it does a different type of relationship from that implied in the more usual terms 'counsellor and client' or 'therapist and patient'.

There is some argument about the right terms to use of the partners in the helping relationship. Some person-centred counsellors find the term 'psychotherapist' too redolent of the power of the helper, and many counsellors prefer not to use the term 'patient', because it suggests not only a model of medical intervention, but also the expertise of the therapist that accompanies that model. I have already indicated that I use the term 'client' for convenience in this book, although not without reservations, since it has connotations of the solicitor's office or even of the brothel! It is difficult to convey in one word just how important it is to meet persons in need as individual people; of course, like other jargon terms, these technical words are seldom used in the counselling session itself.

THE DESIRE TO CONVERT

All that I have included in this chapter applies as much to the pastoral ministry as it does to the use of counselling in any other situation. There is one motive that is less likely to appear in secular settings, and may be explicit or implicit in a religious context.

The trust that people have in their counsellor, as well as the power that a counsellor has to influence clients, means that great care is necessary in relation to validating or suggesting the values that come from religious faith and practice. Counselling should not be seen as a way of persuading people to adopt a particular expression of faith, either directly, or through offering a service that is deliberately designed to show that the Church is 'with it'. Counselling is offered for its own sake, as far as possible free from any strings that might otherwise be attached. The same is true of counselling offered in an educational setting, or in the workplace. Those responsible for paying for such a service may have their own ideas, but their counsellors work for the clients, and not for the employers. This applies just as much to their work with clients, some of whom may be tempted to use counselling to get round the institution or the employers. Counsellors need to try and keep above the use of counselling as an expression of institutional games and politicking.

In the church context, it is important to be aware of the attraction of motives that are other than pure. I have known a client start attending a particular church in order (so it appeared) to be in the same building as his counsellor, even though the counsellor rarely attended the church and certainly did not make a point of talking about her faith. One of the difficulties that some pastoral counsellors may face is that far from encouraging their clients to adopt a particular belief or to attend religious services, they will inevitably find themselves having to challenge some of the versions of faith that their clients express. Ironically, offering pastoral counselling may be more successful in emptying churches than in filling them, since there are developmental points when people need time on their own, away from an institution that has sheltered them for too long, and to which they have handed over their autonomy.

Although these are real concerns for counsellors and counselling facilities situated within obvious religious traditions,
counsellors elsewhere are not free from subtle, or even more
obvious, use of their position to persuade clients to think or act
in particular ways. It is impossible for any counsellor to be
value-free; and it is sometimes difficult to avoid even gently
nudging a client in a particular direction, whether it be towards
a view on faith, on politics, on society, or on an institution. The
desire to convert clients to one's own views and to produce
carbon copies of oneself is another area that helpers need to
give consideration to.

Counselling is a peculiar activity. Truth is stranger than fiction,
and the experiences and the phantasies of clients span the
whole range of human experience, making soap operas, novels
and even psychiatric textbooks appear insignificant against the
real-life dramas that are talked about in sessions. Some of the
issues are also issues for the counsellor, and some of them will
actually involve the feelings of the client towards the counsellor
as well. Others may seem far removed from the counsellor's
life experience. Little of this can ever be shared, except in
supervision, and even then with the greatest care to preserve
confidentiality and the identity of the client. The mixture of
the sensational and the boring, of self-consciousness and self-
denial, of success and failure, of advance and retreat, of feeling
and thinking, makes counselling work and a counselling
ministry both fascinating and exhausting.

Throughout this chapter I have underlined the importance
of a counsellor's self-understanding and self-acceptance as an
integral part of the work; this helps a counsellor assess how
far he or she should be identified and involved with each
client. Concern for parity of power includes the counsellor's
awareness that the client's problem is also to some extent the
counsellor's, so lessening the dangers of confusing self with
the other, and of making unwarranted assumptions. Through
increasing self-knowledge counsellors become less tempted to
project their own difficulties on to their clients, and less inclined
to try and resolve them through other people. At the same
time they become less afraid of exploring the client's problems
simply because they are close to their own. Their personal
insights enhance their sensitivity to and understanding of the

other. Experienced counsellors use themselves more than most of their clients ever realize, and more than most counsellors who are starting out imagine.

Inevitably, as in any other demanding work, disillusion or cynicism can creep in. Far from denying the importance of self, I have argued above that helping others is just as much for oneself as it is for them. If counselling is to be effective it must continue to be personally satisfying. I doubt if there is such a quality as pure altruism and I find no shame in gaining a sense of personal value through counselling. Many therapeutic relationships give pleasure and rewards. What is vital is that these pleasures and rewards are not deliberately sought, especially as a way of trying to avoid some of the more uncomfortable situations that inevitably arise in counselling and therapy, and to which I now turn.

NOTES

1. H. Eadie, 'The psychological health of clergymen', *Contact – Interdisciplinary Journal of Pastoral Studies* (1972), 41, p. 2. See also L. Francis, 'Personality theory and male Anglican clergy: the EPP', *Contact – Interdisciplinary Journal of Pastoral Studies* (2000), 133, pp. 27–36.
2. It is not my intention to discuss the practice of supervision further since there is a companion volume in this series by J. Foskett and D. Lyall, *Helping the Helpers: Supervision and Pastoral Care*. SPCK 1988. See also P. Hawkins and R. Shohet, *Supervision in the Helping Professions*. Open University Press 1989.
3. E. Rayner, *Human Development*. Allen & Unwin 1986 (3rd edn), p. 166.
4. Quoted by P. Roazen, *Freud and His Followers*. Penguin Books 1979, p. 151.
5. S. Freud, *Recommendations to Physicians Practising Psychoanalysis*. Standard Edition, volume XII. Hogarth Press 1951, p. 115.
6. M. Jacobs, 'The therapist's revenge: the law of talion as a motive for caring', *Contact – Interdisciplinary Journal of Pastoral Studies* (1991), 105, pp. 2–11.
7. H. Eadie, 'The helping personality', *Contact – Interdisciplinary Journal of Pastoral Studies* (1975), 49, p. 6.
8. H. Guntrip, *Healing the Sick Mind*. Unwin Books 1964, p. 87.
9. Eadie, 'The helping personality', p. 6.
10. H. Searles, 'Oedipal love in the counter-transference', in H. Searles, *Collected Papers on Schizophrenia and Related Subjects*. Hogarth Press 1965.

11. This theme is expanded in M. Jacobs, 'Naming and labelling', *Contact - Interdisciplinary Journal of Pastoral Studies* (1976), 54, pp. 2–8. See also M. Jacobs, *The Presenting Past*. Open University Press 1998 (2nd edn), pp. 38–46.
12. K. Horney, *The Barefoot Psychoanalyst*. Karen Horney Institute.

CHAPTER FIVE

Some Early Difficulties

There is a delicate balance in the way in which counsellors use their own experiences, feelings and thoughts in working with any one client. In the last chapter I made it clear that a counsellor must not let personal ambitions, motives, problems and conflicts intrude on the client, yet I also hinted at the value of using her or his feelings and thoughts as fully as possible as a guide to understanding the client. I suppose that there is no other way of trying to understand a client's experience that is quite as effective as the counsellor's own reactions to a client, or to part of a client's story. At various times a counsellor will feel excited, surprised, uncomfortable, anxious, sad, bored or even neutral: this is normal, however experienced the counsellor may be. When a counsellor has a strong reaction, it is fairly certain that the client is feeling something too, although not always the same as the counsellor. Counsellors, for example, can experience a session as being very helpful, while the client feels the opposite; or a counsellor may feel despondent, whereas the client's experience is of considerable progress. Where helpers need to be particularly careful is if their reactions to all their clients are invariably the same. Counsellors who never experience clients as angry, for example, probably need to question whether their perceptions are saying more about themselves than their clients.

A balance is also necessary between staying detached enough to look at what might be happening, and involved enough to be experiencing it. The close link between what a counsellor feels and a client feels when they meet provides me, in this chapter, with a way of looking at initial sessions with clients, and reflecting upon the difficulties and anxieties that clients have, particularly if they are new to counselling; and which counsellors similarly experience, especially if they are just starting out. But some of this applies equally to other occasions with long-term clients and seasoned counsellors. I shall also look at ways of responding in such situations.

FIRST SESSIONS

Perhaps the first point of anxiety, especially when a counselling student is about to translate their initial training into counselling real people, is one about competence. This can equally apply to more experienced counsellors when meeting a new client, because the questions that a counsellor has in mind include: 'What sort of person am I about to meet?' 'Will I like them?' 'What will they make of me?' 'What will their problem be?' 'Will I be able to help?' 'Will I know what to say?' There is no way of avoiding such feelings, nor is there any way of answering such questions until the counsellor and client meet and begin to work together. The only consolation is that anxiety about the unknown is usually worse than actually meeting face to face. Once the session is under way, especially if the counsellor concentrates upon listening to the client, such anxieties normally subside. There are occasionally difficult clients, and some of these situations I discuss later in this chapter. But the majority are not difficult, and as long as a counsellor remembers that he or she does not have to come up with answers, and continues to help the client to tell their story, the session will proceed smoothly enough for any sticky points to be discussed in supervision afterwards. If the new counsellor is left wondering whether he or she did or said the right things, so too will an experienced counsellor reflect on this. The only difference is that the experienced counsellor will be less worried about having to get everything right.

If counsellors get worried about first sessions, how do their clients feel? In some situations a client may know who they are going to see, either personally or by reputation. But in most cases they will not, and if they have had, as is increasingly the case, an assessment interview, their counselling will probably not be with the same person. A client's anxieties may also be expressed as questions:

- What does counselling involve?
- What am I expected to say?
- Will I be able to express myself clearly?
- What will the counsellor think of me?
- Will the counsellor be critical?
- Will the counsellor think I'm making a fuss about nothing?

An experienced counsellor's initial anxieties soon subside once the session begins, but clients do not always settle so quickly. The counsellor has to be sensitive to the client's anxiousness, perhaps encouraging it to be expressed; or easing it by creating a calm and accepting atmosphere, in which the counsellor does little more than help the client begin their story, at the same time beginning to trust enough to want to return another time and talk further.

Part of the counsellor's anxiety stems from a sense of responsibility, and the knowledge that the client probably has hopes and expectations of the counsellor. Some people expect the counsellor to have answers; or to give advice; or to be an expert on human relationships; or to be an advocate for them in some institutional settings. Professionals are expected to be 'experts', which has implications of solving problems fast and effectively. The more desperate a person is, the higher their expectations, unless they are at the end of their tether, and giving up hope. Counsellors have a particular difficulty when the expectations are high, in that there are no answers available in the first few minutes, nor perhaps even in the first hour. First meetings for counsellors and first meetings for clients may have quite different objectives. As far as the counsellor is concerned the first meeting is an opportunity to formulate questions, not find answers:

- What brings this person now?
- How long have they felt this way?
- What are they going through at this moment?
- What has triggered this off?
- What can I as a counsellor realistically achieve?
- What does the client want to achieve?
- How serious are they about using the help I can offer?

The client may also be framing questions, but questions that are quite different and often difficult to answer:

- Does counselling work?
- What success do you have?
- How will it help?
- How long will it take?

In answering such questions a counsellor needs to combine honesty, sensitivity and tact: 'My experience is that counselling frequently does help. That's one of the reasons why I am a counsellor. I can't guarantee that it will be helpful for you. I suggest that we could arrange to meet a few times, and then decide together whether it is helping or not.' Openness from the beginning about the possibilities that counselling offers is infinitely preferable to false promises or the creation of high expectations. Such a beginning also conveys a sense of partnership, by underlining that the counsellor is not the one with all the answers, and that each partner in the therapeutic relationship has a contribution to make.

Sometimes clients have other anxieties, and their questions are different:

- What do you want to know?
- What do you want me to talk about?
- Can't you ask me some questions so I can tell you what you need to know?

Their anxiety similarly may be expressed non-verbally, with the client sitting looking intensely at the helper or, alternatively, unable to look at the counsellor, desperately wanting the counsellor to take the initiative and responsibility for the conduct of the interview.

A counsellor does indeed have this responsibility, although it is not necessarily discharged through asking lots of questions. In reply to such questions, or in response to such looks, a counsellor remembers that the client has probably not experienced anything like this type of interview before, and so naturally expects 'the expert' first to ask some questions, and then to give advice. By sharing the responsibility for the session with the client, the counsellor can help the client understand a little more of what it is about, and what the counsellor's role is:

- What would you like to tell me about yourself?
- What do you think it would help me to know?
- I wonder if you can try telling me what you are thinking and feeling, whether it seems relevant or not. There's plenty of time today, and we can always meet again if you want to.
- I know you would like me to ask you questions, but they would tend to be questions I want to ask, and not necessarily what you want to tell me.
- Perhaps you have some questions you ask about yourself.

Others are more direct as they begin, making it clear that they see the counsellor as a doctor or a magician: 'I want you to get rid of my feelings. I want some advice from you. I want you to tell me what's wrong with me.' There may be a flattering tone to such requests, although the counsellor at such a point probably wishes that he or she were as knowledgeable and as powerful as the client wants. Again an honest but sensitive response can begin to correct false expectations: 'I wish I did have a straightforward answer to give you. Unfortunately I don't, because everyone is different and every situation is different. What the two of us want to do is to find what might be the right answer for you.' Or the counsellor might say: 'You know yourself better than me, and I don't know anything about you yet. I wonder if you could tell me more about yourself, so I can begin to understand what it is that's troubling you?'

Explanations, or other ways of answering that match the questions a client asks, are very important in this early stage, since they help the person to learn what counselling can and cannot do, and the part that the client plays in it. Sometimes the answers are accepted as reasonable, and the client begins to talk more freely about herself or himself. Rational explanations do not always work, especially when a client's question covers up a different kind of anxiety. For instance, if the client continues to see the helper as a magician (albeit at times complaining that the counsellor is a wizard with a broken wand), this false expectation might be linked to the childlike wish in the client for a parent-figure who will make everything better.

For a long time children see their parents as capable of anything, and their disillusionment can be great when they are let
down for the first time. Thereafter they may go on looking for
a replacement who will take on the omni-competent role:

> I was once seeing a bulimic woman, whose main wish was
> to be able to stop eating compulsively, and to eat normally
> again. I was drawn into making some suggestions for con-
> trolling her eating, none of which appeared to be tried. In
> one session the client said that she wished I would lock her
> up, control her eating, and stop her from making herself
> sick. I pointed out how she sometimes wanted to be looked
> after like a child, and that she was wanting me there all
> the time, because even if I locked her up and gave her food,
> that was the only way I could stop her from deliberately
> vomiting. At the same time she had rejected as unworkable
> my suggestions to help her plan her eating. She wasn't able
> to take in what I offered her, and so was controlling me
> rather than allowing herself to be controlled.

Because more people now understand what counselling is
about, some of them seem to open the first session with accurate expectations of the counsellor, but in fact underneath
their reasonable outlook they still have similar wishes for
someone to take over: 'I realize you can't help me. I know I
have to help myself, and that you can't tell me what to do.'
With such hints of other underlying expectations, a counsellor
can reflect in this way upon what the client appears to be
saying:

> 'I recognize that you know that, but given what you've been
> through it wouldn't be surprising if you still wished I could
> wave a magic wand and change everything.'

> 'You said when we started today that you knew I couldn't
> tell you what to do; and that's right, because I can't. But
> you're obviously just as worried as you were, so perhaps you
> are wishing that I could have made things better for you.'

Such responses help to distinguish the real responsibility
that counsellor and client each have, including the counsellor's

refusal to manage or direct the client's life. (Of course, if it was absolutely essential for the safety of the client or for others close to the client, a counsellor might have to act differently.) But the counsellor's care and concern for how the client feels at this point, and for any disappointment the client may experience, is still conveyed, partly in the tone of the counsellor's response, as well as in the words. Counsellors need to demonstrate their willingness to work within the limits of their understanding and experience; and clients are helped to see the part they play both in counselling, and for what decisions they take in their own life.

HELPLESSNESS

Inevitably there are times when clients feel no control over what is happening to them. Although they recognize their responsibility for themselves, there is no way in which they can change what they are feeling. Neither is the counsellor ultimately responsible for the way the client feels (although there are occasions when counsellors can make things worse). This does not prevent a counsellor from being very anxious when he or she experiences times of complete helplessness. At such points a counsellor worries lest what he or she says may make things worse, or that by doing nothing and saying nothing the client will be driven to despair. Such feelings of helplessness can occur when clients are very distraught, or if they are withdrawn and passive, or when they talk about matters that the counsellor cannot comprehend. It is tempting in these situations to talk too much, and so thrash around for something helpful to say. The counsellor may give advice prematurely or even unnecessarily; make interpretations that have not been thought out; or act in other ways that have no virtue other than filling the void.

It is at moments like these that a nagging voice inside the counsellor seems to be saying, 'Don't just sit there, do something'; or a pastoral counsellor may wish the New Testament phrase could come true, 'Speak the word only and I shall be healed'. In fact, helpers are generally much more useful when they can do the opposite: not worry about saying anything (at least of importance), and reminding themselves, 'Just sit here.

You don't have to do anything'. Not that this stops counsellors
(even the experienced ones) feeling at this juncture that they
should never have decided to embark on a counselling career;
while beginners think (perhaps rightly!) that no one prepared
them for this, and tend to dwell on their own discomfort
rather than stay with the client's. The counsellor's own sense
of helplessness may be an indication of how strongly the
client feels the same, just as I have suggested that feelings of
responsibility in the counsellor are the counterpart of strong
expectations on the part of the client. At these times the most
effective support that a counsellor can give is to stay with the
helpless feeling, waiting for the 'still small voice of calm' to
speak, as it will do (in time) when the level of anxiety drops in
the counsellor, and then in the client. The following example
illustrates the value of 'just sitting there':

> I had been seeing a young woman student for a number of
> weeks. The client, Dee, had been in considerable distress
> during many of these sessions. On one occasion she arrived
> in a very desperate state. She was going to end it all. There
> was no way out. There was no point in living; and so it went
> on, her despair conveying itself incredibly strongly to me. In
> trying to recall the session afterwards for my notes, I could
> remember little of what Dee had said, or even what I had said.
> I was only left with painful reminders of how ineffective I
> had been, and how helpless I had felt. I had not known what
> to say, and consequently I had said very little. At this distance
> from the session I think I may have encouraged her to
> express her feelings about wishing to 'end it all', because I
> knew that was what I ought to do. But I am not even sure
> about that. I was left deeply concerned for Dee's safety, and
> for my reputation as a counsellor with my colleagues if any-
> thing happened to her. I felt immobilized. My one certain
> memory is that at the end of the session I had said to Dee,
> 'There's nothing I can say which takes away the pain you are
> feeling. Perhaps when we meet next week, something might
> come then.' I do not know whether Dee realized it, but this
> felt like a desperate hope on my part, because I was not at all
> convinced that the next week would be any better.
>
>   After Dee had left the room, I sat in my chair in a rather
> dazed condition, unsure of how I should have dealt with

what she had been saying, and feeling that I did not want to see anyone else that day.

After worrying about her and about my dreadful session for at least an hour I decided that it might be better to go out and get a quick bite to eat. I walked across to the university campus, still feeling awful. On the way I happened to meet one of those people who are always cheerful and full of life, and quite insensitive to how others might be feeling. Although the session with Dee stayed on my mind, I forced myself to join in the conversation and to appear cheerful; then I went on my way. During the week that followed the despair and helplessness of that particular session came back to me, together with my 'promise' that 'something might come then': I still had no idea what I was going to say, or how I was going to help.

The day and the hour of our next meeting came. To my surprise Dee entered the room looking more colourful, both in her complexion and in her dress, than I had ever seen her before. She was smiling. She started by saying that she had wondered whether I would survive after last week's session. But she had seen me afterwards talking to someone and laughing, and she realized that I had survived. She went on to say that it was seeing I could still be cheerful that had been a turning point for her.

It was a turning point for me too, one of those instances in my development as a counsellor that vividly stays with me, even this number of years on. I realized that I had helped, not by saying anything of deep significance, but simply by surviving. We may wonder, of course, what would have happened had Dee not seen me afterwards on the university campus, apparently relaxed and all right. But other examples since have confirmed for me that 'simply' being there the next week is also a potent sign of having survived, without there necessarily having to be any extra contact in the week between. This combination of being able to survive moments of intense personal anxiety without communicating it to the client, but at the same time expressing the client's own sense of helplessness, does more than any hyperactive response, whether in words or by action.

It also has to be said that on occasions, after a particularly difficult session, a client might contact a counsellor before the next scheduled session, and not simply because the client is going through a difficult time; sometimes there is a further reason, albeit a less conscious one, to check that the counsellor is still there and undamaged. Such checking does not mean that the counsellor always has to fit in an extra session (the temptation of many new counsellors, and of some experienced ones too). The phone call is often sufficient for the client's anxiety, as long as the counsellor gently but firmly reminds the client of their next planned meeting.

NOT UNDERSTANDING

Another problem for counsellors seeing their first clients is the expectation that counsellors have that the counsellor should understand everything that the client says. Clients are themselves anxious about this, sometimes desperate to be understood, wishing they could put into words the confusion of feelings they are experiencing. It takes much experience, but also it often takes many sessions, to grasp what a client is trying to struggle with, and perhaps even then this only happens because the client has been able to find a way through sufficiently for the counsellor to follow.

There will be many occasions, especially in early meetings, when a counsellor does not understand a phrase or a muddling description of what clients are feeling, even when they sometimes think they are clear themselves. The urgency of the client's desire to be understood can make a counsellor feel ill at ease. Clients sometimes express the wish that counsellors could read their minds, to make it easier for them, although it has to be said that this is sometimes a wish not to have to speak about matters about which the client feels shame or guilt. There are also clients who are very frightened in case their counsellor can read their mind, or at being too well understood, because they fear the counsellor 'taking them over' and invading their inner boundaries. Indeed, clients of that kind, as well as clients with whom it is impossible to understand anything, might require more experienced help than a new counsellor can give.

There are two types of understanding that a counsellor aims

for: the first is the obvious level of comprehending what a client actually says, while the second is another level, of seeing through the words to what really might be meant. In other words, a client can describe a situation very clearly, so that the counsellor can imagine what happened, but the counsellor remains unsure of what the event actually means to the client. In some cases, however, even the initial description is muddled.

Like new counsellors, experienced counsellors have many occasions of both types of not understanding the client, times when they feel unsure or confused about the obvious content and the deeper meaning. Inexperienced counsellors, anxious to be helpful, and imagining that their seniors know everything, appear to find it less easy to show that they do not understand, as if this implies they have not been listening properly. This is an unrealistic expectation, just as it is unrealistic on the part of clients to expect that they will find a counsellor who will magically understand them, without having to go through the struggle of finding expression for all that is going on in them.

Counsellors who think they have to understand everything often freeze, or switch to a safer subject by asking an unrelated question. In fact, they can share what they are experiencing with the client. If people are not making themselves clear, a counsellor can say, 'I'm not sure I understand that. It may be my confusion, but could you try and describe it again for me?' More simply, the phrase, 'Can you tell me more about that?' invites further explanation. If a client says, 'You know', and the counsellor does *not* know, then say so! 'Sorry, I'm not sure what you do mean. Can you put it another way to help me?' Notice how the counsellor in such responses takes on some of the responsibility for not understanding, so that a client is not made to feel small.

Sometimes, however hard he or she is trying, a counsellor can drift off into her or his own concerns. Even this can be covered tactfully by acknowledging, 'I didn't quite get that: it's me, I'm sure, but could you say that again?' Although it is very important when learning about counselling to cultivate the skill of listening with undivided attention, a more developed approach to listening (to which I also refer in Chapter 3) is the ability to listen to oneself. There are times when I find myself thinking much more about what is going on inside my own head than listening to what the client is saying. When I 'come to' and realize this, I do not stop the client and ask her or him to repeat what they have said. Preferring to follow another of the guidelines, I would rather not interrupt. I would rather say no more than is necessary.

Instead of interrupting, and also instead of suddenly turning back my attention to the client, I sometimes find myself going on to reflect on what I was thinking, and what it might be telling me about the client. All this time, of course, I am continuing to miss, or at best I only half hear what the client is saying. When I have done this little piece of thinking and reflection, I then probably go back to a mood of attentive listening to the client. My attention is then rather more active, because I am aware of having quite a lot to catch up on! I try to look for some clues as to what I might have missed in the client's story. In understanding clients it can be very helpful to listen to our own inner 'still small voice', although I hasten to add at this point, since I am discussing early sessions and beginning counsellors, that this is a much more developed skill, especially since it requires holding on to the space in which the client was speaking, but the counsellor was not hearing, without letting the client realize this.

The second and deeper level of understanding is when the counsellor understands the words and the sense, but not the significance of what a client is saying. Again it is possible to acknowledge this at the time, while storing away the story or the situation described for later use as more material emerges. Often a phrase seems important, but its meaning is unclear. It may fall into place later, or even after the session is over. It is reassuring to recognize that anything that is really important to or in a client will always appear again, sometimes much later and sometimes in another form, but it will push its way into view none the less. It is as if there are aspects in all of us that need to be expressed, and that persistently make attempts to find the light of day, until someone has acknowledged them. Mentally noting such stories, or even little phrases that appear to have some significance, and writing them down after the session acts as a reminder to the counsellor to come back to them at the right moment in later sessions, or lodges them sufficiently for them to ring bells when later references to similar material occur. For the time being, when the client has spoken, the counsellor who wishes to acknowledge at the time that he or she has heard, but has not understood, can say: 'I have heard what you have been saying, but I'm not sure yet what it really means. But it's obviously important, and will become clearer as we go on.' As in all interventions that a counsellor makes, but more especially when there is any anxiety around in the client or counsellor, much of the impact of a response comes from the counsellor's manner and tone of voice. A 'still small voice' often enables a counsellor to express lack of understanding without causing concern or embarrassment to the client.

There is another aspect to not understanding, which I defer until Chapter 8. It is more likely to occur when counselling is more long-term, and is the feeling of being stuck, with either the client or the counsellor (or both) aware that they are going round in circles and getting nowhere. It can be very difficult at such times to know what is happening, but since this may be a sign of defensiveness, the counsellor's interventions often include an attempt to identify the reasons for the resistance as well as providing reassurance to the client that it may take time to understand what is happening.

SILENCE

At some point or other in every series of counselling sessions, there will come a time when silence falls and remains unbroken. It is less likely in a first session, because clients normally have a great deal they want to say. It is more likely to occur in later sessions. Whenever it happens, it can cause feelings of intense discomfort to client and counsellor. As with a client's talking going round in circles, silence can similarly indicate a conscious or unconscious resistance to speaking about uncomfortable things, although identifying its cause is not the same as doing something about it. Furthermore, it would be rash to put it down to any deep defensiveness in the early stages of counselling. Clients take time to get used to an atmosphere where they have permission to pause and think, and where neither side has to be saying anything. Only in close relationships is silence easily tolerated. In the early stages of counselling in particular, even the briefest of silences can be too long for many clients. Counsellors in the early stages of training also frequently find the silences too long when they observe video demonstrations of counselling. Experienced counsellors need to be alive to this anxiety, especially when they themselves grow more comfortable with allowing longer pauses.

Silence can in fact speak volumes. Before breaking it, it is best to try and gauge the particular mood. I vividly remember conducting a group session in which, apart from my own unproductive and, as I now see them, unnecessary interventions, silence reigned for a whole hour and a half. What was fascinating (and the members of the group said this when they were on speaking terms again the next week) was the way the silence moved in mood from embarrassment to anger, bewilderment to dejection, reflection to humour, with at times a very deep sense of peace. On one occasion in a different group that I was facilitating, I did not myself speak for the first seventy minutes. I was aware that I was partly afraid to speak because in the previous session I had been torn to shreds for an intervention I had made. But I was also aware that I was punishing the group who, despite their active conversation, became more and more uncomfortable at my silence.

What therefore does any silence mean? It may be that one client does not know what to say. Another may know what to say but is too embarrassed or frightened to say it. A third may be angry with the counsellor. It may be a battle of wills to see who will break the silence first. The silence may simply be a natural pause while the client thinks what to say next. It may be a time for reflecting upon what has been said, such as when a client sees the significance of their own words, or when a counsellor has offered a particularly poignant insight.

By tolerating a silence for a while, a counsellor has time to gauge what it might mean. If he or she feels a need to break it, which in early sessions may be more necessary than when a client gets used to natural pauses, it can be done in a way that draws out the mood as it appears to the counsellor:

'You seem to be deep in thought – I don't want to interrupt, but is there anything you want to share/find difficult to share with me?'

'You're not sure where to go from here/there?'

'You look puzzled/tense/upset/angry/etc.'

It is not wise to allow silences to go on for too long, especially when a client is obviously uncomfortable, although a counsellor who can pause just a little longer each time before intervening will often find that clients adapt to silences and break them themselves. Sometimes a client makes a direct reference to their discomfort: 'I don't like these silences'; or they may be even more direct: 'Can't you say something?' It is important, again especially in the early stages of counselling, when it is all new to a client, for a counsellor to explain the situation: 'I want to let you go at your own pace – I'm not trying to play a game with you. I am keeping relatively quiet because this time is for you, and I want you to have the chance to speak about what you want. But maybe we can look at what it is that is making that difficult for you at present. Perhaps it's me.' If a client says: 'I feel that you are expecting me to say something', a counsellor can explain: 'This is a time for you, and of course I'd like you to tell me whatever you can. But it's all right for you to be quiet if you want to think about what you might want to say.' In early meetings it is very important to build up trust and to invite a client's co-operation; and a counsellor has to co-operate too when a client is stuck, anxious and silent. Ways of responding to pauses, which consist of reflecting back, paraphrasing, repeating the last few words, and minimal prompts, are discussed more fully in *Swift to Hear*.[1] Only later, when a much firmer relationship has been established, might a counsellor want to interpret what a silence appears to mean.

FORMING A PICTURE

I have suggested that early sessions can be easier in respect of silence than later ones, because clients often have a lot that they are bursting to say. (Groups, incidentally, are often the opposite. Early meetings are full of difficult silences!) It is easier also for a counsellor when seeing a new client, because a counsellor wishes to build up a picture of the client, which means getting as much factual information about the immediate situation, the recent history, and even the earlier history of the client's background. I do not in this book look at the question of assessment, which can involve a detailed history. This is normally carried out by experienced counsellors and therapists, and is a particular specialized way of interviewing, which is used in many counselling settings, from voluntary agencies to private practice, to distinguish the clients who can best use counselling and the type of contract and counsellor they can be offered. I have illustrated in *Swift to Hear*[2] and elsewhere[3] some of the distinctive features of those people who might best use counselling and those who might better be suited for longer-term psychotherapy, as well as those who are probably not suitable for either.

Nevertheless, all counsellors want to know about their clients, and even if a full psychiatric history is inappropriate, early sessions provide the chance to ask pertinent questions when certain subjects are touched upon. A client's history builds up over time, with more of the obvious facts coming in early sessions, and much of the detailed and less obvious information coming in the fullness of time. The temptation in early sessions is to use questions when a client is passive, in order to keep the interview running smoothly. When this happens a counsellor is in danger of becoming an interviewer, or like a doctor taking a history in order to make a diagnosis and/or a prognosis. Questioning too early and too often creates a false impression of what the counsellor's part in the session is, which essentially is someone who listens, and who uses their relative passivity to try and help make sense of what the client is experiencing, feeling and thinking. As I indicated in Chapter 3, it is helpful for a counsellor to have some questions in mind, but it is better to ask them when they can be related to something the client has just said. Asking questions out of context frequently changes the subject. It may help counsellors to find out what they think they ought to know, but probably at the expense of the client's priorities.

OUTSIDE PRESSURES

Much of the anxiety that a counsellor feels in starting counselling stems from a sense of responsibility to the client. It is not made any better when the very essence of the counselling method largely prevents the counsellor from using more active ways of offering help. Even greater pressures can exist when a counsellor is asked to see a person at the request of a third party: sometimes this is a member of the client's family, but often it is another 'authority figure' such as a doctor, a teacher or a senior colleague. The counsellor is seen as the expert, or in some cases as the 'so-called expert' whom the third party wishes to test out. It is less the case than it once was, but some counsellors work within institutions or agencies that expect rapid results, or have third parties who make referrals and yet are sceptical of the value of counselling. Counsellors can feel not only the pressure of the client, but also of others to demonstrate their worth. There may be expectations from a person's relatives, or friends, who have 'sent' the client for counselling. Where there is a high level of anxiety in an institution, an agency or a family, a counsellor often has to deal with phone calls, letters, or even visits from other people, who want to ask the counsellor what he or she is doing, or who want to share their own concerns about the client.

There are all manner of questions raised in such situations, including the real motivation of the client, which I discuss in Chapter 8. There are ethical issues about confidentiality. Unless a person gives express permission, a counsellor (like other professionals) is not in a position to talk about the client with third parties, however close or concerned they may be. If a counsellor has time, he or she may choose to meet or speak with these people, because it can help them to share some of their anxieties. Obviously it is important to demonstrate some understanding of the dilemmas that face relatives, friends or other staff in an institution. It is equally important neither to reveal what the client is saying, nor to attempt to take these third parties on for counselling as well. A counsellor needs to be careful lest he or she becomes a go-between for members of a family, or between a teacher and a student, or a doctor and a patient, preventing what might be appropriate and more direct communication between them.

The clients in question should be informed about all such communications outside the session and with outside persons, so that they do not perceive the counsellor as going behind their back, even though this does not prevent the third parties from being seen that way. Clients have to be assured that their confidentiality has been respected, although such contacts can for a while undermine the therapeutic relationship, leading clients to distrust the counsellor until they have assured themselves that nothing has been revealed. Where a client does give permission for information to be passed on, counsellors need to be sure they know what information the client is prepared to have shared, and what the effects might be of doing so. Giving copies of any letters to the client might be seen as a clear way of assuring him or her of the counsellor's word.

If counsellors feel the stress of this type of third party pressure, this may indicate that particular clients also feel it, becoming suspicious of the counsellor, and fearing what may happen if they speak openly about themselves. What does a third party's referral mean to a client? It may mean the counsellor is seen as being there to enforce the 'powers that be': authorities sometimes send clients for counselling as part of a disciplinary procedure, so that it becomes part of the punishment. The client is often on a kind of 'parole' or 'suspended sentence' – I refer here not to the legal system, but to schools, universities, churches and other institutions. Alternatively, a counsellor may be expected by the client to become an advocate against other authority figures. A counsellor's task may be perceived as making the client 'fit' into a family's or partner's expectations, or as a way of shutting the client up, or as someone who will provide the client with powerful utterances that can be shuttled back to the family as a way of getting at them.

In the face of these and similar pressures, a counsellor needs both to feel independent within himself or herself, and also to ensure that the client is helped to trust and recognize the counsellor's impartiality. Saying it once is unlikely to be enough: indeed, saying anything once in counselling is seldom enough, and counsellors learn to watch out for continuing signs of anxiety long after they have tried to set a client at ease by reassuring them. The situations that I describe here often indicate family or institutional tensions that do not go away just because a client has started counselling. What is particularly difficult, and is made even more so when a counsellor feels antagonized by outside pressures, is trying to combine all that is best in empathy and sympathy for the client, and staying alongside them, with that type of impartiality that enables the counsellor to step back from the client's side. Only in this way can the counsellor initiate looking at the client's own contributions to family or institutional difficulties. Counselling does not mean believing the client is always right. Respect and acceptance does not mean getting enmeshed in the client's view of others. Counselling is most valuable when clients can be helped towards recognizing their own contribution to the tense and difficult situations they describe. What has the teenager said or done that has provoked his parents into being so angry – perhaps he has been testing them out. Why does the young woman who is constantly deceived by her partner stay with him, when experience suggests that he is unlikely to change? What is their part in all of this?

It is impossible to rely on what appears to be, or is made out to be, objective information. When it comes to analysing human relationships, they are too subtle, complex and slippery to get hold of in that straightforward way. In most circumstances a counsellor can only work with what he or she is given, which is the client and the client's story. When a third party intervenes this sometimes clarifies, but just as often it muddles the picture. In longer-term counselling and psychotherapy many of a person's difficulties begin to appear in their relationship with the therapist: it is then that therapist and client can start moving from only talking about the 'outside' situation, where it may not be clear who does what, to the 'inside'. In their immediate relationship it becomes clearer what the client contributes to the process and what the therapist contributes to it – as long as the counsellor or therapist remains as much aware of their own part in the relationship as they would wish clients to be aware of theirs in the outside situations they describe.

There is another outside pressure on a counsellor, which merits some attention. Behind every counsellor in a supportive way, but to some extent more negatively overshadowing any counsellor's work, is the training they have received, the books they have read, and the supervision that they receive. Tutors and books are third parties, authorities perched on the counsellor's shoulder, perceived sometimes as telling him or her what they should be saying or doing. Because a counsellor is supervised, there is always the awareness that what he or she is saying to and feeling with the client is subject to scrutiny. Particularly in sessions prior to presenting work in supervision, there can be tension between what a beginning counsellor would like to say to a client, and what he or she feels would look right when reporting the case. A counsellor can of course not tell a supervisor or a supervision group about particular clients, or 'be economical with the truth', although it would be a pity if supervision became viewed in such a threatening way that it led to secrecy. What this point also illustrates is that in starting in supervision a new counsellor often has many of the same feelings that a client has when starting counselling. Supervisors in turn need to recognize all this going on in their relationship with their supervisees.

BECOMING ONESELF

In a book such as this, which sets out to speak with some authority on the technical aspects of counselling, and to suggest ways of handling difficult counselling situations, it is all too easy for me to give the impression that counselling is really about 'tricks of the trade', and to lead some readers to equate counselling technique with manipulative game-playing. If this were true, it would run counter to the reader's wish to help others through what they can offer of themselves, so helping their clients to become more truly themselves.

If it is not yet clear from what I have written, and from the way that I write, it will become clear in later chapters that I hold the therapeutic relationship to be central to the process of counselling, as it is indeed to all helping work. People normally have to work quite hard at creating and sustaining good relationships, and there are identifiable features that help to make them successful or disastrous. Relationships are built up over a period of time, overcoming various hurdles along the way. The skills and other technical aspects I describe in this book are present, although not always analysed or expressed, in many other normal relationships. One of the distinctive features of the counselling relationship is that it is open to be talked about, much more so than in most other situations. Yet far from being abnormal, it may be that the counselling relationship sets a different norm, which might ultimately be of equal value in many other relationships as well.

To arrive at this way of relating does cause the beginner and the less experienced counsellor certain difficulties. There is room for conflict between the way a counsellor wants to be 'in himself or herself', and the way he or she is recommended to be in a counselling relationship. In the last chapter I suggested that counselling is a strange situation, very artificial in one way, deeply personal and human in another. It is an intimate relationship, yet also a distant one, and normally confined to one hour or less a week, with firm observation on the part of the counsellor of the boundaries of time. There may be intense feelings on the part of the client, but these feelings are limited to verbal expression or to tears; other forms of expression, such as interpersonal physical demonstrations of loving or hating, are expressly forbidden by the majority of authorities on counselling practice. I will show, when I describe the phenomenon of transference, that a counsellor allows perceptions of himself or herself to be made by some clients that may be quite false, staying with them, at least for a while, in order to help a client to understand how the client reacts to others and why. This can be experienced as discomforting to the counsellor, who would prefer to be seen for what he or she really is, especially when the projections or the transference are negative. Instead of answering a client's questions, a counsellor often prefers to put them back to the client to answer, or to look at them from another angle altogether, which sometimes feels as if he or she is being awkward. A counsellor may express certain feelings such as pleasure or laughter with the client, and at the same time hold back other feelings such as disappointment, disagreement or other reactions which might be expressed more readily in other situations. Such examples confirm that counselling is not a normal social meeting, or even a normal business meeting, as many clients themselves observe, especially as they come to value the uniqueness of the situation that provides them with an opportunity to be themselves as they can be in no other setting.

Added to all this, beginning counsellors are told that they must be 'real'. The person-centred approach has correctly identified one of the core conditions of effective counselling as being genuine.[4] Counsellors are rightly encouraged to be in touch with themselves, and to be more spontaneous, and yet at the same time there are what amount to injunctions upon them, that are equally valid, to be very careful about how they respond. They may be taxed by clients who wonder why the counsellor does not talk about him or herself, and who might even express intense frustration at what they see as a complete

lack of response to them. Some even complain quite openly
that what they really want is a friendship. If counsellors have
any feelings at all, they can at such times experience themselves as harsh, depriving and insensitive, unable to respond
to what the client convincingly argues is an ordinary and reasonable request.

Such conflicts and discomfort never completely go away,
particularly when clients have deep needs for closeness that
they wish their counsellor to meet. But much of the initial
conflict that does exist for anyone who is at all human between
the role of being a counsellor and being oneself lessens with
increasing experience of working with clients. As Kennedy
and Charles write: 'Artificiality drops away and the atmosphere
and the exchange become less studied and more genuine . . .
We discover that our best responses match our best potential
as human beings.'[5] As technical skills are assimilated, they are
more naturally expressed. They are more readily adapted to
each situation, and the counsellor experiences a greater sense
of freedom, knowing the value and the importance of the
boundaries which he or she sets, and how to be flexible within them. As long as he or she is not an obsessional personality,
for whom everything must always be done the same way, what
appeared at one time to be rules are seen as the guidelines
they are intended to be, reminders of what often works best for
the majority of clients. Feeling more secure as a counsellor,
her or his unique way of being begins to emerge in a way that
does not intrude upon the client, but that often enhances the
relationship. Technique is tempered with the care and compassion that was always the motive for wishing to be a counsellor
in the first instance. Where accepted counselling skills appear
counter-productive with a particular client, counsellors learn
to use their supervision to reconsider how they might handle
specific situations.

In his book *True and False Experience*,[6] Peter Lomas looks
at the need for psychotherapy and psychotherapists to develop
beyond the necessary first steps which Freud took in his
understanding both of technique and the nature of the therapeutic relationship, to put more emphasis on the real human
relationship between, using his terms, the therapist and the
patient. Lomas recounts how the important and much-respected
psychoanalyst Winnicott suggested that no analyst should depart

from recommended technique until he had ten years' experience of routine practice behind him. But Lomas wishes to put it another way, no doubt drawing upon his own experience. He suggests that 'it takes ten years for most psychoanalysts to gain the confidence to depart from a technical approach which they should never have adopted in the first place.'[7] He has argued elsewhere[8] that new therapists have of course many years of life experience upon which to draw.

Lomas is particularly critical of some aspects of technique, and indeed does not like the term 'technique' at all. Lomas and Winnicott and many others who are important authorities in the field of therapy and counselling are in good company together, since most of them have in some way or other chosen to break away either from the established theory or technique learned in their own training. Indeed, they have become new authorities on therapy partly because they have made distinctive contributions of their own.

New counsellors are frequently like rule-conscious children – although there are a few more dangerous ones who are like boundary-less babies. There is nothing obsessional about observing rules; like children learning the rules of new games, who insist they are stuck to, it is wise to be initially cautious about the adults who try to change them. Unfortunately, students of counselling sometimes elevate what they have learned to the status of inviolable technique or practice, whatever school they have been trained in. They say nothing about themselves, if trained perhaps in a psychodynamic school, even though they are longing to say 'me too'; or they generate all the warmth they can, if trained perhaps in a person-centred approach, even when they do not feel it with a particular client; or they refuse to give any advice, if in one approach or another they have been taught to be non-directive. There is a sense in which they are right, and I for one do not want them to overturn the basic guidelines before they are very well used to practising them, and so have become second nature. In learning about counselling there are some ways of helping and relating that need to be unlearned, because they are not part of a counselling approach. Many of the points that I make in this book work rather well, and help clients to feel more secure, to express themselves and to grow. It is important to keep relatively quiet, to stick to time boundaries, to know how to answer a client's question without being drawn in inappropriately, to know that touching clients is not usual, and in all circumstances to proceed with care as well as caution.[9]

Kennedy and Charles comment that 'maturing counsellors appreciate the fact that what they do in counselling does not ask them to change themselves as much as it invites them to come closer to their best but frequently unrealized selves'.[10] I question them slightly, because I believe that most people learning to be counsellors *are* being asked to change aspects of themselves, *in order to* discover their unrealized potentialities. Counsellors have for a long time realized that much that is beneficial to a good counselling relationship is also the mark of a good human response. What at one time may have appeared to be 'natural' ways of relating can be artificial culturally-determined defences against effective and honest communication.

When clients observe that counselling is a strange situation, it might be appropriate to agree with them, because there is indeed something unique about it. The whole area of therapeutic relationships is a fascinating one, since there are many other relationships that are also therapeutic, and anti-therapeutic. Counselling is not the same as friendship, as those who try to counsel their friends in a more formal way will soon discover. Yet it has something of that quality. Counselling is not the same as marriage or a similar intimate relationship; or the same as the parent–child, the teacher–student, or the work relationship. Yet it has aspects of each, just as each of these has elements that also appear in the therapy relationship.

No amount of experience can take away any of the feelings or situations described in this chapter, which from time to time will be as strong as they were when first starting counselling, and are in any case always somewhere below the surface. They may not always be as disquieting as they are at first, but they will always be around. The counsellor who forgets them, or denies them, or is tempted to say he or she no longer feels them, betrays the fact that they are still only a little way towards becoming a mature counsellor. It is through being able to monitor and recognize these and similar uncomfortable responses, as well as the more positive ones, that an effective counsellor is able to keep in touch with what clients experience both in their relationship with himself or herself, and elsewhere with others.

NOTES

1. M. Jacobs, *Swift to Hear*. SPCK 2000 (2nd edn), pp. 55-7.
2. ibid., pp. 150-6.
3. M. Jacobs, *Psychodynamic Counselling in Action*. Sage Publications 1999 (2nd edn), pp. 63-72.
4. C. B. Truax and R. R. Carkhuff, *Towards Effective Counseling and Psychotherapy Training and Practice*. Chicago: Aldine Press 1967.
5. E. Kennedy and S. Charles, *On Becoming a Counsellor*. Dublin: Gill & Macmillan 1989 (2nd edn), p. 63.
6. P. Lomas, *True and False Experience*. Allen Lane 1973.
7. ibid., p. 147.
8. See my video made with Peter Lomas: *A Conversation with Peter Lomas* (1990), available from Audio-Visual Services, University of Leicester, Medical Sciences Building, University Road, Leicester.
9. I explore the issues in this section at greater depth in M. Jacobs, 'A maturing professional approach', *Contact - Interdisciplinary Journal of Pastoral Studies* (1990), 101, pp. 19-27.
10. Kennedy and Charles, p. 62.

CHAPTER SIX

Boundaries of Time and Space

Those who are asked to help, to give advice or to counsel, frequently respond in one of three unhelpful ways. The first is to plead ignorance, to refer the person vaguely to another source of help, and to retire from the scene as fast as possible. The second, which is particularly tempting to those people who fill their life with frenetic activity, and who appear to need to prove to themselves and to others that they are useful, is to imagine that personal problems can be solved in a matter of minutes. Preferring to give advice than to listen, they only hear the bare bones of the problem before delivering a few comfortable words. Such people probably allay their own anxiety more than that of the person who has approached them. Their need is to 'do something' and to do it quickly.

The third pitfall is more common among those who have begun to learn the value of listening. In this case, the eager counsellor spends not just one hour, but two or even more hours at one sitting, listening, talking, hoping that with time a solution will present itself. What actually happens is very different. Both counsellor and client become more and more tired, and end up going round and round in ever-increasing circles. The helper becomes more desperate to find a way through. Yet his or her tiredness and frustration makes this even less likely the longer they go on.

It is true that time heals, although the time that it takes to adjust to even the most acute situations has to be measured in weeks and not in hours. In all kinds of helping work the time that the helper can spend with a person in distress is necessarily brief, even if it is 'quality' time that can be intense and productive. Clients spend much more of their week on their own or with others, thinking and doing things that in some cases help the work of the counselling session to be carried forward. In order to make the time with the client as special and as productive as possible, it is important to consider how best to structure it.

I have already drawn attention in Chapter 2 to the distinctions that need to be made between counselling and counselling skills or, to put it another way, between formal and informal counselling. When looking at boundaries this distinction must be borne in mind. Much of the work of clergy and of other professional and voluntary helpers involves this latter type of informal counselling where an ongoing series of structured appointment times is either not possible or does not seem appropriate. I look first at these more informal settings before examining the use of time in the more structured and formal counselling. Much of what I suggest about informal settings is equally applicable to formal counselling; and while the latter may not appear immediately relevant to some of my readers, the principles involved in formal counselling have an important bearing on less structured work, especially when counselling skills are used. Indeed, the way time is viewed and used by both the helper and client is often an indication of attitudes and personal wishes and fears in other relationships as well.

TIME BOUNDARIES IN INFORMAL COUNSELLING

Since personal difficulties are rarely resolved after one visit or consultation, it is important to recognize the need for continuing contact with those who seek help. Many helpers have heard complaints about those who have seen these people before: how they only visited once; that they never came back; that they did not want to know; or that they said they would call again and did not. There may have been good reasons for this: the visitor may have felt that one visit was enough. The busy professional person has other demands and emergencies that fill his or her diary, making further visits more difficult. Those who are indeed kept busy trying to meet the demands upon them can easily forget that the client whom they visited might have seen them as the only person to whom they could talk.

All caring work, therefore, whether it be in voluntary agencies, professional settings, the church or secular services, could benefit from the experience about appointments that counsellors have: how there is value in making arrangements to meet again, even if it is some time ahead, and even if it is for a shorter duration, because this gives the client something to look ahead to. It is, of course, very important to be able to keep the appointments. To be reliable is very caring in itself, providing a sense of safety to the person with whom a further appointment has been made. Even where one meeting appears to have been sufficient to resolve immediate issues, the offer of another time, if only to see how the client is coping, may make all the difference in consolidating the help given. Such an offer is not necessarily accepted, but it should none the less be made.

In fact, planning times ahead is not just of benefit to the person who is offered assistance. Such arrangements also help to make the sometimes limitless demands of pastoral and other caring work more manageable. The helper offers time, but with limits set upon it. A meeting arranged for two weeks ahead may make it less necessary for a client to ring beforehand, which is more likely to happen if he or she does not know when the helper will appear again. This means less interruption for the helper. When such a meeting is arranged, a limit can be set on it: 'I'll be able to see you for half an hour.' Here again the specified time can help the client as well as the helper, because they know that they are not taking up more time than the helper can spare.

If there are some clients who are afraid to ask too much, there are others who can be very demanding. These are sometimes the people whom most helpers do not relish meeting, because it is so difficult to get away from them: the thought of an interminable time with them easily acts as a barrier to seeing them again. Stating a time, both date and duration, makes such a meeting more manageable, as long as the helper stays firm with what was originally offered. The limits that counsellors impose on the length of their sessions, and even on their number over a period of weeks or months, provide a useful model that can easily be adapted to many pastoral situations and other caring work.

The frequency and duration of such meetings, whether they involve the client coming to a pastor's office, or to a voluntary agency, or the carer visiting the person's home, depend upon a number of circumstances. In the case of a bereavement, regularly spaced visits may provide a strong sense of structure for the bereaved at a time when their world may have collapsed into pieces. Although later visits may be arranged less frequently, contact might be sustained for a period of months, since grieving is a long process. In highly fraught situations visits may need to be more frequent, though where this is the case they should be for a shorter duration. Caring work and supportive counselling (the next chapter explains how this is different from counselling that explores and uncovers deeper feelings) often necessitate greater flexibility of time and frequency than is customary in formal counselling, although this never means providing limitless time at any point.

Obviously such arrangements have to be agreed, however informally, by the pastor and the parishioner. Times must be mutually convenient, yet certain times of the day might be better avoided, especially when there is the possibility of distractions in a home visit, such as children being home from school. The formal counselling interview is in some respects much more comfortable for the counsellor and the client than many pastoral and other caring situations. There are additional stresses put upon the more informal meetings when they have to take place in the client's own home: apart from unavoidable distractions, it can be less easy for clients to take a step back from their immediate situation and from the pressures around them. On the other hand, the visiting carer, befriender or counsellor sometimes has a clearer picture of what their client has to put up with.

All these practical arrangements have in themselves a stabilizing effect on many of those who are distressed. They know that someone is there; and the next time they can meet is a fixed number of days away. Because this fixed point provides an anchor, those who offer care in pastoral and other settings have to be careful about the way they respect such arrangements. In addition to being reliable in keeping them, they need to give enough warning, and to make an alternative time, if they have to alter dates. Where such alterations have to be made, even if it means keeping the client waiting just a day longer,

the pastor or the caring person must be sensitive to the possibilities of disappointment in the client. The same sensitivity
is necessary in respect of holidays or other times that may make
a longer wait between appointments necessary. This means
listening for hints of the client's feelings, and encouraging
such feelings to be expressed. Unreliability in itself discourages
trust, but so too do altered arrangements when there is no
opportunity to discuss how this affects the client. Although my
experience relates to formal counselling, the following example
illustrates the point and provides a link into time boundaries
in more formal settings.

> I had to alter arrangements with a client, at her request, but
> forgot to check my diary on the day, and so arrived late at
> work to find her waiting. Because she was relieved to see
> me at all, my first attempts to tap her anger at being kept
> waiting, and being forgotten, met with no response. I came
> back to it later in the session, when a reference to being
> let down elsewhere gave me a reminder that I had not yet
> worked through my error. This time my client admitted
> that she had been sitting waiting and fuming, but that she
> found it difficult to hold on to angry feelings for very long.
> She knew, however, from past experience, that such feelings
> would come back when she was walking home.

TIME BOUNDARIES IN FORMAL COUNSELLING

All that I have described about making clear time arrangements, about being reliable, and about altering arrangements,
applies equally to formal counselling. There is another factor
about time that counsellors in more formal practice recognize
as important, relating to decisions about frequency of meetings.
The more frequently a counsellor sees a client, the greater the
likelihood of the creation of a dependent relationship. Some
new counsellors, or those who are suspicious of counselling,
worry about clients becoming dependent and they get very
anxious when clients hint at such feelings. In fact, counselling
requires clients who can trust the counsellor, and who are not
afraid of being somewhat dependent. Clients who are themselves scared of becoming dependent can be the most difficult

to engage. There are some who become very dependent and require the care of more experienced counsellors, although even less experienced carers and counsellors can often provide a stable point for a dependent client to grow towards autonomy, as long as they are utterly reliable, unflappable, firm on keeping to time boundaries, and can offer time ahead for the foreseeable future. I can think of a number of people, some of whom were never trained as counsellors, who have been available, but with clear limits, to some temporarily very dependent people, and who have helped them through to a deeper sense of calm as well as to greater autonomy.

Generally, the less frequently counsellor and client meet, the less chance there is to maintain continuity. In some instances, although not all, it may be difficult to build up any sense of trust. Conversely, the more frequently they meet, the more likelihood there is of deeper dependency, making the meetings more necessary to the client, and disappointment greater when they do not take place, or when the frequency is lessened. Generally speaking, for the type of counselling described in this book, meeting once a week would be the norm, although less formal counselling may take place more infrequently.

Clear boundaries help clients. They know where they are. They value what becomes their own time. They do not feel guilty about using their time in the way they want to. They even know when they can get away! The demarcation of clear boundaries also helps the counsellor, and has the added advantage of providing some protection when working with that small but much-feared minority of people who become very demanding, finding every and any excuse to contact the counsellor or the caring helper. If counsellors have agreed fixed times with their clients when they can meet, extra demands can more easily be met with the reminder that 'perhaps we can talk about that at the time we have arranged to meet'. There are however no simple ways of handling these difficult situations, especially when the helper is pushed on the limits that have already been agreed. Problems with clients such as these should always be taken for discussion in super-vision, so that support for maintaining boundaries can be given, and the possibility of understanding the abuse of them can be attempted.

With a better sense of the use of time – both its availability and its limits – counsellors and their clients come to sense the possibilities that come from having a definite structure within which to work. Most counsellors arrange for their sessions to last for 45 or 50 minutes. Sometimes the opening words of the session have particular significance: they may even act as the 'theme' for the meeting.[1] The first half of the time can often be given over to encouraging clients to relate what they want to say, with the counsellor reflecting and responding to help clients to expand on their concerns, in ways described in Chapter 3. Any comments, links or interpretations that the counsellor thinks it might be helpful to make need to be put while there is still time for the client to understand them and perhaps respond to them. The proximity of the end of the session sometimes needs to be pointed out a few minutes before the actual time of finishing, when feelings associated with ending the session might also be drawn out. Although this is a somewhat stereotypical picture of a counselling session, it is a useful framework to have in mind, including in adapted form in the more informal meetings of pastoral care and other types of help.

The structure of formal counselling is that of a fixed session, with a given length of time that the counsellor works to, and often, although not invariably, for an agreed number of sessions ahead. Counselling, as I explained in Chapter 2, is usually more time-limited than is psychotherapy, where an open-ended contract is more usual. Nevertheless, some counsellors, while still working for a limited number of sessions, do not define the number at the start, but wait for a natural point at which to draw the counselling to an end. Even in this case, they give proper attention to fixing an ending a few weeks ahead. Although the duration of a series of counselling sessions can be extended, if there is need and if the counsellor has the space, a definite contract has advantages, not least in that it helps to concentrate the issues. This also has implications for the handling of endings (for a full discussion of endings, see Chapter 11).

Time, duration and contract are, of course, not legal requirements; they are more in the nature of a commitment and an agreement between counsellor and client. Every counsellor has to learn (often through his or her mistakes) when to relax boundaries compassionately; but also when to hold firm to them. It is obviously irresponsible to finish a session, or bring a contract to an end, when it is obvious that the client cannot cope. When there is a genuine emergency, and when a counsellor has time, it is uncaring not to give an extra appointment. Most isolated calls for extra help are made from genuine motives, when a person has reached the point of not knowing where else to turn. On most occasions there will be reasons external to counselling itself that give rise to such calls, but they are sometimes related to the previous appointment: where, for example, a chance remark by the counsellor may have unnerved the client, who then has to get in touch to check that all is still well.

There are inevitably occasions when a counsellor has no extra time to offer, and with the best will in the world cannot help. Since the solution is not in most cases to tell clients to see someone else, they sometimes have to wait – and they invariably do. The result in some instances is that they feel much stronger for having entered a crisis and yet come out the other side relying mainly on their own resources. Referral to another therapist at such a time, in the middle of a counselling contract, usually only confuses the issue, and is in any case not what the client wants. Nevertheless, it is not good practice for counsellors to work in complete isolation, and for occasional clients it may be necessary for counsellors and other helpers to ask a colleague to provide some kind of cover while they are away – to be ready to take a phone call if necessary, which is preferable to offering a face-to-face session.

What counsellors (and indeed other helpers) need to spot are those clients who are always asking for extra time, since another solution is probably called for than squeezing in further sessions. In such cases greater frequency of sessions may be necessary for a very disturbed client, who has regressed (gone back) to a state of infantile dependency: and obviously other therapeutic resources may be called for in such cases. In every instance, a counsellor should discuss such situations with her or his supervisor before even mentioning the possibility of regular extra appointments to a client. In many cases it is far better to face what may be difficult and demanding clients with a firm reminder of the boundaries, simultaneously trying to help them to look at what it is that pushes them to go on testing the counsellor out.

What becomes clear in discussing boundaries is just how much control a counsellor has over time. Indeed, this is an area where it is possible to use and abuse power over the client. Clients have the power to stay away from sessions: but only counsellors and therapists have the power to provide sessions at certain times and on certain days, to change the length or time of the session, or to give extra sessions. Even within the space of a session, a counsellor is monitoring the progress of the hour to ensure that the session allows a client time to expand, and time to draw things together. It is rare for a well-conducted session to go over time. By keeping an eye on the time (albeit avoiding obviously looking at the clock or a watch) a counsellor can structure the session to allow a person who is very distressed to wind down. Clients can then leave in a relatively calm state, at least in their outward composure. It is often their appearance that is their greatest concern, because they do not want others to see that they are, or have been, distressed.

One example of careful handling of the end occurred with Freda:

The session was coming to a close with only five minutes left. I noticed that the anger that Freda had been expressing had turned to sadness, because her eyes were moist, even though her tone of voice was still bitter. I wondered what I should do. Should I acknowledge that she was also feeling very sad? If she began to cry it might not be so easy to keep her tears in check at the end of those five minutes. Should I keep quiet about my observation, but perhaps lose the opportunity of reaching into this side of her feelings? She was normally angry, and had not yet showed any sign of breaking down. For a moment I kept quiet, weighing up the possibilities, until Freda rather sheepishly smiled at me. I felt she was wanting me to acknowledge something, and I said what I had been thinking: 'It's nearly time to finish, but I'm aware how sad you feel. I'm hesitant about mentioning it with only a few minutes to go.'

Freda nodded, and she began to cry in a restrained way. I went on: 'There's quite a lot of pain there.' She cried more openly, and I did not interrupt for a brief while; but then I gently said: 'It's difficult to stop there, but we must do so soon. Would you like a few minutes here quietly before you leave?' Freda shook her head, dried her tears, and left. The session ended only a few minutes over time. The next week she said how my acknowledging her sadness had helped, because she had taken some steps in the intervening period to help herself with some of the causes of it.

It is not always possible to give more than a few extra minutes. On those occasions when clients get very upset, and want some time to wind down and make themselves feel presentable to the outside world, it helps for a counsellor to have an extra room where the client can rest until he or she is ready to leave. This is not always possible to arrange, especially if counsellors work alone and have little space other than their office; but those who work as part of a team in more spacious premises may wish to consider this type of facility, available to be used when really necessary. It makes ending a difficult session easier for both counsellor and client.

Handling the start of sessions also calls for some thought. Counsellors can learn from the feelings and reactions of their clients about time boundaries, and sometimes understand more about these clients. This is particularly so with clients who are late for sessions. It is possible that a client who is late may have indeed missed the bus, or may have been delayed by a phone call when about to leave home. Such excuses can be taken at face value, although there may be underlying reasons for leaving late or staying on the phone that should not be dismissed out of hand. It is normally only possible to help a client look at lateness when there is some evidence of ulterior motive, such as a difficult last session; or where there is per-sistent lateness. This latter may be a sign of disorganization that affects other areas of a client's life, which has other implications. Here are two examples:

1. 'I'm sorry I'm late. I'm not just late for you, I'm late every-where.' I observed to George that he seemed to be saying that he found it difficult to organize his life, and reminded him that that was one of the things he had initially com-plained of when he had first come to see me.

'It's not just that,' he replied. 'I don't want to look as if I've got to fit in with what others want me to do. I was late this morning for classes too, because I'm blowed if I should do what my tutor wants.'

This helped me to see that one of the reasons why George could not pass his exams was because he was fighting against any sign that he was being made to comply with other people. He compensated by over-asserting his independence, although nearly always in a way that was counter-productive to him, since he got a very poor reputation with authority figures, and it undermined his efforts to stay at university.

2. 'I'm late again,' said Helen in a voice that taunted me. I responded, 'You say that as if you think there's something significant about being late. Are you wanting to draw my attention to how late you always are?'
    'I suppose so – I'm not sure of the value of coming here any more.'

As we explored her feelings about seeing me, Helen related how easily she got into a rut in her relationships with men. She liked relationships that were 'touch and go' – in more senses than one, as I pointed out to her. Because I had laid down the times when we could meet, she saw me as both controlling her and tying her down. With a history of a very dominant father, she found it difficult to relate to any man, such as me, who appeared to be in charge.

In addition to genuine causes for lateness, there are therefore many possible meanings: it can happen if a counsellor keeps a client waiting, or goes on holiday, or alters an appointment – when the client is late it is a kind of 'tit for tat'. Sometimes it may be a way of expressing disappointment or hurt at what a counsellor said, or failed to say, or did not notice the last time they met. Lateness often shows how anxious a client is about coming, because it may mean talking about difficult subjects. It may mean that the client is dissatisfied because nothing is changing, yet cannot express criticism of the counsellor.
    Counselling involves the encouragement to express feelings openly; lateness, or even leaving a session early, may be a form of 'acting out' (as it is known) for clients, rather than actually saying what they feel. Counsellors themselves need to be

careful that they do not 'act out' either; for example, not picking up persistent lateness, or clients regularly leaving the session early, can be a way of avoiding what the counsellor feels, which sometimes is equal anger with the client. If a client is indirectly expressing criticism of a counsellor, the counsellor obviously also needs to be open to accept it, which may involve taking up the misuse of time boundaries.

I have suggested that the end of the session can also give rise to certain situations that may point to meanings other than the obvious. When a client brings up a subject that is interesting, and makes the counsellor want to ask more, this may make him or her unsure about finishing at that point. Such late remarks may be for all manner of reasons: that the client in fact does not want to talk in detail about the topic, even if the counsellor is interested. The client knows there will be no time to do more than register it. Alternatively, a door handle remark can be a message that the client wants more time, and does not want to go, and is trying to claim more attention. In most instances it is wise to avoid being drawn into saying anything other than, 'I wonder if we can take that up next time.' It is risky to try and interpret a client's late remarks at a point when there is no time to pick up the client's response. Sometimes, however, a counsellor does not realize what is happening until afterwards:

I was seeing Joan at her doctor's suggestion. There were some serious family tensions that the doctor knew about, but that the doctor had not told me. In his letter of referral he had hinted at these problems, but since they involved confidential information about other people as well, he felt he should not divulge them. I concurred, not least because I like to start fresh with a client from the beginning, without knowing anything other than what the client wants to tell me.

We had met a dozen times, with the doctor's hints always in the background. I knew that something was there, but I did not know what, and Joan referred from time to time to 'a dark secret'. I tried to help Joan look at what it was that made it difficult for her to tell me more, but we got nowhere that way. Then one day Joan started by saying that she had decided to tell me something which I ought to know. At last!

I sat back, was all ears, and felt pleased that there was now sufficient trust between us to allow her to reveal the mysteries hitherto hidden from me.

Joan said she would start at the beginning, which for her was way back in the family history of those long since dead. For forty-five minutes she went through this history in detail, although none of it seemed to touch upon anything that indicated why she was so depressed, or upon 'the secret' that was too shocking to be told until today. We were due to finish, when she said, 'It's very difficult for me to get it all in today, could we go on now?' By this time I was well and truly hooked. It was my last engagement of the day, so I said that just this once I would go on for another forty-five minutes, if that would help. I was convinced Joan would then tell me everything.

She resumed her story from where she had left off, and continued to cover the minute details of her early life. There was again no hint of anything that could be described as 'a dark secret'. And so it went on for a further forty-five minutes. I was still none the wiser. Or perhaps I was a little wiser, because I realized at that point that it had been a mistake for me to let Joan go on. After she had left the room, I recognized how much this 'secret' had become a game between us. I began to see parallels between what happened between us, and what had always felt like her teasing behaviour towards men. Eventually 'the secret' came out, but it was of little significance even to Joan, who had used it to try and control the therapeutic relationship.

A different situation around the close of the session tended to occur when I was seeing Keith. I began to feel that despite providing a lot of care and showing considerable understanding of him, it was not sufficient. Some clients would have passed through the crisis at this point in a series of sessions, but what seemed to be at issue was difficulty over the limits of time I could give Keith:

His father, to whom he had been very close, had suddenly left home to live with another woman, turning his back on him and on the rest of the family. Naturally Keith was very upset, although he was not living at home, but sharing a flat with two other young men. In his sessions with me Keith was fairly calm until the last minute, when I said it was time to finish. He invariably began at that point to cry hysterically, curling himself up into a tight ball in the chair, and arousing in me a lot of concern. I felt heartless. At first I tried to ease the situation by reminding Keith that we would have to finish, and allowing him to calm down in his own time. This took me as much as ten minutes over the end of the session.

I then began to learn from other people that Keith was leaving my room and casting himself upon them in an equally dramatic way, pouring out all his grief and anger, and clinging to those who offered to listen. He had done this so often and for such a long time that they began to grow impatient with him, and with me, because they began to get in touch to tell me so. I realized that Keith did not show me very much of his intense feeling and certainly not his anger. He did not make me feel angry either, although it was obvious that my own calm acceptance of him was missing something important.

After a particularly irate call from one of the young men in his flat I decided I needed to look at my handling of the situation. When the time drew near for me to announce the end of the session, I said, 'I think you may be feeling annoyed with me for saying we have to finish, when you would like to go on.' 'No,' Keith replied very reasonably. 'I'm very grateful to you for listening to me.' 'But I still think you would like me to go on listening for longer.' I added, 'I think you feel I turn my back on you just as you feel your father has done.' This time Keith left without a fuss.

The next week he came very late for his session, saying he had forgotten about the appointment. I pointed out to him that it was most unusual for him to be late. I wondered if he felt annoyed with me for drawing attention to the limits. Despite his thanks at the time, I still thought he was resentful at having to leave. It is not always possible to know why change occurs, but it was probably not pure coincidence that from that week onwards Keith ceased to take his troubles so obviously elsewhere and began to make some adjustment to the situation with his father.

There is little that occurs in the course of a counselling

relationship, including the counselling contract, that does not throw some light upon the fundamental aspects of a client's inner world or on their other relationships. The following example again shows how significant the time and frequency of meetings can be to a client, and how reactions to a counsellor's setting of limits parallel responses to similar circumstances:

Laura was married to a professional man. She did not need to earn her own income, although she was always busy with all kinds of voluntary work for local charities. She was most unhappy at home. Her husband was not very generous with money, even though he had a large income. He would buy all the books and records that he wanted, but would brush off her own requests for things for herself. She found it difficult to ask him for anything more than the running expenses of the house. It emerged in the course of the first session with me that her father had never given her much encouragement, and that he was distant and stern, although her mother had often slipped her the odd five shillings when she was going out, and had always been caring towards her.

One week, between our scheduled sessions, Laura phoned me to ask if she could have an earlier appointment because she was feeling upset. Unfortunately there was no way in which I was able to make it any earlier. It may also have been bad timing that when she came at her usual time I also had to mention that I would be taking a break for my holiday in a few weeks' time. I did not think to take up her feelings about the impossibility of my arranging an earlier session, until the end of the hour, when I noticed how tearful Laura looked. This reminded me that I should have mentioned it. I said that I thought Laura might still be disappointed in me, for not being able to see her sooner. Laura replied that it did not matter, and I again took this at face value. She looked quite angry as she left the room, and only then did I realize that it would have been better if I had said, 'I think it does matter to you.' As I made notes on the session I also spotted that I had missed the significance of Laura saying that she had met someone at a dinner party who had confided in her that she too was seeing me. Although in her head Laura had realized that I saw other people, it wasn't until she had actually met another client that she had felt jealous. I wondered whether it had been this chance meeting with another of my clients that had led Laura to ask for an earlier session.

Fortunately the opportunities that are missed in one session can often be taken up in another, as long as a counsellor realizes what has been happening:

The next time Laura and I met, much of what I had wondered about was confirmed. Laura started by expressing how angry she had felt last time, because I had not given her any extra time when I could see how upset she was at the end of the session. She felt that I only cared about her while she was with me, and I ignored how she felt in between times. If I was like *her*, she said, if I was *really* involved with helping people like *she* was, I would soon realize that I have to be available to other people whenever they need you. It was indeed a forceful outburst.

Although I was left smarting (and indeed I had made a considerable number of mistakes with her), I was also surprised, and in that sense pleased, that she had been able to voice her discontent openly. In another session, after the one in which Laura was able to tell me what she felt, I pointed out that although I had not given her extra time, she had herself replied that it did not matter when I had suggested that she might be disappointed in me. I also began to look at the way she gave herself away to others without setting any limits, including giving way to all her husband's whims. There was perhaps some merit in setting limits. Laura obviously took this insight to heart, and learned from being able to tell me what she thought of me, because she began to make appropriate demands upon her husband. She discovered to her surprise that if she asked strongly enough he would respond, and that he could be much more generous when asked than she had thought possible. She was none the less, because of the structure of their relationship, still dependent upon him.

It was significant that when our counselling contract was coming to an end, Laura said that my work must be very demanding. She had avoided being demanding herself, and in her home and helping work she had allowed other people to make unreasonable demands upon her. My ability to respond to her (some of the time), as well as (at other times) both to choose not to, and also accidentally to fail to meet her demands, all combined to help Laura look at some of the possibilities for constructive action and change.

Such examples from the arena of formal counselling illustrate the active use that is made of time boundaries. They are treated as more than a set of business-like arrangements (which indeed they are), since they become yet another focus for the relationship between counsellor and client, with its implications for other relationships in the client's life. These particular examples also demonstrate how even with experience counsellors miss signs from and in their clients, although they learn how to recognize their failures and to take up such issues later. Using the boundaries of time and the therapeutic relationship in this way is not typical of the application of counselling skills in less structured settings. There are lessons to be learned about time and limits in formal counselling settings that pastors and other helpers who use counselling skills can adapt to their own work. It is important to become more sensitive to the importance of time and other boundaries, and to understand how precious such spaces become for those for whom such people care.

BOUNDARIES OF PERSONAL SPACE

While there is considerable therapeutic value in the sensitive use of time and contracts in counselling, there are other boundary issues that are just as important to helpers and to clients; these also need addressing. If there is to be proper respect of each other in the therapeutic relationship, counsellors must avoid invading the personal space of their clients, and some clients need to be helped to avoid the temptation of invading the personal space of their counsellors.

Counsellors and other helpers are in considerable demand. Laura in the example above was right: caring is often exhausting work. Counsellors need to protect the boundaries of their own personal space, by ensuring that their workloads are manageable, and managed so that they do not invade their private lives. If clients need to make contact between sessions, they should be encouraged to do this at particular times. Only very rarely should they be given a private phone number. Discriminating counsellors learn to recognize those clients who have to be kept at arm's length, particularly outside the counselling session, as well as to recognize those who will make intelligent use of an emergency number – indeed, the only clients to whom such a number should be given should be those who are unlikely ever to use it, but for whom possessing it acts as a type of necessary talisman.

Counsellors need to protect themselves against overwork and against clients who do not know how to control their demands. It is equally important that counsellors and therapists are alive to the personal space of their clients. Here I refer partly to the extreme care with which a counsellor makes any kind of intervention, so as not to frighten a client away, as well as not to take advantage of a client who is willing to answer everything a counsellor asks. Ways of intervening that accurately assess the client's limits of tolerance are examined in the next chapter.

The particular boundary about which there is need for real caution is that of body space. Counsellors starting out inevitably raise the question of touch. I imagine that discussions about its place in counselling will continue for as long as therapy is practised. I may recommend that counsellors do not touch their clients, because of the danger of intrusiveness, but there are other respected therapists who recommend that counsellors learn how to use touch appropriately to avoid the danger of being seen as cold and distant.

These are particular issues for helpers who wish to make use of counselling skills in circumstances where they are normally used to touching their patients or clients: doctors and nurses clearly have to use touch most of the time, sometimes in most intimate parts of the body; clergy may use touch as an expression of a blessing or in the course of their own type of healing ministry; other helpers may be accustomed to shaking hands, or touching an arm or shoulder, as a natural and spontaneous part of relating that does not normally merit a second thought.

Nevertheless, in counselling in medical settings it has long been accepted that doctors who have patients in psychotherapy need to pass physical care of the patient to a colleague. It is when doctors and paramedical staff in such settings use counselling skills that the boundaries are more blurred, and need to be extremely carefully monitored. Similarly, clergy who normally use touch in their pastoral and spiritual ministry need to be careful of its place when they make active use of counselling skills with the same persons. These warnings apply as much to those using counselling skills in other settings. The boundaries are unclear, and whenever this is so there is a danger.

Concern about the use of touch in formal counselling and therapy arises from a variety of circumstances. Although some would subscribe to the value of allowing clients to experience their pain without prematurely reassuring them, there are dangers implicit in such reasoning: such arguments do not support coldness or distance, but they imply the danger of technique for technique's sake. My own arguments are different. They partly stem from the observation that there is too much evidence about abuse of clients by counsellors and therapists to feel confident that helpers naturally know the right limits. My reservations partly come from the necessity of not repeating the slightest hint of anything that acts as a reminder of sexual or physical abuse that may have taken place in the client's past. Since more clients have been abused than say so early on in therapy, there is the further danger that arises from not knowing whether or not this may apply in any particular circumstance. My anxiety about touch also comes from knowing counsellors who have had the utmost difficulty with clients who have interpreted such gestures as permission to become literally very clinging – not as a sexual wish, but in huge need of comfort, like a baby to its mother.

Three examples illustrate my own wrestling with such issues:

> I was due to see a blind client. Access to my room was a little difficult, and I asked her whether she wished to take my arm up the stairs. I must have asked in such a way that she could not refuse, because a couple of sessions later, when she was talking about the difficulty of relating to me (linked by then to difficulties in her family of origin, including some

sexual abuse) she said that she couldn't stand being touched by anyone, and that she certainly did not want me helping her up the stairs. The session after that she failed to come, and we never met again.

I had been seeing a woman in mid-life for about a year, during which time she had been able to express deep feelings about surgery she had undergone for a serious condition. This had left her feeling disfigured. The relationship between us was a close one, and on a number of occasions I made good observations which supported her and helped her grow in her self-esteem. Her attractiveness came up from time to time, as well as the way in the past she had allowed partners to take advantage of her, so that she had rarely experienced much physical pleasure. There were times when I was aware that had I held a different view on touch, comforting her when she cried might have been a possibility, although I would nevertheless have been concerned about the way men had treated her in the past. When we got up at the end of our last session, she was clearly finding it difficult to have to finish, and she said, 'What do we do now? Shake hands?' It felt fine at that point to give each other a hug, sealing what clearly had been a good relationship. Earlier in therapy such a gesture would not have felt so appropriate.

I once agreed to see for counselling a woman whom I had met on a conference, and who later had been present at the same church service as myself. At the point at which the 'peace' is given (when members of the congregation embrace or shake hands) I gently embraced her since this is what she had obviously wanted. I learned from her afterwards, when she started counselling, that she found it very difficult to get close to other people, women and men. She began to express a desperate need for me to give her a hug in the session. There were all sorts of reasons in her history that made me feel extremely cautious about this, as well as my concern lest I become a substitute for the physical closeness she wanted but feared in outside relationships. It was a very painful time for her, and a difficult one for me, because she made me feel very callous. At the same time I was not unsympathetic to her plea that what I had done once in a church service, surely I could do in counselling. Although in my own mind the boundaries were quite distinct in the different settings in which we had been involved, she rightly showed how confusing it can be to cross them. What I could do was accept the confusion, underline my own boundaries as a counsellor, and show how these deep concerns reflected so much of her family history. But it would have been better had the 'promise' not been hinted at in the first instance.

Since I know from colleagues of examples where (particularly woman to woman) touch is a natural end to a session, or a hand on the client's arm is a helpful gesture, there are obviously no simple answers. There should always be caution in any cross-gender pairings of client and counsellor (with some consideration too for gay and lesbian pairings), as well as extreme caution where there is any hint of sexual or physical abuse in the client's history. It is because these situations carry so much risk, and because touch that is inappropriate or misused is often disastrous, that the answer must be not to cross physical boundaries where there is any doubt.

BOUNDARIES OF ROLE IN PASTORAL COUNSELLING

There is one other major complication concerning a rather different type of boundary; this applies to clergy in particular, though it may be relevant to other helpers. Because clergy and other ministers frequently have other functions to perform, principally in the conduct of worship and the administering of the sacraments, they are perceived in other ways by some of their congregation and by many of their parishioners. This influences all their pastoral work, including their pastoral counselling. A pastoral counsellor, and a pastor who uses counselling skills, may at one time be experienced as a quiet and attentive listener, and at other times as the confident leader of worship; as the person who preaches about good and evil; as the minister who pronounces the forgiveness of sins; as the priest who baptizes, marries and buries; as the idealized parent-figure and representative of God (by some church-going men and women); or as the denigrated and feared parent-figure (by some who are antagonistic to the Church). The boundaries of the one role and function cannot help overlapping the boundaries of the other.

What happens, for example, if a minister is preaching upon the need for profound respect of persons, and in the congregation there is a person who has been talking in counselling to the same minister about his hatred of his parents? It is difficult enough if the minister is not this person's counsellor, but it is at least possible to split off one from the other. That is impossible when they are the same person. A preacher or a teacher inevitably puts forward ideas more clearly and with greater certainty than when struggling with more personalized issues in a pastoral counselling session. Similarly, the minister who is preaching or teaching reveals opinions about ethical, theological, social and even political issues. Some of this may cause disagreement between counsellor and client, in such a way as would not normally interfere with the counselling process at all. Those who engage in pastoral work (and other helping work) are more actively 'up front', and more revealing of themselves than counsellors tend to be. Although I do not subscribe to counsellors becoming like 'blank screens', there is much to the therapeutic style of relating that makes the counsellor unobtrusive and held back.

Similarly, when a pastor is involved in administering the sacraments, particularly communion and the sacrament of reconciliation (what was once called penance), these are psychologically very powerful acts. What does it mean to have sins forgiven, particularly face to face in an individual meeting such as the sacrament of reconciliation involves? Whatever the theological qualifications (of which I am aware), it is an extremely important and powerful act for one human being to forgive another human being their sins. And what does it mean to receive communion, especially if such an important priestly figure is the same person who is caring for you and helping you in counselling? Might it carry with it associations of being fed as a baby by your mother – which is indeed the symbol of Corpus Christi – the pelican feeding its young from the blood of the breast? An example illustrates the complications:

Eve was seeing a pastoral counsellor who was also a priest.

Normally the counsellor would not have seen Eve in other circumstances, because the referral had been made by her own minister to a counsellor at some distance. But on this occasion the counsellor, as a priest, came to Eve's church to help out when the minister was ill; and was therefore the one who gave her communion. At their next meeting Eve described how she had felt that she wanted to take the chalice from him at the communion and throw it down on the ground. In fact on this occasion the symbolism in this phantasy tied in remarkably well with something she had told him on another occasion. Eve's mother had told her that as a baby she constantly pushed away the milk which was offered her at the breast. But it clearly had made it hard for Eve, and had it not been carefully handled by both of them it could have been very difficult for the counsellor too.

Situations such as these suggest that clergy in parishes, or indeed others such as teachers in schools, need to be careful about engaging in counselling with those whom they will inevitably see in other roles. Yet such is the widespread acceptance of the value of counselling skills in pastoral and other caring functions that it would be foolish and unrealistic to suggest that the two functions cannot coincide at all. Using counselling skills, or even some forms of brief counselling, is not the same as practising psychotherapy. With experience it is possible to make use of many situations that arise elsewhere outside the counselling interview, as Eve and her counsellor did in the example above. This includes the distortions in the relationship that arise from other forms of meeting in different situations. However, where a pastor or any other helper is seen in more than one role, there is greater complexity to the relationship between care-giver and client, which may need to be handled with considerable finesse.

Those engaged in pastoral ministry, and those who use counselling skills alongside their normal work functions, need to be aware of the issues of confusion of boundaries, such as are illustrated from the examples in church ministry. Such awareness involves remembering what has been said and what has happened in counselling (or counselling-type) interviews, as well as what is said and happens on both sides when each meets the other in different circumstances. A counsellor meeting a client outside counselling, or a person who uses counselling skills in other contexts, particularly has to remember who said what, where and when, so that nothing confidential from the counselling is shared in the non-counselling situation. Despite these difficulties, there are advantages, as in the case of visiting people in their own homes. Seeing clients in other circumstances, as long as they do not feel spied upon, adds new dimensions to the picture the counsellor has of them. So too does it add to the picture that clients have of their counsellors, who may not feel quite so able to relax without wondering what their off-the-cuff remarks might have meant to those whom they will later see face to face.

Training in counselling and therapy sharpens the helper's awareness of all the dimensions involved in personal interactions. In addition to listening, and responding carefully, monitoring one's own responses and motives, this chapter has shown the necessity of maintaining safe boundaries for the client and counsellor to work within. All these are vital foundations and walls for the development of the counselling relationship, which the next chapter begins to examine.

NOTE

1. See the exercise 'First and last words' with its explanation of this aspect of the session in M. Jacobs, *Swift to Hear*. SPCK 2000 (2nd edn), pp. 112–16.

CHAPTER SEVEN

Levels of Intervention

It will be clear from all that I have described about the foundations and boundaries of counselling that this is far from being a purely passive way of helping, even though much of what a counsellor does is aimed at providing the right milieu, and a safe enough relationship for the 'still small voice' in the client to be expressed and for the 'still small voice' in the counsellor to be heard. Counsellors tend not to say very much, but they are active in their thinking, in monitoring their feelings, and in keeping an eye on what is happening in the therapeutic relationship. When they speak, these observations contribute greatly to what they say, while how they frame what they wish to communicate is thought through carefully, because what a counsellor (or indeed anyone in a position of authority) says can make considerable impact upon a client's self-perception. While it holds true throughout counselling that each particular client sets their own agenda, and provides in their contribution the substance of each session, the counsellor's manner and spoken contribution is also vital: clients want to be listened to, but they also want to hear what their counsellor thinks.

At one stage the person-centred approach stressed the non-directive stance of the counsellor. Indeed, many people still use this term to describe counselling, sometimes in praise of it, sometimes to denigrate it as a way of helping. In fact Rogers, who originally used the term 'non-directive', dropped it in favour of 'client-centred', which in turn became 'person-centred' counselling. It was an important change, because it is impossible to be totally non-directive, but it is essential to remain centred on what the client is saying (and not saying). Inasmuch as counsellors do not give advice, and do not introduce their own items for discussion, their contribution is non-directive. They listen carefully, they accept whatever is said or expressed, they demonstrate a warm and genuine concern, and they reflect what they hear and observe in their clients. In other ways, counsellors are more directive: as the last chapter demonstrated, every interview has a beginning and an end, and it is the counsellor who plays the larger part in setting and keeping these boundaries. The sheer presence and personality of a counsellor is bound to impinge upon the client, and therefore to some extent influences what a person chooses to talk about. Simply by being there, a counsellor exercises a pull or a push on what the client chooses to speak about or not to speak about, and the way that they frame it. For example, a male counsellor may evoke one set of issues, and a female counsellor another. This suggests that even passivity influences direction.

As soon as a counsellor intervenes, which he or she cannot avoid doing, the intervention inevitably shifts the course of counselling, either in the same direction that the client is taking, or in another one. It is highly unlikely that a counsellor could sustain total silence, even if it were desirable, but even the counsellor's silence evokes feelings, and can shift the direction (see the example of Mark below). The moment a counsellor speaks, he or she actively contributes to the direction of the interview, because the counsellor chooses to reflect back one phrase rather than another, or stresses one word in a sentence instead of another, or highlights one feeling rather than another. The caricature of counselling is that of the parrot response; indeed, unless a counsellor were to repeat word for word all that a client says with precisely the same inflection, every reflection of the client's words suggests one emphasis rather than another.

Counsellors are not non-directive. It is better to admit this as an impossibility, and to exercise care over what direction any intervention might suggest, than to believe in the outdated myth of not influencing the client. In some respects counselling is the same as any conversation. One person speaks, the second responds, providing a cue that is taken up, missed, contradicted, etc. The first person responds to the second's cue and takes it further; the second switches back to an earlier phrase, or chooses a new tack, which the first can accept to follow or not. Each person offers direction to the other. The same is true of the counselling interview. Normally the client begins while the counsellor listens. The counsellor takes up what he or she believes is most important to the client. The client responds, sometimes by agreeing, sometimes by rejecting, sometimes by accepting part of the reply, sometimes by changing the subject. In an open counselling relationship (what I later describe as a 'working' relationship) each party takes the initiative, each listens to the other, and each learns to respond, to agree and to disagree.

There are, of course, differences between the counselling interview and an ordinary conversation. Clients are encouraged to do most of the talking, to express themselves spontaneously and openly, and without holding too much back. Counsellors say much less than they might in most social settings, and when they speak they probably weigh their words more carefully than they would in normal conversations. They make special efforts to concentrate on the client more than upon themselves, and they try hard to understand. When they speak they are careful, trying to ensure that what they say does not hurt, and that it will not be taken the wrong way. But counsellors also say things that they would never say in a polite conversation!

In weighing up how best to respond, counsellors have a number of choices. Some of these responses have been outlined in Chapter 3. Within many of these styles of response there are different levels of intervention, which this chapter describes. The choice of which level of intervention depends upon a number of factors, such as the skill and experience of the counsellor, the time available for the whole counselling contract, and more specifically the remaining time left in any one session. Levels of intervention also depend upon the relationship that the counsellor has with the client, and the psychological strength of the client. With new clients, especially when they are very distressed, or if they are very disturbed people, it is essential to spend time slowly building up trust and providing a supportive milieu that contains their anxiety. As clients engage more deeply in the therapeutic relationship, and trust the process more, the level of intervention can move to a more exploratory one – although with very disturbed clients a counsellor proceeds very cautiously indeed. When trust is well established, and client and counsellor can be more honest with each other, and when it is clear that the client is strong enough to take more incisive reflections and remarks, then it may be possible to engage on a level that involves interpreting what may be happening for the client. This is a process that is designed to help clients look more closely at what they are thinking and feeling, and how their experience connects with other aspects of their past and present relationships; or this deeper level may take the form of confrontation and challenge: facing clients with something that they find difficult to look at. It is part of a counsellor's responsibility to decide with which clients and at which times it is most appropriate to support, to explore, to interpret or to confront.

Another way of distinguishing these levels of intervention is by looking at the way each handles anxiety, which is in some ways a negative feeling, although it is also a useful indicator of points of difficulty. A counsellor who chooses to intervene by offering reassurance and support does so in order to suppress or ease the client's anxiety (and sometimes the counsellor's as well!). At that juncture the counsellor wants the client to feel as positive as possible both about himself or herself, and about the counsellor. When a counsellor decides to explore an issue, he or she tries to do this without causing undue anxiety, although recognizing that digging a little deeper probably will be less comfortable in the short term. When a counsellor believes that it could be helpful to interpret or challenge the client in some way, he or she does so with the awareness that such an intervention will probably provoke anxiety, but that in doing so there should be more chance in the long run of clarifying the client's insight and strengthening the client's own inner resources. These levels of intervention require progressively more counselling experience for them to be handled well.

LEVELS OF RESPONSE

Each of the kinds of response suggested in earlier chapters are capable of being adapted to these different levels of intervention. In Chapter 5 it was suggested that in the early stages of counselling new clients, it helps those who are anxious if they can be told a little of how the counsellor works and what is expected of them. Let us suppose that a client has been coming for a number of sessions, and has previously appeared untroubled as to what to say. Early reassurance has not been necessary, but today he starts by saying, 'Where shall I begin? I don't know what I'm going to talk about today.' A counsellor can take this simple opening up at one of a number of levels:

1. It is possible to allay the client's anxiety, in much the same way as a counsellor might choose to do in a first session, but in this instance saying, 'It is difficult sometimes: it doesn't seem to have worried you before, and you needn't worry about it now. Perhaps you can try to tell me anything that comes to mind, even if it doesn't immediately seem relevant.'

2. It is equally possible to explore the difficulty: 'You seem to be feeling anxious about that today. What do you think the difficulty might be about?' Here the counsellor invites the client to look at the problem together with the counsellor.

3. It is possible that the counsellor has an idea that might explain the client's difficulty in speaking. This could either be an interpretation, or take the form of a confrontation. A supportive interpretation might be: 'One of the things I've noticed about you is that you sometimes think you're not interesting enough. I wonder if you're afraid that I won't be interested enough in you if you go on talking to me?' A different response, which is more challenging but still invites an explanation, might be: 'You mentioned at the end of our last session that you wanted to talk about something embarrassing. Perhaps it's that which is stopping you from saying anything else today.' In both these examples the counsellor is suggesting reasons for the client's hesitation. The interventions try to interpret the block that has appeared in the client's ability to use the session.

Similarly, there are different levels of intervening when there is an awkward silence. One obvious level is to relieve the anxiety building up in the silence by breaking it, perhaps by reminding the client of what she said just before she paused and went quiet. Alternatively, aware that it raises the temperature a little, the client can be asked what she is feeling, and then perhaps what it was that made her fall silent. A third level is to interpret the silence – 'You've gone very quiet. I wonder whether there's something about what you were telling me that has upset you?' Yet another level is deliberately to heighten the anxiety for as long as is necessary and effective, and let the silence continue. In this case, a counsellor has to be careful not to get into a cat-and-mouse game with the client:

> Mark said rather hesitantly: 'I have these dreadful thoughts. I'm not sure I want to talk about them.' He lapsed into silence. I had a good idea that the thoughts were negative feelings about me; but I was partly unsure, and I partly felt that even if I was right that this was one occasion when Mark could own his feelings for himself. I had protected him too much in the past, and felt this made him somewhat like a 'little boy'. I therefore fell in with the silence. The atmosphere became quite tense. Mark shifted in his seat, knowing (I thought) what he might tell me, but not yet wanting to. Had I thought he did not know what it was that was troubling him, I might have intervened to reassure or explore. But I chose to leave it without saying anything. I knew that if he wished, he could change the subject. After a few minutes he blurted out, with considerable anguish: 'I wish I wasn't thinking these things.' I said quietly: 'But you are, and you won't tell me.' There was another pause, this time a much briefer one, before Mark exploded, telling me just how angry he was with me, and just how much he'd like to see me suffer. When he finished he seemed very relieved that he had said all this with such force, and that I had not responded in kind. We went on to look at what it was about me that made him feel that way, and why his reaction to me was such a strong one.

I could have handled it differently, but I knew that Mark could tolerate the tension and that if I had given him any excuse he would have put off saying what he did. With a different person I might have said: 'Thoughts are only thoughts, they don't harm anyone. It's up to you whether you want to tell me or not.' I could have asked what made it so difficult for him to tell me. Choosing to maintain a high level of tension with Mark helped him express what he wanted to say, with all the forcefulness that he was feeling. Given his difficulty getting angry in case he hurt other people, raising the anxiety level in this particular instance seemed to be appropriate.

Asking questions can also be used to support, explore or even to confront a client. Suppose a client starts the session by saying that the last week has had its ups and downs, and then pauses. If a question is called for at that point, a counsellor can ask what the 'ups' were: such a question invites the client to talk about the positive aspects of the week, and hopefully is supportive. The counsellor can ask about the 'downs', which may raise anxiety, but could help set an agenda of the difficult issues. There is also a less directed response, which asks the client whether he or she wishes to talk about the 'ups' or the 'downs' or both.

It is also important to recognize that in asking questions, a counsellor may be probing insensitively into areas of a client's life that are extremely difficult to talk about. Questions need to be put delicately, but sometimes not put at all, at least until the client has broached the topic. This particularly applies to the area of sexual abuse or sexual attack, and other intimate subjects:

> I had been on a day's course on sex therapy, and had been told that in cases of sexual difficulty it was important to take a full history of sexual attitudes and behaviour. This is because some people have misinformation about sex which needs to be clarified so that a programme of re-education can be started. I recognized the importance of this soon afterwards, after a number of unproductive sessions, using a behavioural approach with a couple from a different cultural background. They explained that their religious beliefs forbade them to touch each other's genitals in foreplay. I understood rather too late why my attempts to help them had so far got nowhere, and I wished I had taken the advice of looking at sexual attitudes, as the course tutor had recommended.
>
> My next client that same day had a sexual difficulty, which I imagined would now provide me with the opportunity to get it right. I decided I would not let this one pass without taking a full sexual history. The young man was

quite naturally somewhat hesitant about talking about sex. He seemed to want to talk about his most recent unsatisfactory relationship. I ignored this, eager to do the task properly. I kept questioning the young man about his first sexual experience, because I thought that the details were important, and I did not let him talk about his present experience. I then proceeded to ask similar questions about the second relationship, and all the time the young man was urgently hurrying on, wanting to know what was wrong with him. I cleverly thought that his urgency threw light on his problem, which was premature ejaculation. I suggested to him that in his anxiety to get on he was unable to relax. I took up one of the young man's phrases, about being 'a bull in a china shop'. It may not be surprising that my client did not come back for a second appointment. It soon became clear to me as I thought about it that, if anything, it was me who had been unable to relax. The questions I asked were too clumsy and provocative, and they made me, not the client, the bull in a china shop.

SUPPORTING AND UNCOVERING

Most counselling sessions include supporting and encouraging responses to the client, and questions or reflections that are not afraid to highlight the difficulties that the client talks about. From time to time a counsellor may also wish to challenge or confront some thinking or behaviour in the client, in order to look for other possibilities. And in the course of each session, a counsellor may make connections and interpret what may lie behind some of the difficult thoughts or feelings that the client expresses. With many clients the levels of intervention move from listening through exploring to challenging and interpreting. Brown and Pedder have tabulated some of the different levels of psychotherapy, although the identification of these levels depends on a clearer distinction between counselling and psychotherapy than some would feel able to make. Nevertheless, their list is a useful guide for levels of intervention in counselling as well, with new counsellors probably more at ease with the top levels, and more experienced counsellors more capable of engaging at the 'deeper' levels. Brown and

Pedder suggest that the top layers of support and counselling involve:

1. unburdening of problems to a sympathetic listener;
2. ventilation of feelings within a supportive relationship;
3. discussion of current problems with a non-judgemental helper.

An intermediate level of work additionally involves, in the context of a deepening relationship:

4. clarification of problems, their nature and origin;
5. confrontation of defences;
6. interpretation of unconscious motives and transference.

The deepest levels of exploration and analysis are:

7. repeating the past, remembering and reconstructing;
8. regression to less adult functioning;
9. re-experiencing and resolving conflicts and working them through.[1]

In addition to careful and deliberate choices of levels of intervention, as they develop from a counsellor's experience, counsellors need to be aware of clients where only the one style of being supportive is appropriate. While a counsellor can be alert to the possibility that some clients might move to deeper levels, with clients in more exploratory mode it is also important to watch for times when it might be necessary to pull them back on to safer ground. Supporting a client can sometimes help develop enough inner strength for that person to move into more exploratory work; while working with anxieties at times necessitates a healthy retreat into supportive work. The following two examples demonstrate a shift in each direction:

A young woman had come to university, but was missing home dreadfully, and was clinging on to her family by going home every weekend. In her counselling sessions with me it was clear that each essay, each lecture, each failed friendship made her feel very low. I worked very hard to support her in staying, and in the progress she slowly made in set-tling. For the first term she hardly shifted, but in the second term she began to show signs of a different side of herself. She said in one session that when she was at home, she would sometimes swear if she dropped something. Her parents would laugh at her in a playful way, as if she were a little child who did not know what she was saying. She seemed quite angry about this. It appeared to me that any efforts she made at home to be more independent were humoured. I realized that here was a potentially stronger character than the one I had seen when we met in the first term. She happened to mention that her parents worried about her, and I began to see more clearly that it was per-haps her parents who were keeping her tied to them, and preventing her from developing away from them. I therefore changed the tenor of my interventions, ceasing to concen-trate so much on supporting her efforts to stay at college, and instead pointing out to her that she seemed to be saying that her parents were reluctant to let her go; and that I thought she was playing along with them so as not to offend them. As these ideas were discussed, there was quite a change in the descriptions the young woman gave of her feelings at home. Previously she had felt 'stranded' when away from them, whereas now she talked of being 'swamped' by her parents. In the first term she had feared her parents dying while she was away, but now she began to say that she would miss them, of course, if anything happened to them, but that she could live without them. What had started as a supportive relationship, aimed at helping the student to stand by her efforts to stay at university, turned into one in which I helped the young woman look at issues that made it difficult for her to leave home.

Norman had found his counselling sessions with me very helpful, and seemed to value the opportunities they gave him to think about himself. He was obviously making advances in his work, getting more confident week by week. Because it was my area of interest, I was pleased to see how he was exploring past and present relationships in the sessions. However, after a while the way in which he talked about the past shifted. The valuable progress he had made seemed to take a turn for the worse. It began when Norman was rejected by a young woman he had tried to get to know at work, and to whom he had presented himself in a very facile way. After this point, he came to his appointments with so many thoughts in his head that there was never enough time to explore them, and I felt that he was showing signs of considerable confusion. He denied that he was at all worried, and said how much he liked to talk about himself. From what he said, it was clear that he was behind with his work, and was using too much time at the office in writing his life history. It seemed as if what had started as useful uncovering work had turned into a very introverted, obsessive and narcissistic exploration of his life. I felt that he was in considerable danger of losing his job, but I also feared that he might even lose his grip on reality.

I decided to change my approach, and I became much more directive. I supportively reflected that I could see how much Norman valued thinking about himself, but I went on to say that this monumental task of writing his life history was taking up so much of his time that he was putting other aspects of his work and his social life at risk. I advised him to try and put the life history on one side for the time being. I worked with Norman to structure his day better, so that he was able to give more time to this job, and had less time to write about himself. Counselling had started with the promise of being able to foster his insight, but it was obviously no longer working to Norman's advantage. Given the constraints on my time, and my hesitation about working with a client with such an obsessive interest in himself, the change of tack felt essential.

There are often early indications in the manner of those who might be potential clients, in their history, in the way they present themselves, and in their initial relationship with their counsellor, that give clues as to the most appropriate level of approach to use. It may also be that counselling is not the most suitable way of helping. There is a great danger in counselling becoming so popular that it will be looked upon as a 'catch-all'. Those who are obviously bizarre in their thoughts, or are so disturbing that they make the counsellor feel more than usually uncomfortable, are likely to need a different kind of help: very skilled psychotherapy, or a psychiatric assessment. When faced with such people, the counsellor is often aware of a type of discomfort that bears little resemblance to that which he or she normally feels with someone who is in deep distress, but is only temporarily incapacitated.

Counsellors do not have to take on every person who approaches them for help. It is particularly dangerous to attempt counselling with people who appear to believe that all is well with them, when it is obvious to the counsellor and to others that it is not; or with those who have no insight at all into themselves. If a person talks in a confused way, jumping from topic to topic, with ideas that are clearly out of touch with reality, or shows feelings that are inappropriate to the circumstances described, referral to a general practitioner or a psychiatrist is probably indicated. Without usurping the role of the psychiatrist, a counsellor can ask questions to see how long the feelings and thoughts have been present; whether there has been previous medical and psychiatric treatment; or whether this is a more immediate crisis that may be extreme, but is out of the ordinary in a person who has previously had largely normal reactions to their experiences. These questions may clarify whether or not a second opinion should be sought.

There could be difficulty working with clients who have a history of very poor relationships, and show little sign of having related even to one person properly (even if it was a stormy relationship). They are equally unlikely to relate to the counsellor sufficiently well to make use of an approach that aims at exploring problems. If such people have experienced difficulties for a very long time, especially in coping with normal fluctuations in circumstances, or if they speak of emotional difficulties that have been with them for many years, a counsellor may again want to consider referral to a psychotherapist, who can probably offer a long-term contract and special expertise to such a client.

Some people should only be seen supportively, especially when the counsellor feels uneasy about handling the material they bring. It is possible to offer a short contract, helping someone through a particular crisis, but not in any way entertaining therapeutic ambitions of shifting the underlying difficulties. If a counsellor chooses a supportive approach with those who are seriously disturbed, greater flexibility of time might be necessary – a few minutes on some occasions, longer periods at other times, with greater frequency of contact sometimes necessary. A good example of such work can be found at the beginning of Chapter 1, where I arranged to see Alan, who had had a severe breakdown, for two half-hours a week instead of one hour a week; and to use the time supportively, rather than attempting to look too deeply at the underlying issues.

Supportive work with people who are or who have been very disturbed involves strengthening the defences that appear to be most effective against a client's fears, feelings and painful memories and thoughts; it may mean helping to manage external pressures, so that they do not become overpowering; and it often involves supporting the reasonable and central core of the client (what is sometimes called the 'ego') against the harsh demands of an over-strict conscience (sometimes called the 'super-ego'). Freud once described the task of the ego as having to mediate between the demands of the external world, inner drives (sometimes called the 'id'), and the super-ego. 'Life is not easy', he wrote.[2] He believed that in mature functioning 'the ego is as it should be if it satisfies simultaneously the demands of the id, of the super-ego and of reality – that is to say, if it is able to reconcile their demands with one another.'[3] Technical though this phrase may appear, it neatly expresses the task of a counsellor when supporting a client, since in supporting the ego, a counsellor tries to mediate, alongside the client, all the other pressures that threaten to invade and overwhelm.

Encouragement is therefore given for every positive action, and affirmation for each sign of coping. Reassurance may not always be enough, and sometimes supportive work (as with Norman in the example above) means being more directive, giving advice, or helping decisions to be made that are realistic and responsible. If management of a client's environment is necessary, it can be helpful to encourage the client to ask others to assist in this task.

CONFRONTATION

The levels of intervention in counselling and therapy range from listening and supporting to working with deeply regressed clients (which it is possible Norman might have become had I not stopped his spiral downwards into himself). One of the most delicate skills a psychodynamic therapist uses, which experienced counsellors also practise, is that of interpreting what clients express in their words, thoughts and feelings, through linking past and present, through identifying defensiveness, and through working closely with the therapeutic relationship itself. Sometimes interpretations try to draw out what the therapist or counsellor believes may be thoughts and feelings of which the client is unconscious. I explain how some types of interpretation are made in the course of the next two chapters.

An equally difficult skill to practise, but one that counsellors of different schools use, is confrontation. Here a counsellor deliberately draws attention to a more conscious feeling, idea or topic that the client appears to be avoiding. A confronting intervention tries to make the person more explicit and honest in expressing their real thoughts and feelings. It may mean the counsellor being direct in the first instance, to encourage the client to be direct:

1. *Client*: This girl came round to see me last night. We talked all night.
   Counsellor: You just talked?
   Client: Well . . . yes.
   Counsellor: You mean 'no'?
   Client: Mm. Well, you see, whenever she comes to talk to me she always finishes up by wanting to go to bed with me.
   Counsellor: Sounds like it's not just her that wants to go to bed?
   Client: Well, no . . . but then I feel awful about it the next day.
   Counsellor: But you might enjoy it too?
   Client: I suppose I do, if I'm honest.
   Counsellor: It seems quite a difficult situation for you.

2. *Client*: My friend was going on and on about her aches and pains, how she'd been to see the doctor, and he was no good, how unsympathetic her husband was; she went on about her children – and there was me trying to rush to catch the bus into town, and I was getting more and

more fussed – so I nearly said to her – well, no, what I
actually said was . . .

Counsellor: What you *nearly* said was . . . ?

Client: No, it doesn't matter.

Counsellor: Go on. You can say it. She's not here.

Client: Well, what I wanted to say was, 'It's all bloody well
for you to go moaning on, but what about me? You don't
know the half of it. You don't know what a bloody mess
I'm in . . .'

These are examples of spontaneous dialogue about specific
events, where a counsellor actively draws the client out. Sometimes a confrontation concerns a more general trait, and is
expressed at a point in the session when the counsellor hopes
the client may give some thought to the observation. The
following examples are taken out of context, but illustrate
other ways in which confrontation might be used:

'Every time I suggest something you tell me I'm wrong, as if
you're afraid of me getting close to what you're feeling.'

'You often talk about your children but you never mention
your wife.'

'You've been looking as if you want to cry, but you are afraid
to let go.'

Although there are clearly times when clients resist expressing themselves fully, many of them, eager to talk to someone
whom they believe will understand, express themselves very
fully. Indeed, it is sometimes the counsellor who is less able to
take up difficult issues, however plainly they are dropped in
front of him or her. When starting counselling, some students
avoid taking up painful remarks and hints. They are perhaps
afraid that they will not be able to handle the emotional
impact of the client's story and feelings. They are perhaps afraid
of the client getting hurt, when the client is of course already
hurt and wants to share some of the pain. There certainly
seems to be some fear in new counsellors which leads them to
avoid confronting in themselves the areas of pain that the
client appears to wish to talk about. Opening up an issue with

confidence, which a client can only hint at somewhat nervously, often brings with it relief. For example, this is what happened after the example of brief confrontation above:

> 'You've been looking as if you want to cry, but you are afraid to let go.'
>
> The client sighed, wept quietly, and then broke into profuse tears. After a while, having gently quietened from the deep sobbing, he looked at the counsellor and said: 'That's better: I haven't cried for years: I've been fighting it back all this time.'

Confrontation is not a way of trying to catch clients out, of making them appear small, or of judging and punishing them. If a counsellor is aware of feeling angry towards a particular client, he or she needs to exercise great caution, because any remark might be wounding, but confrontation could be especially damaging when used as an excuse to 'get at' the client. It is also vital to understand that everyone has natural defences and that such defences serve a purpose, as I explain in the next chapter. Confrontation must respect defences, and not be used to go at them like a battering-ram; nor is it an iron fist in a velvet glove. Kennedy uses similar images, in warning against the improper use of this type of intervention. 'It is not a hit-and-run operation. It is not a blunt instrument . . . [It is not] clubbing the other person through immediate and massive direct attack . . . A search and destroy expedition against the defences of others is a sad but unfortunately popular form of confrontation.'[4] What is interesting is that in the second edition of Kennedy's book, the chapter on confrontation has been removed, and replaced at the same point with one on supportive psychotherapy.[5] As much as any other intervention, confrontation needs to respect, support and use the 'still small voice' which always speaks more effectively and deeply than the blusterings of interventions that sound more like earthquake, wind and fire. Unless rapport and trust have been built between counsellor and client, inept and unthoughtful confrontation may drive the client away.

In the hands of a clumsy counsellor, confrontation is a dangerous weapon. In the hands of the skilful counsellor, it is like a surgeon's scalpel, delicately opening up areas of pain or

shame. At all times, but especially when a counsellor has intervened in a more confronting way, he or she must be ready to
stem too great a flood of pain or feeling. Incisiveness and
sensitivity go hand in hand with flexibility, as counsellors
gauge the possible reactions of their clients to their different
interventions.

I have sketched earlier a picture of those clients who might
be most suited to a supportive level of counselling. What of
those who can make good use of exploratory work, including
interventions that are confronting and interpretative? In a first
interview, particularly in assessing new clients, a counsellor
can often spot certain signs that are good indicators of clients
who may work well at uncovering what it is that causes them
difficulty. There should be indications that the client has
functioned adequately before the onset of the present crisis;
that the client has had some success in relating to others, and
preferably to at least one person closely. A good work-record
(where work has been available to them) may also be a sign of
underlying strength. In assessing a client, a counsellor looks for
signs of a conscious wish to change, and of sufficient discomfort
with what is wrong to want to give up counter-productive
patterns of behaviour and reactions. At the same time, the
wish to change needs to be accompanied by a recognition that
there are no magical answers, and that the client has to play a
part in this: the person who persists in expecting others to do
all the work or do all the changing is unlikely to be suitable for
counselling. A more uncovering approach looks for in clients
an ability to keep in touch with what they experience and feel,
and a facility for putting all this into words. Clients need to
show some capacity to relate to their counsellor, and to be
sufficiently responsive to take in what the counsellor says –
although not always to agree with it as a compliant person
might. Clients ideally should show some recognition of their
effect on others, and the effect of others on them. They need
to be sensitive to what others feel. Finally, exploratory work
requires clients who can accept the length of time that is
involved in counselling. The person who wants results by
yesterday will find little help unless such a driving demand
can be challenged early on in counselling. In effect, clients
have to go on bearing their problems for quite a while. It
obviously helps if the therapeutic relationship eases them, and

provides a place where they can be temporarily off-loaded; but counselling rarely yields rapid results, and sometimes it ends up with an outcome that is quite different from that which the client wished for in the first instance.

Such a client is clearly an idealized picture, and possibly a person for whom counselling may seem unnecessary! This list of qualities is, of course, a selection of the aspects that single out clients who might make good use of a more exploratory and open level of intervention.

MAKING REFERRALS

There are other people who ask for help who do not fit readily into either of the two categories of client described as suitable for supportive or exploratory work. They are neither bizarre nor seriously disturbed, so there is no question of confining the help to support or of referring them to a psychiatrist. On the other hand, they do not seem suitable for more exploratory counselling either. Sometimes they are people with life difficulties that clearly need other skilled help and not counselling – or at least not counselling in the first instance. This is where counsellors find knowledge of other resources, statutory and voluntary agencies, an immense asset. Sometimes such people are very quiet and extremely passive, unable to sustain a lengthy conversation, let alone take the initiative in the way clients do in counselling. It is possible that some supportive counselling might help, but it is unlikely to be the best help available to them. More active forms of intervention still, such as social skills training or cognitive-behavioural therapy, might be preferable, and referral to a clinical psychologist indicated.[6]

For one reason or another, counsellors need to refer on some of those who ask them for help: to other counsellors, to agencies, to psychotherapists, psychologists or psychiatrists. There is an art in making referrals, from the first suggestion that the counsellor may not be able to help, to the information that the client is given and the details that (with permission) may be passed on. To be referred may be experienced as a rejection – especially if the client has specifically approached a particular counsellor, or has already been shunted from pillar to post in the past. Referral may worry the client, as if it is a sure indication that something really disturbing is around – which in a few instances will be the case. If too much resentment or anxiety is aroused, the client may not accept the idea of referral, or may not keep the appointment with the helper they are referred to. Being referred to another helper also means starting again, inevitably repeating one's story. If a client has had to pluck up courage to tell it once, he or she may shrink from the thought of having to start all over again. Having been let down (as it might feel) by the first counsellor, it may take longer to build up trust with the second source of help.

Perhaps the most difficult referrals are of clients who make it clear, in the way they speak of doctors, psychiatrists or other types of helper, that they have received bad treatment in the past. Sometimes this is true; and where people have had bad experiences of professional help, they should not be dismissed as paranoid. When referring them to similar kinds of help, a counsellor has to take the utmost care, firstly to select the best help available (where previous mistakes will not be repeated), and secondly to gain the trust of the client to enable the suggestion to be accepted and acted upon. Offering a second appointment, after the referral appointment, might be a way of ensuring the client does not feel that he or she is being sent out to fend for himself or herself in what feels like the lion's den.

Nevertheless, counsellors and other helpers need to recognize that they are not omni-competent, and to feel comfortable with declining to take some clients on. The earlier this can be detected in the first interview the better, since the ground can be prepared straightaway, without giving false hopes and impressions to the client. It is also important to monitor the client's reactions to mention of referral, and to allow time for the feelings about it to be expressed: disappointment expressed to the first counsellor will make the second therapist's task a little easier, since the feelings will not be so obviously carried over into the next relationship. It is important also to be confident and positive in suggesting another source of help, rather than give the negative impression that the client has made the counsellor feel anxious.

In my time I have received many referrals, some of which were made well. Even before the client saw the first counsellor the client was told that the appointment was to assess the situation, and find the most suitable person to help. The interview was kept short so that the relationship did not have much chance to flower. The client was asked whether a male or a female counsellor was preferable. The client was told how long he or she might have to wait before counselling could begin. Other referrals have been handled less well. The following is a composite example of several clients' opening words and illustrates the most common errors in making a referral:

I was told to come and see you. I don't think Mr Smith had time to see me. I don't know why I'm here. Is there something really wrong with me? I never thought I'd have to see a psychiatrist. What do you want me to do? Do I have to start all over again?

It is not difficult to see how this referral could have been handled better. This client has come to see me to please Mr Smith rather than because he sees the benefits for himself. He sees the referral as a rejection and rationalizes what is perhaps an anxiety that the person referring did not wish to go on seeing him. The client has not been given the reason for the referral, leaving him to imagine the worst about himself. The remark about seeing a psychiatrist confirms his fears, and the person referring this client has not clarified my true role. Neither has Mr Smith explained to the client the possible value of counselling and what to expect of the interview with me. Therefore, what started perhaps as an informal approach to Mr Smith has become a more formal process, and the course of this has raised even more anxiety. Neither is the client sure of what I already know (although I could tell him this when I introduce myself). Indeed, I have no indication from Mr Smith what the client's difficulties might be. It could have been made easier for the client and for me if Mr Smith had asked the client's permission to communicate a few simple facts about him in order to break the ice.

Counselling and therapy involve different levels of intervention, the use of which depends on the skill of the counsellor and the suitability of the client. Counsellors often work with a very broad range of clients: they are in some ways the equivalent of primary care in the medical field. It is counselling services and agencies that are on the front line, and increasingly used by other professional helpers as a dumping ground for all the clients they cannot handle. Counsellors, perhaps more than psychotherapists, need to become flexible in the approaches they use, the contracts they offer, and the levels of intervention that they incorporate in their work with a wide variety of clients. With some of their clients, and within a few sessions, counsellors create a working relationship in which insight and exploration help get behind the presenting problems. In the context of a containing therapeutic relationship, clients are helped to experiment with changes and to develop greater self-understanding. When this happens it is often rewarding for client and counsellor, although it is seldom straightforward. Defences and resistances often appear, and the relationship itself is recognized as having many layers to it. It is these deeper areas of the therapeutic engagement that the next two chapters address.

NOTES

1. D. Brown and J. Pedder, *Introduction to Psychotherapy*. Tavistock Publications 1979.
2. S. Freud, *New Introductory Lectures on Psychoanalysis*. Penguin Freud Library, volume 2, pp. 110–11.
3. S. Freud, *An Outline of Psychoanalysis*. Penguin Freud Library, volume 15, pp. 377–8.
4. E. Kennedy, *On Becoming a Counsellor*. Dublin: Gill & Macmillan 1977 (1st edn), pp. 128–33 *passim*.
5. E. Kennedy and S. Charles, *On Becoming a Counsellor*. Dublin: Gill & Macmillan 1989 (2nd edn), pp. 159–63.
6. See the exercise on referral in M. Jacobs, *Swift to Hear*. SPCK 2000 (2nd edn), pp. 156–60.

CHAPTER EIGHT

Meeting Resistance

Counselling has a number of different aims. Clearly a principal one is to relieve suffering. Another is to promote more permanent changes so that suffering is less intense in the future. A third is to enable people to understand more fully what makes them the way they are, why they react as they do in particular situations, or what makes them provoke certain situations. Change and insight go hand in hand, although it is not clear exactly which takes the lead: some would say that insight promotes change; others that change provides the opportunity for insight (and hindsight).

One of the strengths of the use of counselling as a way of helping people in distress is that it sees the client as central to all these goals: counselling is not what is done to the client. Clients are not 'counselled' as some people mistakenly say. It is what a client is able to do and to see for himself or herself that makes the difference, even though the counsellor is a very important part of the process. Counsellors provide a second perspective, an outside view, a sounding board, a mirror that reflects other situations. All these images express the value of another person in the process of individual change. One of the tasks of a counsellor is to help open up a path towards change and insight, especially when the client feels stuck and does not know how to begin or where to go.

It soon becomes clear in any piece of counselling work that there are barriers to progress. We have examined some of the early difficulties. These are not always barriers; they are sometimes lack of knowledge. But they may be an indication of barriers that will arise. Sometimes the blocks to change are external and difficult to alter without radical upheaval. Someone who is in an unhappy relationship, if all else fails, can leave the relationship. There may also be situations that are impossible to change at all. The person who has no job, and stands no chance of getting a job, may not be able to alter their situation. Sometimes the barriers in counselling are caused by the counsellor, who is insensitive or blind to difficulties in the client, and makes the client feel reluctant to proceed any further. Indeed, it is worth considering first of all whether it is the counsellor who is the 'problem' – in other words, 'Is there something about me that makes it difficult for you to talk to me?'

Sometimes the barriers to movement in the session and to change outside it appear to be located within the client: there is something about the client that is the sticking point. This chapter looks at some examples of these indications. In the last chapter I cited Freud's view that being a person is like a balancing act between different internal and external demands. There are occasions when one or other 'part' of a person appears to be unable to allow further progress. This may be expressed in terms such as 'There's something stopping me', 'I can't think what makes me do it', 'I can't help it'. People sometimes express this sense of internal struggle as 'one part of me' feeling at odds with 'another part of me', or 'I feel torn inside', or 'I can feel a conflict going on inside me'. The apostle Paul in one of his letters describes the sense of war that there can be within the personality. 'I see another law in my limbs warring against the law of my mind.'[1] These expressions are examples of what Freud also meant when he used more abstract terms of the ego trying to handle the id (inner drives and needs), the super-ego (the conscience), and reality (other people and the outside world).[2]

When these conflicts and difficulties get in the way of counselling itself, or prevent change being put into effect by the client, counsellors try to look for and understand the cause of the resistance. This is a special and advanced skill. In addressing it I move beyond the more immediate and pressing concerns that a client initially brings to counselling into the deeper levels of intervention outlined from Brown and Pedder's work in the last chapter.[3]

In that chapter I made it clear that there is no value in trying to confront by bulldozing a way through the difficulties and barriers that a client appears to present. A counselling session should never become a battleground between counsellor and client, although on occasions it will. At such times a counsellor needs to retreat and look at what is happening. If the image of a battle has any value at all (and Freud favoured the military image), it more aptly describes a struggle going on within the person who has asked for help. What a counsellor tries to do is to take sides with the central rational 'ego' of the client – in other words, supporting the reasonable, conscious self. Part of the assistance given to the ego is to help the client to feel that any thought and any feeling is acceptable and controllable if it can be expressed verbally, and that the ego or self will not be submerged by such expression. This is difficult when a client feels frightened of feelings and ideas and would prefer to have nothing to do with the painful thoughts and emotions. Clients often see themselves as coming for counselling to 'get rid' of all that, not to give expression to it! They urgently want the counsellor to restore the status quo. Sometimes this is indeed what counselling does – supportive counselling is largely aimed at relieving distress and restoring equilibrium.

Counselling that explores more deeply, though, attempts to uncover both hidden feelings, and behind them the sources of them, so that when the feelings come again they are not so threatening and uncontrollable as before. Initially it sometimes appears to clients that the counsellor is taking sides with the less desirable part of themselves, which they would prefer to suppress or forget. There are other aspects of a person that also want to be addressed. Although I use a metaphor to personify these parts, psychodynamic therapists believe there is validity in thinking about each individual as having a number of 'internal' persons within them (seen with greatest clarity in cases of multiple personality, where writ large is something of what is present in everyone). These other selves may also be afraid of the counsellor, seeing him or her as a fifth columnist, who will get inside on trust and then force an unconditional and absolute surrender. Such an analogy is clearly a dramatic one and it is no doubt over-simplified; but it does convey the deep sense of struggle that goes on within many people, and that a counsellor or therapist has to contend with.

HANDLING RESISTANCE

When a counsellor becomes aware that a client is in one way or another feeling 'stuck' or in some kind of disabling internal conflict, the first step is to try and see just what is happening: what is the form of resistance? What type of defence is the client employing? The second task is to accept the defensiveness as being a natural way of warding off anxiety. Only then can a counsellor begin to look for what the client may be defending against, what feeling or thought he or she is experiencing (often unconsciously) that they are frightened to see and express. It may be possible for the counsellor to suggest the difficulty of getting in touch with that feeling or idea. As a client is then able to give expression to ideas and feelings, a counsellor has to show he or she accepts without blame or shock everything the client says, and that he or she does not judge such feelings or ideas to be bad or inappropriate (there is a reason for them, even if the counsellor cannot yet see it). A counsellor is a type of mediator, supporting the client's central self, but also able to accept the need in the client for expression of other parts of the self. Sometimes 'bad' feelings turn out not to be so bad after all: the client has a distorted view of what is bad (some people feel anger is bad, or that weakness is shameful). Sometimes the feelings and thoughts can be understood as appropriate within a particular context, although needing some adaptation before they are appropriately expressed in external situations.

A simple example of this way of handling resistance comes from the end of my first interview with Pat, a young student who had shed a lot of tears in the session because her boyfriend had just left her. When I asked Pat whether she would like to return next week and talk further she hesitated. 'You're not sure,' I observed. 'No, I'm not. I don't want to be silly.' Since she had earlier murmured something about being silly when she had started to cry, I picked up her phrase and suggested: 'Perhaps you are not sure about coming back, because you're afraid I will think you're silly if you get upset?' 'I'll come,' Pat quickly replied.

Notice here how I framed this observation: I started by describing her resistance (not coming back) and suggested it was because of her anxiety (that I will think she is 'silly') at showing her real feeling (by crying). Rather than simply identifying what a client is trying to avoid (being upset, shame, embarrassment, feeling angry, getting too close), a counsellor also tries to show what the resistance is and why it is there in the first place. Simply observing resistance alone in a stereotypical confrontation ('You don't want to come back – I think you're resisting') is often an attack by the counsellor on the client, and experienced as such, giving rise to the very resistance that the counsellor is trying to get the client to remove.

This particular sensitivity to resistance and skill in facing it is not one of rapid discernment and immediate insight. When a client feels or shows some form of resistance it can be a long task getting through it. Clients are trapped sometimes in prisons of their own making: so afraid of looking at themselves and facing what they are feeling that they are unable to move forward. Invariably, in the end it turns out that they are far more afraid than they need be, but they do not know that at the time. Often it is their super-ego or conscience that makes it very hard to talk about themselves: they denigrate themselves, see themselves as bad, weak, vulnerable; and even fear that they are damaging, dangerous, immoral. Such self-criticism makes it scarcely surprising that despite their wish to feel better, clients will put up barriers and are often unaware that they are doing so. Even the counsellor's best efforts to help are resisted. Some people are terrified, given the bad image they have of themselves already, that if anything else in them sees the light of day they will be deluged with overwhelming feelings.

The barriers that all people in one way or another put up against exposing difficult feelings and thoughts to themselves and others, in fact serve an important function. Just as what they protect is not in itself 'bad', so defences are not a sign of weakness. In some ways they are a sign of strength, and it is only when defences become weak that a person feels helpless. They are the natural defences of the mind, just as the body has its natural defences, rejecting anything that is alien and that might harm it. In an illness such as cancer some of these defences fail in their task. Or, to use another parallel, in transplant surgery the body's natural defences are a hindrance to the surgeon, because an implant will be rejected unless the immune system can be put on hold. The mind/psyche/self has similar defences, which serve as a protection when thoughts and feelings and experiences are too much for the person to bear. One example of such a psychological defence is seen if a person is faced with a shocking event. Following a sudden blow to the system, the mind appears to anaesthetize itself against too high a level of pain (both physical and psychological) in order to function temporarily in other necessary ways. It may be semi-automatic functioning, as in a road accident, for example, when the bystander summons aid, gives assistance, and shows remarkable signs of coping. It is only later that the full effects begin to be felt. The helper might begin to shake as her body reacts; her mind starts to comprehend the horror of what she has experienced; and other forms of physical and psychological discomfort begin to be felt. A little while later this person may begin to go over the incident in her own mind, getting some sort of 'handle' or control upon it. Perhaps she will talk to others, sometimes many times, until the experience can be recalled without the initial deep sense of anguish.

One of the values of counselling following traumatic shock (as in accidents, major disasters, or other examples of sudden death) is that it gives time for a person to come through the shock and the numbness, and to be with someone as they begin to re-experience what they have been through or to realize the full impact of loss. A counsellor provides a chance for someone in such a state to tell their story, bit by bit, sometimes over and over again, until the trauma has become less threatening and time begins to heal.

When we talk of defences that are put up against the process of counselling, these too are the same natural defences that are employed in the face of unwelcome or shocking thoughts. They may similarly include numbness, or denial as it is more technically known; and there are many other ways in which we try to cope with the unacceptable. A counsellor learns to recognize these defences from the way people describe themselves and others, from the way they talk, and from their different attitudes. The term 'defence' describes broad styles of warding off unacceptable ideas and feelings. The term 'resistance' is one that is more often used of specific expressions or examples of defence as seen particularly in the counselling process. In my description I try to illustrate the main defence mechanisms that people adopt with examples of resistance in practice.

A difficulty in explaining these defences is that while I wish to foster recognition of defences, and consequent care in handling them, I run the risk of setting down a set of 'labels'. These terms should not of course be used with clients except in instances where such jargon has become part of common use: the terms 'projection' and 'denial' are either known or readily understood by people who have some smattering of popular psychology. The other danger is that counsellors may be so worried about identifying the defence, as if they were bird-watching, that they will miss the importance of the defence. In practice, defences often overlap and so defy neat categorization. Any value in my explanation of the defences that psychologists and psychoanalysts have identified lies in studying their richness in protecting people against excessive pain. It is not necessary to trouble overmuch about precise labels when working with clients. They may, however, be useful for shorthand communication in supervision and case discussion.

In the last chapter I described how important it is in supportive counselling to take steps as and when necessary to reinforce a client's defences, especially if the defences are working relatively satisfactorily. Only certain examples of resistance may need to be looked at – such as missing appointments, and not coming on time. When counselling moves into a more exploratory level there is more reason to consider trying to identify inner conflicts. It is then that it might be helpful to try and put defences to one side and look at various expressions of resistance. In doing this a counsellor needs to work in such a way as to invite the co-operation of the client, who (as I have suggested above) is helped to understand the value of their defensiveness as well as its function. It is important also to distinguish those forms of resistance that clients are aware of in themselves from those that they are not conscious of. In the latter instance even greater care is necessary if a counsellor's observations are going to be heard. Such an approach often makes a client more ready to lower their defences, inch by inch, until it becomes safe to face the feelings and thoughts that they would in many ways sooner hide from themselves and the counsellor. The gentle approach of the counsellor, the 'still small voice' that appeals to the often timid 'still small voice' of the client, enables these changes to take place. It can take a very long time.

ACTING OUT

I have at several points alluded to time boundaries, and to the implicit messages there may be in a client arriving late or missing a session. These are examples of a particular form of resistance that is called 'acting out'. In other words, instead of telling their counsellor directly, clients express their anxiety or their anger and disappointment with their counsellor by actions rather than words. They may also do this by taking out their feelings on other people (see 'displacement' below). Reactions like this are not necessarily signs of a client's own difficulties: they are sometimes the result of incompetent counselling. The counsellor may have said or done something that caused offence, or even missed something that the client was trying to express. Sometimes clients act out their disappointment when their counsellor has inadvertently let them down: for example, if a counsellor has to cancel or postpone a session, a client may respond by doing the same. To call this a type of 'tit for tat' on the part of the client is not to diminish the seriousness of the client's feelings at being let down, and in wanting (perhaps unconsciously) to give the counsellor a taste of their own medicine. Such acting out can also occur after (or even just before) a counsellor's holiday break.

A somewhat different form of acting out is seen in some psychosomatic conditions, or even in some emotional states, where there is in some sense a 'gain from illness'. In no way am I siding here with those who criticize the sick and mentally ill as 'layabouts'. I am acknowledging that sometimes there is more to be gained from being ill than from being well. Distress can become a powerful way of mobilizing care and attention (which the person actually needs), of deterring anger, or of passively expressing anger by making other people feel guilty. What needs to be questioned is whether being 'sick' or 'depressed' is the only way of getting a response from others or of expressing difficult feelings. Even in counselling itself there are times when 'getting worse' can be an indirect message to the counsellor. When a contract is coming to an end and a client seems to get worse, perhaps with the original difficulties returning, or through the onset of new problems, the client is giving out messages about the prospect of 'going it alone'. His or her new or resurgent difficulties may be a way of saying,

'Can't you see that I need to go on seeing you? I can't let you go. How can you stop seeing me when you can see I'm no better?' Counsellors should never deny the reality of such physical or emotional pain (indeed in psychosomatic symptoms it is an important first step to acknowledge the actual pain as real); but they should also recognize that these feelings are unconsciously a way of resisting (as well as in some way expressing) other, even more painful, emotions.

The opposite of 'the gain from illness' is another form of acting out: 'the flight into health'. It is seen most dramatically when people are genuinely desperate at the first counselling session, but come to the second completely better. It is sometimes like a miracle, and there is no obvious reason for the change. The client feels 'so much better'; or, as in one psychosomatic presentation I remember, the skin rash of many months had completely disappeared. By 'getting better' so quickly, clients may be saying something about their fears about talking and where it is likely to lead them. Their worries are genuine. They may be terrified of what they will uncover if they pause to look within. In most cases their fear is out of all proportion to what they will actually find if they go on, but they obviously do not know that.

The threat of what change may bring is another reason for people 'getting better'. As a client begins to see that there are difficulties in relationships that need facing, which may threaten the stability of those relationships, he or she may prefer either to stay ill or to take flight into health rather than acknowledge what is happening. The acceptance of the counsellor in a first session may highlight the lack of support in a partnership or family, and put those relationships under the microscope in a way in which the client had not anticipated.

Although some clients come to a second session 'feeling better', skilful handling of this subtle resistance by the counsellor often enables them, later in the second session, to acknowledge that not all is well. Supporting change, underlining the strength coming from feeling better, gently enquiring into what may have helped, not infrequently leads to a client saying: 'Actually, there is something else...', and taking the counselling on further than before. Once through a second session, this type of resistance is less evident.

SPLITTING

I have already used the metaphor of a battle or a conflict within, between feelings and conscience, or between opposing feelings. Splitting is a defence against what are called 'ambivalent' feelings towards the same person. Splitting is also a way of trying to cope with confusing experiences at the hands of one person. It is called an early or primitive defence, although this is a natural defence and not so much an avoidance in the context of the first months of life, where splitting is thought to be the necessary way a baby copes with the confusion of good and bad experiences.

A baby has none of an adult's more balanced view of her surroundings. Adults learn how to order experience, but it is difficult for a baby to equate the good feelings that come from the times when Mother is available with the bad feelings that come from her not being there. There is a world of difference between the heaven of being fed, warm, secure, held and loved, and the hell of being hungry, cold, uncomfortable and all over the place. Unlike an adult, a baby is not yet aware that these good experiences and bad experiences are related to one and the same person. To cope with such a mystifying world (and to protect the good feelings towards Mother from the infant's rage), a baby has a split set of images: there is a good mother who is associated with fulfilment and good feelings, and a bad mother who is associated with frustration and bad feelings. During the first few months these two images gradually blend into one. A child learns that those who offer satisfaction can also be frustrating, and that those who frustrate can also satisfy. The process is a complex one, which I over-simplify here. The healing of the split comes about through the nurturing figure providing good enough care for the baby to have confidence in the power of good over bad, and in loving feelings being able to survive hateful feelings.

These powerful images are reflected in many myths and fairy stories, with their symbols of the primeval or ultimate conflict between good and evil. They demonstrate the universality of these issues, and perhaps the most fundamental of all human problems, stemming, appropriately, from the very first moments of an individual's life.

Since no one ever grows up perfectly (whatever 'perfect'

means) it is not surprising that evidence of splitting remains in all adults, and in some cases reflects deep-seated difficulties with ambivalence ('on the one hand . . . on the other hand' feelings). Some people show very black-and-white attitudes: one race or one country is seen as warlike and aggressive, while another is seen as only wanting peace and prosperity. The Cold War between the Soviet Union and the United States typified such attitudes. It can be seen in politics, where politicians and their followers brand each other in stereotypical ways, often forcing open splits that need not be as severe as they are. (There is often relief in the electorate when so-called 'bipartisan' attitudes prevail.) In families one parent may be endowed with all the good qualities, while the other parent is seen as a tyrant. Children can carry different parts of family dynamics: sometimes one sibling shouldering one set of images, and a second representing different qualities. In working partnerships, one person may be set off against another, so that in church life one member of the clergy is supported by one faction, and a second by another group. Similar phenomena can take place in teaching or in training groups: one teacher may be idolized, another seen as incompetent. I recall being a member of a training group where we split our two consultants into 'goody' and 'baddy', while a second group with the same two leaders saw them in completely the opposite way.

One of the problems with identifying splitting is that there are elements of truth in the grounds for the split, and those who are split in this way can take some pleasure in being identified as standing out against their 'rival'. Those who find themselves set up as representatives of the different factions often value the identity this gives them, and fall in with the expectations on them. In a family one parent may prefer to be seen as good, leaving the other to clear up the mess and take on the anger of the family; one leader may like to adopt 'the caring image', forcing the other into picking up the harder authoritarian role.

The examples of the defence known as splitting show the frequency with which a counsellor may detect and observe the client's experience of close relationships as well as of the wider world. A husband who is only described as 'bad' must have some good qualities as well. A mother who is always described as caring and understanding must also at times be experienced as selfish and possessive. In the counselling relationship too, splitting may be seen as a resistance. For example, a client may reject most of what the counsellor says, but at the same time talk about how helpful a former counsellor was. More commonly, the split is reversed, with the client flattering or idealizing the present counsellor and denigrating the former one, thus provoking or even promoting feelings of rivalry between helpers. In such situations, counsellors (who do not get many obvious rewards in their work) are prone to accepting such flattery, little realizing that the previous helper may have been told the same; or that perhaps both of them will be disparaged when the client leaves and sees another helper! Similarly, a counsellor who is flattered face to face can never be sure of what is being said behind her or his back, particularly when other helpers are involved. Whenever possible, the counsellor tries to lead a client to express both good and bad feelings, positive and negative reactions, towards the counsellor as well as others. Counsellors need to heal this split and encourage greater acceptance of ambivalent feelings, so that clients are helped to see and experience 'the whole'. By encouraging the acknowledgement and expression of good and bad feelings towards one person – and often this person is the counsellor – this particular defence pattern begins to shift.

In any counselling practice, but even more particularly in the application of counselling skills in other caring settings, counsellors have clients who 'split' by seeing two or more helpers simultaneously. Sometimes they divide up what they say, so that one helper is given one half of the story and the other is told a different aspect. It is important not to go along with such splitting when a client sees several helpers for what is in effect exactly the same kind of help. While it may be necessary for a client to see a doctor for physical complaints, and an advice worker for welfare guidance, and a counsellor for emotional difficulties, a counsellor would hope that the interaction with the other helpers in this instance could also be brought to the counselling session – and that the other helpers would not try to engage the client in a counselling relationship. Where a client is seeing another counsellor as well, all three people involved (the client and the two counsellors) have to consult in order to decide which of the counsellors the client is going to see. Once decided, the other should not become involved in any counselling (or similar) relationship with the client.

ISOLATION AND DENIAL

Isolation is similar to splitting, although in this case a particular feeling is withheld from its true object, and sometimes split off so that it is expressed towards another. A man who has sex with prostitutes may only be able to feel sexually alive with a woman for whom he feels nothing; at the same time he may only relate to his wife when their relationship is non-sexual. This defence is also seen in what is called *intellectualization*. Here a situation is talked about, but there is none of the feeling one might expect from it; or feelings are talked about but not actually experienced ('I am very angry' said without any passion). In extreme cases, inappropriate emotions may be expressed, isolating the person completely from the threatening and overwhelming power of his or her true feeling. Some people talk in a detached way about themselves as if they are analysing a machine. Others may discuss one area that is interesting (or even potentially seductive and exciting), while drawing the counsellor away from aspects that they would prefer to steer clear of. Isolation of feeling can also take the form of joking about everything, chatting about trivial matters, talking in a generalized way, or even trying to get the counsellor to talk about himself or herself.

Such situations can sometimes be very frustrating, almost as if there is a lack of serious intent on the part of the client to work in counselling. Yet a counsellor looks for reasons why there may be such resistance: perhaps the client is afraid of being overwhelmed by particular feelings, or afraid that acknowledgement of such feelings will damage others. Counsellor responses in such situations might include:

'You seem to find it amusing, but I wasn't feeling that. I wonder if it is difficult to admit any other feelings in case they hurt you too much.'

'We seem to be going round and round on this same point, as though there's something about it we're not getting to. I wonder if there is anything else you are finding difficult to tell me, because you are afraid I'll disapprove of you.'

Denial bears some resemblance to isolation, although it is usually much more explicit and obvious, but for all that harder to contradict. Vehement denial is particularly obvious, and often looks to the observer like fear of acknowledging an idea that is too close to the truth: 'the lady doth protest too much'. Counsellors have to be very careful not to presume that every denial on the part of the client indicates the opposite; this 'heads I win, tails you lose' argument was used too much in early psychoanalytic polemics, and was indeed condemned by Freud.[4] A counsellor must try to distinguish different expressions of denial: those when a client's denial is genuine, and where in some circumstances the counsellor is clearly wrong; those when the counsellor's remark is premature, and there is as yet no clear evidence who is right; and those where the counsellor may well be right, but a client is not yet ready or able to accept it. Suppose a man who works for a company that is about to go bankrupt says: 'I'm not worried', or the counsellor comments: 'Perhaps you are worried about losing your job.' If the client denies any worry it may mean that he cannot face the anxiety of the situation. On the other hand, it might be that he knows he has another job to go to, or that he is more relieved than worried at the prospect of early retirement from an unsatisfactory job. In instances of denial, other clues may determine whether or not there is any resistance:

My client Olive was telling me about taking her little boy to the doctor. She had been told that her child would have to see a consultant at the local hospital. 'But I'm not worried about him,' Olive said to me, looking (I thought) rather anxious as her eyes darted around the room. As she went on, she mentioned several people whom she knew. They had all been to doctors and been told that nothing was wrong, but discovered later that they had serious physical conditions. By this time I felt I had enough confirmation of my earlier suspicion that Olive was denying how worried she was about her child. I said: 'I think in view of what you're saying about these other people, that you can't help being a little worried about your son, even though it is difficult to admit that to yourself. Of course, I hope the doctor was right in saying that it's just routine; but these other people have made you worry; and as a mother it's bound to be worrying, when you care as much as you obviously do about your son.'

There is a different response that some clients make to a counsellor's interventions, and which is apparently the opposite of denial: they accept everything the counsellor says, and swallow it up. In fact, they do not always take time to digest it, and they do not really let the counsellor get too near to what they are feeling. Although such clients may be afraid to challenge or to disagree, they also seem to be afraid of looking more closely at themselves. Such passive acceptance can be as frustrating to the counsellor as outright rejection.

The forerunner of denial, and indeed the 'arch' defence which lies at the root of most other defences, is *repression*. In this case, feelings, thoughts and experiences are so completely forgotten that it is as if they had never existed. Repression may be of feelings that a person is fleetingly aware of, but then rapidly pushes away. It may be of impulses that are not permitted to see the light of day, because they are felt to be so threatening. In everyday life we can forget names and details about people, but the repression is only partial because we *know* we have forgotten. Where repression is total, we have even forgotten that we have forgotten! Painful or uncomfortable memories are hidden away, although repressed feelings have a way of slipping out sideways – such as in slips of the tongue or, more seriously, in psychosomatic symptoms. Freud described 'the return of the repressed' and suggested that much that was repressed found an alternative method of expression, sometimes seen even in the very defences that people put up against repressed thoughts and feelings.[5] For example, compulsive handwashing when used as a defence against recognizing 'unclean' thoughts provides some of the sensuous pleasure that the thoughts themselves would, if permitted into consciousness.

INTROJECTION AND PROJECTION

Splitting and repression have been identified as defences that derive from the early months of life. Introjection and projection fall into the same category, and can perhaps best be understood as 'taking in' and 'spitting out'. These are important ways of being in their own right, but taken to extremes they can diminish the whole person. A negative example of *introjection* is seen in some of the psychosomatic symptoms that people develop in grief: they can resemble the symptoms that were present in the person who died. But introjection can be a healthy means of incorporating and identifying with significant others. Indeed, when it works well, healthy aspects of others can be assimilated, thus strengthening the person who 'takes them in'. Introjection is an important positive feature of grieving.

Problems tend to arise when it is negative features of significant others that are introjected, because these can damage the person who takes them in. This sometimes arises when hostile feelings towards the significant other cannot be acknowledged, and are instead taken back into the self by identifying with 'bad' aspects in the other. Hence in bereavement the grieving person may begin to suffer what the lost one suffered, damaging the grieving client. A client with a pain in her chest had a relative who had recently died of a heart attack. Another client with recent severe headaches turned out to have lost her closest friend who had died as a result of a brain tumour. Introjection, or identification in this negative sense, is also seen when a person who has been criticized in turn attacks the next person in line. This is called 'identification with the aggressor' – taking in and taking on the role of the one who has been persecutory, because there is no means of retaliating. A child had been to the dentist and had had a painful filling. When she came home she was very aggressive towards her younger sister: although less harmfully, she displayed the phenomenon of introjection by playing at being dentist to one of her dolls. These are ways of coping with painful feelings (and in these examples with hostile feelings).

A variation of introjection, already apparent in the psychosomatic symptoms in the examples above, is *turning against the self*. Masochistic tendencies may be a substitute for the expression of sadistic or aggressive wishes towards another person. Suicide attempts are sometimes a desperate attempt to cope with hateful feelings towards a person who is also deeply loved. In their fear of hurting the other, or their fear of losing their love, people who attempt suicide may only be able to turn their anger against the self. At the same time (the return of the repressed) they do hurt others, by making them feel guilty. They partly succeed in expressing their hostility, and if they survive the suicide attempts they may feel even more guilty because of this.

Turning against self is also seen in the self-hatred of some people when they get depressed. Sometimes the efforts of everyone offering them help flounder against this rock of self-contempt, and it has a depressing effect on the helpers as well. In some instances of depression, the anger is not just turned on self, but is passively and effectively expressed while the person manages to remain blameless: 'What are you getting so angry for? I can't help it. I haven't done anything. I'm just depressed.'

Projection is very common and is perhaps the best-known type of defence. When I am unable to acknowledge my own feeling, I can attribute it to another person and condemn her or him for it into the bargain. We often find it less uncomfortable to say, 'He is angry with me' than to admit, 'I am angry with him'; 'She is jealous of me' when in fact, 'I am jealous of her'.

Projections are not made at random. They often have some basis in reality, because 'the cap fits' the person on to whom the projection is made. This makes projection a powerful and cogent defence, and one that is hard to recognize and own. Yet in counselling it is sometimes harder for a client to have any evidence for their projections on to their counsellor, which makes such projections especially useful in demonstrating both the defence and, more importantly, the unacknowledged feelings in the client. A client says, for example: 'You must dislike me after what I said last week.' It is more likely that this is the client's own view of themselves, since the counsellor has said nothing. Nevertheless, just as with denials, it is important that a counsellor does not arrogantly presume that there is no basis in reality for the client's remark. It is often helpful to clarify the apparent projection: 'What makes you think that? Did I appear to show dislike for you last week?' Only when the client says 'Nothing', is it safe to wonder whether the client is not saying something about himself or herself. Clients can readily project their own critical parts on to their counsellor.

There is another common remark that is particularly heard

in hesitant clients in the early stages of counselling: 'I think I must be wasting your time.' Although this sometimes indicates a difficulty in allowing themselves to claim attention (such people were or are often the carers in their own families), clients making this remark can also disguise their feeling that counselling is a waste of time, because it apparently achieved nothing in the initial meeting. A counsellor's reply in such a case can be: 'I wonder whether you feel I'm wasting yours?'

REACTION FORMATION AND RATIONALIZATION

These two defences have their origins in later stages of child development, particularly as children acquire the ability to use action and language to express themselves. *Reaction formation* is an over-reaction to thoughts and feelings that must not be allowed to surface. In some cases this reaction has earlier origins. A person who is afraid of closeness may react against any such feelings by becoming belligerent or distant. Idealization, which is involved in the defence of splitting, also involves idolizing figures who are in positions of authority or fame (often with a 'parental' position like a doctor or a member of the clergy). Sometimes such idealization is a reaction against acknowledging such a person's imperfections. The greater the idealization, the greater the buried feelings. Reaction formation is also seen in the rebellious person who reacts against the fears of being made to conform; this may be linked to earlier anxieties about dependency. Other examples include obsessional people, who are extreme in their cleanliness or tidiness, who may in fact be reacting against their wish to be able to make a mess.

In the obsessional person, such reaction formation is sometimes taken a stage further into another defensive manoeuvre called *undoing*. Undoing tries to get rid of the damage or threat that a person fears. It is seen in compulsive behaviour, which may be recognized by those suffering from it as being irrational, but they feel unable to stop it. Examples include frequent handwashing, checking light switches, door latches, avoidance of certain numbers, and superstitious rituals. It is as if the performance of such rituals exerts magical influence, temporarily easing feelings of anxiety, relieving guilt and deterring the threat of punishment. *Asceticism*, although it may for some people have positive religious associations, is also a technical term for a defence that is another form of undoing. It is a compulsive reaction most commonly seen in adolescents, where in some individuals there are swings between the ardent expression of sexual feelings (in masturbation in particular) and periods of abstinence and great purity. In young women (and indeed in some older women) asceticism more frequently takes the form of strict dieting. Problems with eating, such as anorexia and bulimia, appear to have their origins more in issues of control than of dependency. Although eating disorders are partly reactions against wishes to eat, and partly against developing into a mature sexual adult, there are clear authority issues as well. Although behavioural therapy is sometimes recommended as the most appropriate treatment for obsessional disorders (suggesting that referral to a clinical psychologist might be useful), in the case of eating disorders the evidence for behavioural therapy is not nearly so clear. When working with eating disorders, as with other obsessional problems, counselling requires special experience and expertise so that the symptom itself is not ignored in the therapy, but also not allowed to dominate it.

Rationalization describes the remarkable ability many people have to convince themselves that all is well, when it is quite clear it is not; or to explain away a feeling that normally would be much better fully expressed. In cases of anorexia, for example, a strict diet can be rationalized on the grounds of the wish to be fashionably slim and attractive, and that the person is already overweight, when it is plain for all to see that the anorexic has become thin and wasted. Others may rationalize their grief by claiming heartily, 'Well, he had a good innings! He wouldn't have wanted us to mourn.' Rationalization is closely related to intellectualization, which I described earlier as an example of isolation.

REGRESSION AND FIXATION

These two terms describe both a psychological state as well as a defence. We talk about some people 'becoming regressed'. This is going back to an earlier stage of development, often a child-like reaction or way of being. We also describe others as

being 'fixated', as if they are in some respects glued to a
particular immature spot in their psychological development
and unable to move beyond it. These defences are sometimes
related to stages of development, and can be seen more clearly
in their many forms of expression when a counsellor has
working knowledge of life stage theory such as that proposed
by Erikson or Rayner.[6]

The developmental stage of adolescence, for example, may
be a point to which a person may in some aspects return in
mid-life as a defence against ageing: he or she can be said to
regress to being adolescent. Others appear to find it difficult to
move beyond adolescence in the first place, as in Peter Pan
characters who do not wish to grow any older (although Peter
Pan was probably a little younger); the playboy type stays
adolescent because the next stage of life, which involves intimacy and responsibility, is seen to be too threatening. In cases
of regression and fixation, a counsellor is faced with a more
generalized defence, which will probably take more than
interpretation to work through. Indeed it may be the whole
purpose of therapy or counselling to help a person grow or
re-grow through the developing therapeutic relationship.

DISPLACEMENT AND SUBLIMATION

The last two defences are so similar that the two terms need to
be taken together. In the way they work they are identical,
although their function is different. Since all defences have
positive as well as negative results, it may not be immediately
obvious why sublimation is used as a separate term for healthy
displacement. Since the term is often used, I stay with the
convention – although in practice successful displacement
may be impossible at the time to distinguish from sublimation.
Perhaps it is only failed sublimation that can be recognized as
actually being displacement.

Displacement and sublimation describe the redirection of
feelings and impulses away from their original object and on
to another, or into a different form of expression. It is displacement when, instead of being angry with his child, the father
kicks the cat. As far as the cat is concerned, it might have been
better had the father kicked a door or gone out to play football.

In the latter case, his anger could have been redirected in a more socially acceptable way. Whatever the form of expression, the father's anger is displaced, either successfully (he scores a goal) or unsuccessfully (he hurts the cat or knocks paint off the door), and in a socially acceptable form (football) or in a socially unacceptable manner (kicking the cat or the door).

Sublimation is of a different order. In fact telling his child off, and not having to kick anyone or anything, might have been appropriate sublimation. Alternatively, playing football, but not out of any prior angry feelings, might be called sublimation – using normal drives and impulses in ways that are constructive and creative and socially useful. Sublimation describes a stage of personal development in which a person is able to express his or her feelings in appropriate places to appropriate people and to an appropriate degree; and where he or she can also direct energy into socially and culturally acceptable forms of expression. Freud believed that civilization is built upon the sublimation of basic human emotions and desires into wider activities, such as science, technology, art, literature and religion – and, we may wish to add, into caring for others. He thought religion was one of the least successful forms of sublimation and that art was one of the most successful forms.[7] He also saw clearly (and there is plenty of evidence in the twentieth century that he was right) that civilization is all too often a thin veneer where sublimation hides raw emotions. Take away some of the veneer, and people can behave towards one another in ways that are subhuman. Given the fragility of all sublimation, it may yet be that displacement is still the better overall term to use.

Displacement is seen in the counselling process when clients talk about expressing their feelings towards the wrong persons: especially when various negative feelings are directed at those people who do not deserve to be given them. Displacement is also seen when clients talk about events and relationships outside the counselling session, yet are often describing what they are experiencing within the therapeutic relationship. In this form displacement is one of the most common expressions that a psychodynamic counsellor picks up, since in psychodynamic counselling the link between the world outside the session and the relationship within the session is a vital one, and displacement is the clearest bridge between the two:

Client: I'm feeling really angry with my boss at work today.
Counsellor: I think you may be feeling angry with me too.

Client: I dreamed last night that I was running away from an operating theatre just as the surgeon was cutting me up.
Counsellor: I wonder if that means that you are wanting to get out of here in case what we do here involves cutting you up?

These brief examples make it look as if the counsellor normally has a snap response. In fact, such interpretations of displaced feelings and thoughts are very carefully weighed before the counsellor decides whether and how to suggest them.

THE RELUCTANT CLIENT

Kennedy and Charles make a useful distinction between resistance and reluctance.[8] They use reluctance of an attitude in those who come for counselling at someone else's insistence. They may come under duress, and with pressure to please a third party. Resistance is not such an appropriate term to use of those who are fully aware that they have not chosen to come, and do not wish to be there at all. Resistant clients want help, and for the most part wish to make use of their counselling session. But there are some aspects about themselves that they do not want to see or accept. Reluctant clients do not really want help at all, except to satisfy someone else. As with resistant clients, counselling will not shift such situations unless the counsellor can show that he or she wishes to co-operate with the reluctant person – in this case not against the barriers and other signs of resistance, but against the pressure to be there. The first hurdle is to get over the reluctant client's suspicions of the counsellor.

Rapport and trust can sometimes be achieved by openly acknowledging the compulsion to come and the threat held over them that such clients feel. The client's own feelings about this must be tapped. Analysing the resistance in any other way will be dismissed as irrelevant and may confirm suspicions. Reluctant clients are sometimes surprised by such understanding, and decide to go on seeing the counsellor from their own choice. If they do go on, confidentiality, especially with regard to any third party, must be underlined. Alternatively, some clients realize that the counsellor refuses to force them into counselling; and although they choose not to return at that point, the way has been made smoother for them to come back at a later date, or to see another helper in the future – from choice, and not simply to please or propitiate others.

Working with reluctant people confirms the cardinal principles of working with defences and facing resistance:

1. accept that there is a good reason for the defence or the particular form of resistance;

2. draw attention to the defence, perhaps providing an example of resistance as experienced in the counselling session;

3. suggest or attempt to discover why there is resistance – particularly concentrating on the anxiety that the client feels at strange thoughts, painful feelings or embarrassing ideas;

4. create a sense of trust which enables the barriers to be lowered, in order to allow the particular feelings and thoughts to come to the surface, where they can be expressed, accepted, and a start made towards understanding them.[9]

It should not be assumed that resistance is bound to intrude in every counselling session. Much valuable counselling is done through providing the opportunity for clients to express themselves more fully than they do elsewhere. Many are helped because their helper listens carefully, and reflects back accurately. Some clients are so much in need of a person to listen to them that they show little sign of resistance: they are desperate to have the chance to pour it all out. With some of them resistance occurs at certain points only, and when it is overcome leads into more openness and insight.

Inevitably there are some clients with whom there is little

sign of change. Instead of working through different issues, moving further all the time, the sessions appear to go round and round in circles. This may indicate a limit to what can be achieved with that counsellor; it may mean alternative approaches need to be considered, depending upon the particular circumstances. Some resistance is not just against the expression of thoughts and feelings, but resistance to change itself. This is another place where supervision is invaluable and where referral to other types of help, including psychotherapy, might be necessary.

DEFENSIVE RELIGION

Religious belief and practice, like any other form of human activity, is capable of being used positively or negatively. The defences that I have outlined in this chapter can also be given expression in religious language and in religious ritual. This is not to say that all religious practice is defensive, although Freud clearly thought there was a strong case for a parallel with obsessional practices.[10] At its best, however, religion both supports and challenges defences. In Becker's words, which I quoted in Chapter 1, religion is an 'ideal of strength and of potentiality for growth, of what man might become by assuming the burden of his life, as well as being partly relieved of it'.[11]

Nevertheless, in pastoral care, and in pastoral counselling in particular, it is important to recognize how defensive some religious beliefs and practices can be. (It is also valuable for counsellors in other settings to understand this, since some of their clients will show evidence of similar thinking and behaviour.) I am aware that in this particular field, as in politics, there are many ways of seeing truth and delusion, and my own examples may be contentious to some. I happen to believe they are good examples of defensive religion:

1. Rituals can be felt to be so important that they have to be performed in particular ways, and people feel anxious and guilty if they do not perform them or see them performed correctly. This is particularly true of some Anglo-Catholic or pre-Vatican II Roman Catholic clergy and laypeople, some of

whom feel that lack of proper observance is as sinful as viola-
tions of codes of personal conduct.

2. In other quarters of the churches, particularly those that
are Bible-based, any questioning of literal interpretation or of
divine authorship of the Bible is similarly greeted with horror
and extreme defensiveness.

3. In the Church, as in other spheres of life, rationalizations
can disguise deep unconscious fears. Debates about the ordi-
nation of women, for example, which appeared to revolve
around scriptural and theological precedents, often disguised
the threat to men in authority (and indeed to some of the
women who wanted to keep them so) of the Church allowing
women to become fully equal with men.

4. God and other major figures to whom devotion is offered
(such as the persons of the godhead, other gods in different
faiths, or saints) can be used for projections of the wishes and
fears of believers, who sometimes then justify their own views
on the grounds that God has qualities and characteristics they
have given him (or her – just as much a projection as a father
god!). Sometimes these projections become the basis for actions
that are then rationalized on the basis of previous projections.

5. Prayer and confession can be used as a quick way of suppressing difficult and undesirable thoughts, or of trying to
resolve issues involving human relationships, without accepting
personal responsibility, and without being prepared to take a
proper look at deeper causes for behaviours and attitudes.

6. Sublimation may be used as a way of trying to cope with
sexual and other feelings, through vows of chastity or celibacy;
or as a way of trying to overcome other unwanted feelings such
as anger, jealousy and all 'seven deadly sins'. In fact, the religious life (I mean here in religious orders *and* in the secular
ministry) can be an attempt to suppress rather than sublimate,
with consequent misery for some priests and religious, and for
the members of their congregations whom in some cases they
abuse.

What constitutes mature and immature religion is bound to include a number of contentious issues and difficult boundaries. This clearly raises questions about pastoral counsellors' own values and spiritual objectives, and about models of maturity, which I come back to in Chapter 10.

What needs to be borne in mind, both by pastoral and also by secular counsellors, is that as with any other form of resistance, these particular defences, which make use of religious ideas and principles, are vital and precious to the person who employs them. They will probably not recognize them as defences at all, but as part of their true religion. Neither will they lightly give them up, because the defences cover up areas of pain and difficulty. Perhaps this is even more true of defences that have a religious content to them, since the full weight and authority that a person ascribes to their church or to the Bible is thrown behind the defence, justifying it and rationalizing it; and supporting it sometimes with deep emotional commitment. It is not just a defence that is being faced: nor is it the feelings and thoughts that the defence keeps at bay. In confronting religious defences, a person's whole faith may feel under challenge. Working with some religious people may be one of the most difficult areas of all.

NOTES

1. Romans 7.23.
2. S. Freud, *An Outline of Psychoanalysis*. Penguin Freud Library, volume 15, pp. 377-8.
3. D. Brown and J. Pedder, *Introduction to Psychotherapy*. Tavistock Publications 1979.
4. S. Freud, *Constructions in Analysis*. Standard Edition, volume XXIII. Hogarth Press 1951, p. 257.
5. S. Freud, *Repression*. Penguin Freud Library, volume 11.
6. E. Erikson, *Childhood and Society*. Penguin Books 1965, ch. 7; E. Rayner, *Human Development*. Allen & Unwin 1986 (3rd edn). I have myself moved away from stage theory in M. Jacobs, *The Presenting Past*. Open University Press 1998 (2nd edn).
7. S. Freud, *Formulations on the Two Principles of Mental Functioning*. Penguin Freud Library, volume 11.
8. E. Kennedy and S. Charles, *On Becoming a Counsellor*. Dublin: Gill & Macmillan 1989 (2nd edn), pp. 112-19.
9. For extensive exercises in the skills of identifying defences and

resistance and in framing interpretations of both, see M. Jacobs, *Swift to Hear*. SPCK 2000 (2nd edn), pp. 125–38.

10. S. Freud, *Obsessive Actions and Religious Practices*. Penguin Freud Library, volume 13.

11. E. Becker, *The Birth and Death of Meaning*. Penguin Books 1972, p. 196.

CHAPTER NINE

The Counselling Relationship

Time and again in this book I find myself coming back to the crucial importance in counselling of the relationship between the counsellor and each individual client; and to a therapeutic relationship that is based not upon knowledge, or forcefulness of character, but on what can well be described as a 'still small voice'. In manner, in tone of voice, and in the choice of words that a counsellor uses, he or she conveys both gentle acceptance and an incisive purposefulness. Prepared to be carried along on the wind and tide of a client's deepest concerns, a counsellor both responds to the direction, but also carefully steers a way through the fiercest waters. In an effective counselling relationship, a counsellor and client feel part of each other, responding to each other as much as the yachtsman responds to the pull of the boat and the elements.

There are many other vocations and occupations where the character of the relationship between 'service provider' and client also matters. Those who need to communicate directly with their 'customers' do much better when they can relate well. Not for nothing do service organizations now employ counselling trainers to teach customer skills. In some situations, such as teaching, the Church, and probably also in medicine, the personal factor makes all the difference in communicating knowledge, faith or healing. There is, however, one major difference between counselling and therapy and these other areas. It is a difference that becomes even more significant at the deeper levels of intervention outlined in Chapter 7. In most working relationships, once a good rapport has been established (and as long as it is maintained), the relationship itself takes a back seat while other matters come to the fore: the sale of the item the customer wants, the examination and advice of the doctor, the conduct of worship by a minister, the content of the lesson by a teacher. The relationship itself, once formed, can be taken for granted.

This may also be true of a counselling relationship where the work is on a supportive level, and in more insight-oriented counselling this may also be true as long as the relationship remains clearly positive. Research into the effectiveness of counsellors appears to confirm the necessity for counsellors to meet the core conditions that Rogers and others have set out, which essentially are personal qualities such as warmth, empathy, sensitivity, congruence and non-possessive love.[1] However, where a counsellor works with a client at the deeper levels of intervention, and in the practice of psychotherapy (which essentially is what counselling becomes at these levels), there is much more significance attached to the relationship between counsellor and client. Most counselling approaches would have counsellors monitor the feelings evoked in them by a client, and would expect counsellors to reflect such feelings back (sensitively, and at the right time), partly to help a client see how he or she may appear to others. The psychodynamic model goes even further, and suggests that the way a client feels about the counsellor or therapist can act as an important guide to understanding the attitudes and perceptions the client has towards others, especially to those who are most significant currently, or who were central figures in the client's childhood and adolescence. It is often in monitoring, and in using the more negative or difficult feelings that the counsellor and client have towards each other and working on them in the counselling relationship, that opportunities arise for self-knowledge and consequent change. Counselling and therapy relationships clearly differ from all other working relationships in the constructive use that is made in counselling of what in other professional relationships might be considered counter-productive attitudes.

This therapeutic relationship is a good deal more complex than is suggested in some books about counselling. This does not mean that it is felt to be complex with all clients. In much supportive or short-term counselling the complexities do not obtrude, even though they are still present beneath the surface. Nevertheless, my assessment of what counsellors have to work with now in terms of presenting problems, compared to a generation ago, is that counsellors in all types of agency, voluntary, institutional or private practice, are working with client difficulties that two generations ago would have been the province of psychotherapists and psychiatrists only. It is this increasing depth of difficulty that calls for an even clearer understanding of the nature of the therapeutic relationship.

In this chapter I take five different perspectives. In practice there is an overlap between them all, since it is the same relationship I am describing, but from various viewpoints. There are also some clear differences, which sometimes it is helpful to point out to clients, who struggle with appropriate and inappropriate ways of seeing others and of relating to them. Other relationships also have these complex perspectives, which is what frequently makes close relationships difficult and confusing. The difference between these outside situations and counselling and therapy is that in the latter situation the various elements can sometimes be seen more clearly, and they are actually talked about.

These five perspectives are:

1. the 'working' relationship between counsellor and client, as two people with a definite task, which they undertake together, each accepting responsibility for the work;

2. the 'real' relationship of two people, who are equally human;

3. the 'transference' relationship in which a client repeats patterns of relations to others, even when they are not always *appropriate* responses to the counsellor;

4. the 'counter-transference' relationship in which the counsellor responds to a client;

5. the 'reparative' relationship in which client and counsellor experience some repair to what has gone wrong and some restoration of what has been missing in past and present relationships.

1. THE 'WORKING' RELATIONSHIP

Although a good relationship may be important to other forms of helping, counselling, which deliberately follows a client in the direction in which the client wishes to go, obviously requires a rather special kind of working relationship in which the client is fully involved. The wish to 'get rid of my depression' or 'for you to give me advice' is not in itself enough to form a basis for this working partnership. For a good alliance, especially in deeper exploratory work, clients need to learn that counselling involves working with inner fears and feelings. I have already outlined in Chapter 7 some of the characteristics of those people who are most suited to counselling, whether in supportive or uncovering mode.

I have also touched upon the motivation that brings a person for counselling. Unless clients are able to learn (with the help of their counsellor) how to use the 'hour' they have each week, and unless they feel comfortable with the space to talk and think about themselves, it is probable that both client and counsellor will soon feel frustrated at the lack of active help each gives the other. One hour a week, which is the usual time given to the majority of counselling clients, is not long. During the other 167 hours of the week clients have much time and sometimes space in which to go on working and reflecting upon themselves. Those who use some of this time have much to gain: they take the therapeutic task on for themselves, based on the model that their counsellor offers. Karen Horney's description of the relationship as worker (the client) and assistant (the counsellor), to which I referred in Chapter 4, is worth repeating.

An American psychoanalyst, Greenson, was one of the first to write about the importance of the working alliance.[2] He lists features in the client and in the therapist that are necessary for fostering the work they undertake together. The contribution of the client to the working alliance consists of the capacity to communicate freely in words, with feelings, being able to let go, but also being able to use a sense of order, logic and thoughtfulness. The client needs to be able to contain the wish to act out feelings with regard to the therapist (see Chapter 8). Clients should be capable of listening, reflecting, observing, responding to, agreeing with and contradicting the counsellor; and they should be able to learn to form their own ideas and interpretations, outside the session as well as within it. Part of this comes from a wish to know, to understand and to find

answers, causes and solutions. Such a contribution from the
client is perhaps summed up in the capacity to take the initiative, and to share responsibility with the therapist or counsellor.

Of equal importance are the contributions therapists and
counsellors make to the working alliance. They need to be
good at providing order and structure, and keeping to routine
– good timekeeping, proper notice of breaks, alterations of
times, etc. They should be committed both to the client and to
the pursuit of insight. They must be realistic and reasonable,
acknowledging, for example, the strangeness of the relationship and the process; and helping clients to understand what
is required of them when they are puzzled. Explanations are
important, both of the process and also of any unfamiliar
terms or jargon. Greenson encourages therapists to use phrases
to indicate the sharing of the task: 'Let *us* look at this . . . *we* can
see . . . I wonder what *you* make of this idea'. All this nurtures
the more mature aspects of the client.

Greenson insists that therapists (and counsellors) are concerned for the rights of the client. He is clearly aware of the
dangers of the powerful position in which some therapists put
themselves. It is important to be able to admit to being wrong
in handling a situation, or in not understanding something a
client has said. It is also important to affirm the correctness of
a client's perceptions of the counsellor when the client is right:
'You're right, I don't feel well . . . Yes, I was annoyed . . . Yes, I
did speak somewhat sharply then.' It is then essential to look
at how the client *feels* about the counsellor being that way. He
suggests from time to time reflecting with clients on how they
think they are working with the counsellor, and the counsellor
with them, and how counselling is progressing. Greenson also
states that part of the therapist's contribution to the working
alliance is knowledge of the theory of personal development,
training in the practice of therapy, and ongoing training that
informs empathy and intuition.

In listing these qualities in counsellor and client, I do not
suggest that they should all be present at the very first point of
contact. It is partly the potentiality for such an alliance that a
counsellor is looking for (just as a careful client may be checking this out in the counsellor). The working alliance is built up
throughout counselling, and particularly in the early sessions,
as the counsellor supports each indication of the client's wish

to speak freely, to reflect, to disagree, and all the other abilities listed. One of the long-term aims of any counselling is to assist clients to care for and think about themselves. In the working alliance they learn ways of doing this that can continue long after the end of the contract. Counsellors, especially those who work under the pressure of long waiting lists, know they only have contact with people for a relatively short time. The dialogue between them in the session can be internalized, so that the 'still small voice' of the counsellor is joined by, and eventually totally replaced by, the 'still small voice' in the client. Clients sometimes speak of holding conversations with themselves, as if they were talking inside their heads with their counsellors. A successful working relationship leads to clients taking on the major part of the task, allowing the therapist to step back, to contain, and to provide the incentive and encouragement for this process through regular sessions. If this working relationship is internalized (a good example of introjection discussed in the last chapter), clients may in the future work through new crises with their own strength, and with the support of good relationships made with other people.

This is not an unattainable goal, although brief counselling and counselling skills used in other more time-limited helping work may not allow this internalization to take place. This does not detract from the need for a good working alliance in brief counselling and in related work. One of my clients, after a relatively short time in counselling, told me of his answer to a friend who asked him what went on in counselling. He had perceptively replied: 'It's not like having crutches. It's rather that the counsellor is there, while you struggle to learn how to walk. He doesn't stop you from falling, but he stays with you until you can use your feet.' This is a fine description in itself, but it is more than that. It is an illustration of a good working alliance in which my client became as insightful as me, because his description shows an understanding of counselling that is as good as any I could give.

There is one complication to this perspective: a good working alliance is not necessarily present when clients are able to agree or disagree with the counsellor. The working relationship can be influenced or even hampered by the 'transference' or the 'counter-transference' relationship, which I have yet to explain. Clients can be defensive about co-operating too strongly with their counsellor, perhaps because of some deep suspicion that has its origins in past relationships. Some counsellors find it difficult to accept their clients as full partners in the task. The working relationship is an alliance of the reasonable (thinking) aspects of both parties, but transference or counter-transference (as therapists know only too well) can interfere with reasonable thinking. Although it therefore seems right to start with the working alliance, and to make it one of the foundation blocks for the counselling relationship, there is a chicken-and-egg situation here. It may be necessary to look at the transference relationship in order to help the working alliance to function better, although the working alliance is necessary in order to look at the transference! Similarly, a good and reasonable working alliance can be used as a resistance to avoid feeling. Intellectualization is one of therapy's most frequent defences!

2. THE 'REAL' RELATIONSHIP

Person-centred counsellors have for a long time stressed the importance of the real relationship. The term they use is 'genuine', one of the core conditions needed in the counsellor for effective counselling. Psychodynamic therapists and counsellors have been slower in identifying this perspective, although Greenson, whose description of the working alliance is so valuable, also writes about the real relationship, albeit more briefly.[3] Lomas in Britain has laid particular stress on this part of the relationship, and looked at the value of self-disclosure.[4]

There is a semantic problem, however, over the word 'real', or even over the term 'genuine'. What is real? What is not real? When I explain the transference and counter-transference perspectives it will be clear that some of the distortions that clients (and counsellors) have in their perceptions are only distortions as viewed by an outside observer. They are vividly *real* for the client or the counsellor. The working relationship is also *real*: indeed, Greenson makes it clear that there must be a *real* sharing of responsibility.

By 'real' relationship I mean two human beings, who in any other setting would be just two ordinary men or women. In therapy and counselling, the client and counsellor, for the most part, set this ordinary way of relating to one side. So, for example, clients do not *normally* expect to make a different kind of relationship such as friendship with their counsellor, even though they may sometimes wish to; nor do they expect to learn much about their counsellor's life outside the session, even though they may be interested and sometimes try to find things out. Likewise, counsellors do not expect the working relationship to become a friendship, nor the transference relationship to be acted out. This does not mean that counsellors do not have real feelings about their clients, which are sometimes quite validly expressed, or in some instances *could* be expressed if the client were more ready to receive them.

Apart from the absolute necessity of counsellors to be as fully in touch with themselves as is possible, in order to meet clients at all levels of their humanity, what is important about this perspective? First, counsellors need to recognize the point at which what is called for is not just sensitivity, not just good listening, not just accurate reflection, and not even just empathy: but a plain human response. It is not always appropriate or necessary to share an immediate feeling. It is possible to sympathize inwardly with a client, but in replying to make an empathic response that tries to get in touch with a different feeling altogether. But there are also times when good counselling skills are appropriately forgotten and a counsellor simply replies: 'I *am* sorry' or even 'How dreadful!' When a counsellor expresses compassion or concern when things have gone badly wrong for the client; or client and counsellor laugh together at something they both find amusing; when a counsellor expresses sadness at the end of a counselling relationship; or when he or she congratulates a client on a real achievement – at all such points a counsellor shifts from the working alliance to an ordinary human response.

It is important to distinguish real and appropriate feelings in the counsellor and the client from other (equally real but in one sense inappropriate) feelings that might be signs of transference reactions. For example, people often get close to their counsellor, and feel very sad when they have to stop coming. Their reaction is an appropriately real response. It would be more unreal if there were no such feelings. It would be wrong for a counsellor to interpret the sadness as indicating a problem about leaving. On the other hand, if a client shows intense grief, or immense anger at ending, a counsellor might with greater justification think that problems about endings are distorting the present situation; and that such feelings are an indication that the counselling has not dealt with them.

It is also probable in a good counselling relationship that the people involved will feel really warm towards, and involved with, each other. These are signs of a real and appropriate relationship. Each party will have the normal thoughts and phantasies about the other, but they will not intrude upon the work. If these feelings, thoughts and phantasies (on either side) become too intense or continuous (for instance, a counsellor constantly phantasizing about a sexual relationship with the client or a client getting angry because the counsellor is not expressing physical affection) there is clearly a different way of understanding the relationship. Transference and countertransference have got in the way of the real relationship.

The second reason for awareness of the real relationship is related to Greenson's requirement of the working alliance that a therapist can acknowledge when a client has correctly perceived something about the therapist. Indeed, I would go so far as to say that until a counsellor or therapist knows (or thinks he or she knows) what is happening in the real relationship, transference interpretations are presumptuous. The three different examples that follow illustrate what I mean.

I am normally a calm and relaxed counsellor, and I remain fairly quiet in sessions. I like clients to take the initiative. With most people this works well enough, although there are some who are so passive that I have to adapt my stance and become more active. I suspect this makes me feel more tense, perhaps because I sense the client's anxiety as well.

> Quentin responded quite easily to my quiet manner. He talked freely, he reflected on what I said. It felt like a good working relationship. One day he observed: 'You're very quiet. You don't say much, do you?' It would have been ridiculous for me to 'interpret' this. I replied: 'That's right. I do keep quiet, as you've noticed, because I want to listen to what you are saying. I hadn't felt that worried you, but I wonder why you're saying that at this point?' I acknowledged Quentin's accurate perception, explained the reason, and explored why he had raised it.

Ian, on the other hand, was one of those clients with whom I have to intervene actively. I said almost as much as Ian did. When Ian said to me: 'You're quiet, aren't you? I don't like these silences', I felt his perception to be a distorted one. It was, of course, real to Ian, who was distinctly uncomfortable. I thought about his observation. What was Ian expecting of me? Advice perhaps? Was he afraid of the threat of the empty space? Might he be saying more about himself than about me, because he *is* a quiet person? Here was an occasion when I could only pick up the inaccurate perception of himself, and use it to try and clarify what Ian was thinking or feeling. I said: 'I wonder what leads you to say that? I actually feel I am talking a lot. You seem to be feeling very uncomfortable.'

Ralph was training as a clinical psychologist. He had seen me for a while because he had problems about close relationships. One day he told me that my consulting room was not as colourful as his supervisor's office. I knew the supervisor. What Ralph said was true: she had a lot of bright pictures and interesting table decorations, and my own room, by comparison, was quite restrained. Ralph's perception was an accurate one. However, Ralph went on to say that I was a very cold and distant person and that my room reflected this. My perception of my relationship with Ralph was a different one. I felt warm towards him, and I had shared quite a bit of humour with him. I am reasonably socially skilled, and with Ralph I had felt quite relaxed. Because he was training for a similar profession, I had shared some of my more theoretical thinking with him, so that he had a 'special' relationship with me. Although his description of my room might be accurate, his description of me was not. I thought Ralph was having to push me into coldness and distance (which his remark might easily have done as well), and that he was resisting his wish to be warm and close to me. If I was right, this mirrored Ralph's description of what happened to him in intimate relationships; and echoed his father leaving home when he was very small, never to make contact again.

If I am told by many of my clients that I am quiet and reflective, I can only agree: and I have no wish to change this. If I am
told by many of my clients that I am cold and distant, I would
need to re-think my perception of myself, because it could
mean I have difficulties of my own (counter-transference). Since
Ralph's particular comment was an unusual one, I was more
justified in trusting my own perception of our relationship,
and using Ralph's distorted one to look at its meaning.

The 'real' relationship described here differs from the
'working' alliance, because it includes other aspects of human
relationships that are clearly normal and appropriate for
people to experience with one another. The real relationship is
the second and equal part of the foundation upon which all
counselling and therapy takes place. Without it, other facets of
the counselling process are unlikely to develop or succeed. It
is a very important part of the reparative relationship. It also
acts as a backcloth against which transference and counter-
transference projections can be seen more clearly. But it is not
by itself sufficient for counselling, which is not the same as
friendship or any other close partnership. Without the working
alliance the real relationship will go nowhere, and will probably
get confused with the transference relationship.

3. THE 'TRANSFERENCE' RELATIONSHIP

Some counsellors think that transference only applies to psychodynamic counselling. If the concept of transference has any
validity at all, it cannot be confined to one model of working.
It may not be openly referred to, but it is just as present in
other counselling relationships. It is also part of all helping or
caring work, whether professionally or in a voluntary capacity.
Indeed, at the risk of diluting it out of existence, transference
is part of all human relationships. Although this is not the
place to argue it, transference might be said to be at the root of
every human interaction; but here I shall confine myself to the
more usual understanding of this phenomenon.

When a person falls in love we see transference at work.
Indeed, if one person falls in love with another, but the feelings
are not returned, the example becomes even clearer. The lover
endows the beloved with every ideal, and sees her or him as
beyond compare. Life is nothing outside the presence of the

other. Even if the feelings are not reciprocated, the love feels as strong. The adoring relationship of a baby towards its mother is transferred on to the beloved. In time (whether or not the feelings are mutual and whether or not they are acted upon) the 'reality' becomes clearer, as the lover realizes that the beloved is not quite so ideal, that he or she has other less desirable features, and that they can be apart, and enjoy being apart, without fear of loss.

Another example of transference in everyday life is reactions to people who remind us of someone we don't like: we immediately dislike the new acquaintance even though we do not really know them. When we know them better, we discover that our initial reaction might have been premature, and indeed too heavily based upon our earlier experience of similar people.

Transference reactions are particularly strong in relation to authority figures, and they are far more extensive than the clichéd 'falling in love with the analyst'. People fall in love, hate, fear, rebel against, feel envious of, idealize and denigrate priests, doctors, teachers, lovers, film and television stars as well as their therapist. Counsellors soon become aware that some clients fear their criticism and punishment as if they were harsh parents; that a few clients hold them in awe as if they were Superman or Superwoman with no human weaknesses; or that some are suspicious of accepting help because they fear becoming dependent. If such distorted perceptions, transferred from other earlier relationships, are not always evident towards the helper, they will almost certainly be seen in the way a client relates to significant others. Transference relationships are indeed ubiquitous.

A student whom I was seeing called Sue used to talk about her difficulties in making a break from her mother, who was very possessive. In one session she told me that she would have to go and see her tutor and tell her how things were going. 'If I don't tell her I know she will worry about me.'

It might seem reasonable to keep a tutor informed, although I had been told by this tutor that Sue reported her progress to her far more than was necessary. Had the tutor asked to see Sue regularly, it might have been reasonable for Sue to visit her so often. But in view of her mother's propensity to worry, it was more likely that Sue was attributing characteristics to her tutor that were more appropriate to the situation with her mother. Sue may even have wanted her tutor to worry about her like her mother did.

On another occasion Sue said to me: 'I was very concerned after I left you last time, in case you were worried about me.' The same transference pattern seemed to be at work. I replied: 'You seem to feel that both your tutor and I are going to worry about you like your mother does. It seems to me that you almost need to have someone worrying about you, in case you get forgotten. Perhaps that's why you ring home so often – not just because, as you say, your mother is a worrier, but to check that she hasn't forgotten about you?'

A transference relationship is like viewing someone through a coloured lens that transforms perceptions. But unlike looking through coloured glass, transference distortions are not normally obvious to the person who has them. Also, they are not always obvious to the person who is seen in such ways, who feels misunderstood but does not understand why. These false perceptions often start in childhood and, if they go uncorrected, they continue to pervade the rest of a person's life – especially their most significant relationships. Even people who try to present a different picture and to correct such misperceptions can be 'tarred with the same brush'.

For example, a young boy experiences his mother as harsh, critical and generally uncaring. She obviously provides his first and most crucial model of what women are like, making it difficult for him to alter this image. He might be helped at his primary school (through what I later describe as a reparative relationship) by having women teachers who treat him more kindly and positively, but let us complicate the situation and imagine that his teacher is unusually extrovert, and does not work well with children like him who are withdrawn from the start. Our unfortunate boy has no correcting experience, and he reads her confident brashness as critical and threatening: he is confirmed in his view that all women are to be feared. He enters adolescence with a distorted view, seeing only what he has learned to see. Fearing women, he bungles his attempts to relate to girls of his own age, and fastens on those occasions when he is rejected by them to confirm his views. He is now blind to the more positive messages offered to him. He even begins to treat women as enemies, and therefore invites critical responses from them.

As a young adult, our young man recognizes that he needs help and makes an appointment at the local counselling centre. The person assessing him realizes that it would be better for him to see a woman counsellor, because this may in time challenge some of his assumptions about women. In his first session he is immediately suspicious of her. He takes everything she says as an attack upon him, and he becomes very defensive. He expects her to be hostile and he rejects her attempts to care. This makes his counsellor feel quite angry, although she tries not to show him. It is a hard task for her to create a relationship in which he can trust her, accept what she says, and communicate openly with her.

There are two ways in which the relationship with the counsellor might help this prejudiced young man. First, the perseverance and patience of the counsellor may win his confidence. She provides a new style of relationship, one that corrects what he expected from his mother, and therefore expects from women in general; and she persists in not being put off by him. This is the reparative relationship. Without her having to draw attention to it, the experience of being with her and talking to her changes this young man's attitude to women. Counselling often succeeds because it provides a new model of relating.

The weak point in this perspective, used on its own, is that the client could say to himself: 'I've learned to trust my counsellor, but she is doing this as a job; I've no reason to think that other women are like her. She may be the first woman I've met who's not against me, but I've no guarantee that others aren't still going to do me down.'

There is less chance of this type of reaction if the counsellor has offered an additional perspective in her work with the client, in which she has made explicit parallels between his initial views of her and his view of his mother. If she can show him how he reacts to her, thinking everything she says is critical, she can help him see that he sees her *as if* she were his mother, although she is not. She might also show him that not only are his feelings about women taken unchecked from past experience; but that he also behaves towards her as if he were trying to provoke rejection. This may be a more thorough way of helping the client look beyond the counselling relationship to its parallels in past and present relationships.

Counsellors most need to draw upon the insights of transference phenomena when the therapeutic relationship is partially or wholly perceived as negative, thus (in one way) creating a barrier to counselling. Freud called this 'transference resistance'. At the same time the barrier becomes a pointer ('the return of the repressed'), which Freud was the first person to recognize. Positive transference feelings, as long as they are not counter-productive, can usually be left unspoken, since they do not interfere with the course of counselling: they usually enhance it. There are some positive feelings that are so intense that they constitute a barrier to ongoing work: what is known as the 'erotic transference' is one example, where what seems like intense love and admiration is invariably a resistance towards acknowledging deep-seated need and emptiness, envy, hatred and other extremely difficult feelings. Although in counselling practice such a phenomenon is rare, it is common for counsellors to work with clients who are too ready to accept what the counsellor says. This is neither a good working relationship, nor is it a genuinely positive transference. A counsellor may have to interpret such a response in transference terms:

> Tom came to see me, having the previous year seen a psychiatrist for several weeks. He explained his problems, and reeled off a list of reasons for them that he said his psychiatrist had told him. He included, amongst other things, that his parents had always ruled his life for him, and that he had always felt they were very good to him. The psychiatrist had told him that he should feel some resentment towards them. Tom asked me what I thought. I replied (as I indeed felt by that time in the session) that I thought Tom wanted me to be like his parents, telling him what to think. A little later I came back to the same point: 'You seem to want someone who can give you all the answers like your parents and like your psychiatrist did. It is much more difficult for you to believe that with help you can work things out for yourself.'

Tom's expectation of me, transferred from previous relationships, could have hindered the course of counselling. Such interpretations pave the way for more effective use of counselling: they also point out the influence of past patterns on present behaviour. Transference interpretations, like interpretations about resistance, need to be made sensitively and at the right time. Some people are initially very surprised that a counsellor or therapist refers to the actual relationship in the session. They are used to experts talking at them and over them, and unaccustomed to such personal references. It is important also not to appear critical of people's false assumptions or misperceptions.

I referred, in Chapter 2, to 'the triangle of insight', in which a therapist or counsellor tries to make a link between the past, the present and the counselling itself. Interpretation is not a substitute for careful listening and accurate reflection, and it does not shortcut the healing effects of time; but it fosters insight and self-knowledge. Transference references frequently have to be made time and again, as they arise in different (yet similar) examples, and in the process of working through persistent patterns of behaviour and perception they begin to shift. This takes time, and one difference between long-term and brief work is that there is more opportunity in the former to work through such insights. What may be understood rationally at a relatively early stage normally takes much longer to be translated into deeper change.

New ways of responding and relating can be tried out in counselling, and in turn translated or transferred back to other life situations. A client, for example, learns that he can disagree with his counsellor, and does not have to remain meek and passive. He may then begin to express disagreement more openly in outside relationships, especially when he realizes that his meekness and passivity are inappropriate responses that are more relevant to the past than the present.

Since there is this constant interplay between past and present, and between the present inside and outside the counselling relationship, a counsellor watches for links. In counselling these links are more often between any two points of the triangle of insight: here and there, now and then, there and then. As the level of intervention deepens, and counselling approaches the parallel processes of psychotherapy, full 'three-point' transference interpretations might be made. The following brief examples demonstrate some of these different connections:

There and here:
Client: I'm concerned with what my boss thinks about me.
Counsellor: Perhaps you are also concerned with what I think about you.
[an outside relationship linked to the one with the counsellor, which is strictly called displacement, rather than transference]

Here and there:
Counsellor: I notice that you often get anxious when I suggest you are angry with me. It makes me wonder whether you find it difficult to admit how angry you might be with other people as well.
[the counselling relationship linked to current situations]

Now and then:
Client: I keep thinking you are trying to ridicule me.
Counsellor: That sounds as if you see me like your father, who used to run you down.
[the counselling relationship linked to the past]

There and then:
Counsellor: Isn't the criticism you fear from your tutor when you present a piece of work just like the criticism you used to get as a youngster, when you felt you could never do anything right in your parents' eyes?
[feelings in a current outside situation linked to past feelings]

Here and there, now and then:
Counsellor: You say you feel embarrassed talking about sex with me, and that reminds me of the embarrassment you felt when you met that exciting girl you told me about last week. I wonder whether both those feelings are what you felt when you were younger, when your mother insisted on telling you about her sex life. You said

that was embarrassing. Perhaps there was something exciting about being told things like that too.
[all three points of the triangle linked together]

One of the potential indicators of transference is when statements seem inappropriate and have an *as if* quality to them. It is *as if* the client is confusing the counsellor or another person with someone else – often a parent or parental figure from earlier experience. Since clients tend to see their own perceptions as correct and real, and not *as if* and to some extent phantasy, a counsellor has to show some evidence for such an interpretation:

> Ursula had told me, in an earlier session, that her boyfriend had told her to go out and enjoy herself when she was at college. That remark made all the difference to the following interpretation. In a later session she talked about her father, and how he was restrictive on her as a teenager. He said she had to stay in most of the time to work, and he only let her go out at weekends providing he took her and fetched her home. On yet another occasion she said that she could not go out to discos because her boyfriend wouldn't like it, in case she met another man. Putting these different statements together, I reminded her that her boyfriend had said to go out, and suggested that she was projecting her own anxiety about meeting someone else on to him, seeing her boyfriend as if he was as restrictive as her father.
>
> I only drew attention to the way her boyfriend was seen as if he were the father, using her earlier words as evidence. Had there been any indication that Ursula also felt anxious about talking to me (another man) because her boyfriend would not like it, I might have completed the 'triangle of insight'.

In short-term work in particular, counsellors need to take particular care about remarks that might draw attention to the client's feelings towards themselves. Transference interpretations that are related to the counsellor or the therapist have a tendency to lead to a deepening of the relationship, sometimes evoking even stronger feelings. No one should open up the possibility of such feelings unless they feel experienced enough to handle them, and are sure the feelings will not make the client too anxious. Helpers who use counselling skills, but are not trained or supervised in the handling of transference feelings, should confine the links they make to past and present relationships outside the session. It is possible to refer to defensive feelings in counselling, and less highly-charged emotions, but other personal references should be made with caution. Even such carefulness will not always prevent clients from expressing such feelings – in which case, of course, they should not be ignored. Supervision may be valuable in trying to locate what such feelings in the client might be about, and where else they might relate.

4. THE 'COUNTER-TRANSFERENCE' RELATIONSHIP

Given the complexity of the therapeutic relationship, I hesitate to complicate matters further, but the term counter-transference is now used to describe somewhat different aspects of a counsellor's relationship to a client. The term was originally used of feelings in a therapist or counsellor, transferred from their past experience, in much the same way as transference occurs in the client. Such feelings might distort the therapist's perceptions of the client, or interfere with the therapeutic relationship, sometimes making it difficult to work with a particular client. The advice in such circumstances was often to have more therapy and get rid of such 'neurotic' counter-transference reactions.

As an example of this type of counter-transference, suppose that at school you were bullied badly by a boy with red hair. Ever since then you have found it difficult to get on with red-headed people, since they still make you feel threatened. Since your own therapist was grey-haired this memory and situation never arose and you still feel anxious about it. Your new client is a person with red hair. You may find yourself reacting against him because of your past experience, and feel determined to punish him. Alternatively, you may be so aware of your bias that you become extra-cautious about saying anything that could be construed as negative (notice your defensive reaction-formation!). Either way, this transference from the past makes it difficult to work easily and spontaneously. It is situations such as these, both obvious and less apparent, that make personal therapy and counselling so valuable for anyone who works in a caring capacity, partly to discover where their own difficulties lie.

Counter-transference can also take the form of blind spots. A counsellor may be a strong believer in helping people to become independent. For much of the time such a firmly-held value is useful in counselling, because this counsellor encourages people to take initiatives, and to work at their problems. However, these strong views may not just come from a background where positive independence was encouraged. It may also come from the counsellor's difficulty in co-operating with others, especially when there is a threat of rivalry. Our imaginary counsellor may therefore have a blind spot both about the need and value of being appropriately dependent, and even more so about the value of being inter-dependent. This counter-transference weakness may also prevent the counsellor from allowing people to become dependent on him or her, or it may even make it difficult for him or her to understand the problems of people who work in teams. Inevitably every counsellor has such blind spots: counter-transference in this negative sense is inevitable since everyone has areas of understanding where they are *less* sensitive – or perhaps in other ways *too* sensitive. The original sense in which the term counter-transference was used still holds good.

The second meaning of counter-transference, which now tends to be the more commonly used definition (sometimes called 'concordant counter-transference'[5]), refers to feelings and reactions in the therapist and counsellor that are evoked (often unconsciously) by the client. As counsellors monitor their own thoughts and feelings, they may find some of their own experience with a client is a reflection of what the client is feeling, or what the client makes other people feel. Racker goes so far as to suggest that 'every transference situation provokes a counter-transference situation, which arises out of the analyst's identification of himself with the analysand's (internal) objects. These counter-transference situations may be repressed or emotionally blocked, but probably cannot be avoided: certainly they should not be avoided if full understanding is to be achieved.'[6]

The following examples illustrate how concordant counter-transference might be used in counselling:

One of my clients made me feel extremely careful about saying anything which could possibly hurt. I felt I had to handle the client with kid gloves. When he talked about 'people always shying away from me' I began to realize why this might be so. I used my own feelings about him to understand both the client, and what others felt in his company.

Another client aroused strong feelings of protectiveness in me. That helped me see how she presented herself to others so that they instinctively mothered her. I then began to look for reasons why she needed this reaction from others.

A third client was telling me about events that made me feel very sad, although the client showed no sign of being upset. It was my own reaction that led me to observe just how upsetting the impact of the events the client monotonously described might be.

A different client described an incident that had made her cry, and she wept as she told me about it. What had happened to her made me feel angry, and I wondered where my feeling came from. I thought that perhaps my client was also furious, but unable as yet to allow herself to feel or express that particular response.

In this last example, either of the two meanings of counter-transference might apply. I needed to determine what belonged to me and what belonged to the client. The anger I felt might have been my own difficulty, transferred inappropriately into this situation. I noticed how I called her '*my* client' and she may have reminded me of one of my children, and feeling angry for them. I might have been falsely over-protective to 'my client'. That is the first meaning of counter-transference. Alternatively, I may have picked up the client's repressed feelings accurately, and could use my concordant counter-transference as a reliable guide. In this example (and that preceding it) my concordant counter-transference was also close to accurate empathy.

There is a close link between these two terms, although I tend to experience empathy as a conscious act of trying to identify with the client, and counter-transference as a feeling or thought that pushes itself into consciousness. Both ways of responding are based upon forms of identification, although in counter-transference the client appears to play a more (unconsciously) pro-active role, almost forcing on the counsellor a dimension that the client cannot see. The same caution about the two types of counter-transference applies to empathy. Counsellors need to check that their empathy is accurate and not *simply* the result of their own past experience.

When empathy or counter-transference reactions put a counsellor in touch with what a *client* might be feeling, it is often easier to express this than when counter-transference gives clues to what the client makes *other people* feel. It is easier to say 'I wonder if you might have felt very angry about that' than 'I wonder whether you might make people feel angry'; again it is easier to say 'you make me feel very angry on your behalf' than 'you are making me feel very angry with you'. Where there is a high degree of trust and rapport, the second in these pairs of remarks can be made, although only with the greatest care is it right to say them, and with the aim of understanding why such feelings are evoked. Sometimes it is only later that a counsellor can tell a client how he or she once made the counsellor feel.

It is possible to avoid over-direct and inappropriately timed feedback of counter-transference by slight but significant disguises: 'It feels as if you are trying to make me angry with you.' This distances the anger a little, and the more tentative approach does not presume that the counsellor's reaction is the right one. An alternative is to make observations at one remove, by relating the counter-transference feelings to reactions that others might have:

I had one client who tried my patience to the utmost. Everything I said was made into a joke, and I found it very difficult to refrain from being vindictive, or from ending with the client. At one point I said: 'You tell me that you find it difficult to keep friends. I've noticed you tend to be rather sarcastic in many of the things you say. I wonder if that puts them off? If I'm right, I wonder what it is that makes you push people away like that, when you say you want to have friends?'

Positive counter-transference feelings towards clients seldom need to be expressed, although it is sometimes appropriate, without being seductive or flattering, to share such feelings with a client who seems self-critical: 'You say you are very timid: I have to say that you make me feel that you are very brave, facing all those issues as you have done.' It is more difficult when clients ask direct questions such as 'Do you like me?' Even if a counsellor does, a direct answer might well miss the point of the question. Why does this person ask? What is it about the counsellor's manner that makes this client feel he is not liked? Or what is it in herself that makes the client feel the counsellor does not like her? It may be preferable to put the question back, and look at what it means. A simple reply, such as 'What makes you think I don't like you?', could provide more openings than answering 'Yes', or, even worse, 'No'.

5. THE 'REPARATIVE' RELATIONSHIP

There is some debate about whether counselling and therapy make up for the past, or repeat the past. A psychodynamic view holds that in the transference, past difficulties are re-enacted within the therapeutic relationship. In some instances these transference reactions are worked through, and clients are able to experience that the counsellor is *not* like their father, or mother, or any of the other people who might have hurt them or neglected them in the past. In other instances (such as inability of the counsellor to enter into a more permanent and continuous loving relationship) clients who wish for a different type of relationship come to accept that although this situation repeats their past experience, the counsellor's lack of availability is not intentionally aimed at them in particular – it is simply the nature of the therapeutic contract. Negative feelings about this can be linked to negative feelings in the client about past disappointments, and worked through sufficiently for the client to move forward, less held back by past failures. It is in this sense that it can be said the past cannot be corrected by the therapeutic relationship. Rycroft, for example, after considering the idea of 'a form of replacement therapy' and the effective agent as the therapist's 'concern, devotion and love', adds that 'this leaves unexplained why the analyst should consider himself to be the possessor of a store of *agape* or *caritas* so much greater than that of his patient's parents'.[7] Rycroft underestimates just how abusive and destructive some parents can be, although Winnicott probably states the same point rather more accurately when he writes that the therapist 'can never make up to clients for what they have suffered in the past, but what he *can* do is to repeat the failure to love them enough . . . and then share with them and help them work through their feelings about his failure'.[8]

On the other hand, it is also clear that in some respects therapists and counsellors do make up for what was lacking in the past. Here it is the person-centred approach that has emphasized this equally crucial aspect of the therapeutic relationship. It has claimed that it is *only* by providing the necessary conditions that were lacking in the past that clients can begin to grow, perhaps for the first time, and so develop their innate potential for positive growth.

This disagreement has become less necessary with Clarkson's proposal that there is a fifth aspect to the therapeutic relationship, which she calls the reparative or the developmentally-needed relationship.[9] It is not a question of 'either . . . or' but of 'both . . . and'. Whereas the transference relationship (in the eyes of the client, but also to some extent in reality too) repeats the past damage and failures (though not all) that a client has experienced, the reparative relationship provides some (though not all) of what the client needs in order to develop into a more mature and complete person. The counsellor is able to provide, for example, non-judgemental acceptance whereas in the past the client may have so feared criticism and rebuke that he or she was never able to make the moves towards adult relationships that a different kind of parenting might have helped. In the reparative relationship a client may experience a secure and containing relationship with the counsellor, which helps to repair past relationships where they have been chaotic and boundary-less; or a client is able to express both angry and loving feelings towards the counsellor, and not have them rejected or squashed as in the past; or the client experiences for the first time someone who genuinely cares for them without expectations or conditions, when in the past it always felt as if the client was only loved for being a certain way or for doing the right things; or a counsellor of the opposite gender is able to provide a reparative relationship for a client who might have been abused as a child or as an adult.

Clarkson almost equates the reparative relationship with positive transference feelings, and she observes how therapists are poor at being able to accept the positive feelings clients show them without in one way or another having to interpret them.[10] The difference is that the positive transference essentially comes from the ability to transfer positive features, already present in the client from past relationships (such as trust, hope, and indeed those qualities that make good relationships possible), into the present counselling relationship. The positive transference provides a foundation for the counselling relationship in the first instance, and supports it through its most difficult times in later sessions. Positive transference is equally present in the mature adult who is able to take the healthy elements of their past experience into new situations, enabling them to engage in them more confidently.

The reparative relationship differs from positive transference in that clients experience something with the counsellor or therapist that they have not felt or had before. In time, this therapeutic experience may be positively transferred into other relationships; but for the moment their experience is brand new, and what they need in order to develop further. The reparative relationship also has some similarities to the real relationship, except that in the case of the reparative relationship the emphasis is on the client's experience of the counsellor, and not on the equal level of relating and sharing that is the principal feature of being 'real' with the client. This reparative relationship nevertheless requires a counsellor who can be real, who can accept how genuine the client's positive experiences and feelings are, and who can validate them.

Like every other perspective that this chapter has examined, the reparative relationship is seldom sufficient in itself. One of the complications about the counselling relationship is that what is offered by way of reparation can also be experienced as threatening. Negative transference can interfere even with this positive stance. An example that illustrates this well is working with some victims of abuse, who have not only been abused by one parent, but who also feel that the other parent did nothing to help. At times the reparative relationship, where concern and care is offered in place of abuse on the one hand and in place of lack of care on the other, is itself seen as a threat. If the counsellor gets too close it feels in transference terms like repeating the incestuous nature of the former relationship; if the counsellor deliberately holds back to avoid this, it feels in the transference like repeating the lack of concern. This situation is but one example of the complex interaction of these five perspectives of the counselling relationship.

Every counselling relationship, whether it is of the formal type that this chapter has concentrated upon, or of the more informal type where counselling skills are used in pastoral care or other caring work, contains in differing degrees of intensity all five perspectives that this chapter has described. While the distinction between the perspectives is not always as clear as may appear from this chapter, separately and together they make a major contribution to the counselling process. They provide the basis for insight and growth and change, not only for those who seek help, but also for those who offer themselves as counsellors and therapists. Searles has suggested that clients try to make the counsellors into better therapists, because clients know the help they want, and they try to help their therapists to give it to them.[11] This startlingly original insight is yet another dimension of the helping relationship, which space forbids me to develop here. What it confirms, if it is true, is that the therapeutic relationship is never one-sided. Counsellor and client stand equally to gain much from the work they engage upon together.

NOTES

1. C. B. Truax and R. R. Carkhuff, *Towards Effective Counseling and Psychotherapy Training and Practice*. Chicago: Aldine Press 1967.
2. R. R. Greenson, *The Technique and Practice of Psychoanalysis, Vol. 1*. Hogarth Press 1967.
3. ibid., pp. 216–24.
4. P. Lomas, *The Case for a Personal Psychotherapy*. Oxford University Press 1981; P. Lomas, *The Limits of Interpretation: What's Wrong with Psychoanalysis?* Penguin Books 1987.
5. H. Racker, *Transference and Counter-transference*. Hogarth Press 1968, p. 146.
6. ibid., p. 137.
7. C. Rycroft, ed., *Psychoanalysis Observed*. Penguin Books 1968, p. 17.

8. D. W. Winnicott quoted in D. H. Malan, *Individual Psychotherapy and the Science of Psychodynamics*. Butterworth 1979, p. 14.
9. P. Clarkson, *The Therapeutic Relationship*. Whurr Publishers 1995. A summary of her position can be found in P. Clarkson, 'A multiplicity of therapeutic relationships', *British Journal of Psychotherapy*, 1991, 7 (2), pp. 148–63. Note that although she sets out five aspects to the therapeutic relationship as I do in this chapter, they are not identical to those which I have listed. She conflates transference and counter-transference as one dimension, and as the fifth adds the idea of the transpersonal relationship, one which may well appeal to readers interested in the spiritual dimension.
10. P. Clarkson in W. Dryden, ed., *Hard-Earned Lessons from Counselling in Action*. Sage Publications 1992, pp. 10–11.
11. H. Searles, 'The patient as therapist to his analyst', in H. Searles, *Countertransference and Related Subjects*. New York: International Universities Press 1979.

CHAPTER TEN

Beliefs and Values

The question of the place of beliefs in counselling practice is one that (if I am not careful) will make me many enemies! Those who are interested in or working in religious pastoral contexts might have been waiting for some clear reference to these matters – and I may disappoint them if I do not say what they want to hear. Such is the power of belief, that all else can be judged by its standards. Those who find religion difficult or even impossible may not even have read this chapter, uncomfortable at finding such lengthy reference to the subject. Religion, like sex and politics, was never polite talk, and is more likely to divide myself and the reader than it is to unite us. In fact, I hold that everyone has some type of belief system, even if it is an apparently negating or agnostic one. But that may not be enough to please anyone!

At the same time it is essential in a book in this series to look at conventional religious belief and practice, since those who work in a pastoral setting will have many clients for whom this is an important and even central part of their lives. Indeed, counsellors who work in secular settings, including those who have no identifiable religious beliefs, work from time to time with clients who have strong religious commitments. They need to be relaxed enough with this whole dimension of personal experience to be able to work effectively with such material when it is presented to them. Too many secular (and agnostic or atheist) counsellors are frightened of religious faith, and do not know how to handle it when it arises. They are antagonistic on the one hand, because of their own views, yet they do not want to question what they recognize to be someone else's deeply-held beliefs. The result is that the religious dimension tends to get left out, and a major part of the client's way of thinking is passed over, when there is as much to be learned about people from their religious views as from any other aspect of their experience. Those who wish to may of course pass over this chapter, but I fear that they may be missing out on one of the relevant dimensions of some clients' lives.

I write from a perspective that is informed about (though critical of) the Christian tradition, but I acknowledge the importance of other religions to those who are a settled part of Britain's varied population, and contributors to Britain's cultural richness. Unfortunately I am unable to provide examples from their own traditions and religious life, although I am aware that Jews, Muslims, Hindus, Sikhs, Buddhists, and indeed members of many different groups within the Christian compass, may be reading this chapter. I have to ask every reader to see whether what I say from one perspective has any relevance to their own. I believe many of the general issues are equally important, even if they are expressed in different language and using other religious names and terms.

One definition of 'pastoral counselling' is that it is an activity carried out within the context of a religious community.[1] There is another definition of pastoral counselling that overlaps this: of counselling that recognizes the importance of ultimate concerns to human beings, and that accepts questions about life and death, about existence, values and meaning as valid topics for counselling – as important to people as relationships, sex or work. Counsellors in secular settings do not often experience direct reference to such questions except as expressions of despair: 'I can't see the point of life. I wake up every morning and just feel the futility of it all.' When the mood is one of depression rather than philosophical enquiry, it is clearly more appropriate to take up the depression first. It is probably only in long-term counselling and therapy, as clients move beyond their concerns with the immediate impact of events and feelings, that they may pause to ask some of the questions of existence that existentialist philosophers, counsellors and therapists rightly say affect us all.[2]

Those who work in pastoral settings probably have more clients who raise religious questions, although (like Alan's questions in Chapter 1) even these are sometimes a 'way in' to talking about other issues. Similarly, patients often use medical symptoms as a way of raising personal difficulties with their doctor.

Where the counsellor is known to have some religious commitment or sympathy, clients may feel free to voice questions about their faith and their experience that are inseparable to them, such as: 'I don't know what he [i.e. God] is playing at, making me suffer like this.' When such questions are raised a counsellor who has religious views has to decide whether (and how) to respond to them, or to the feelings that are attached to them. There are no clear answers, even for those who hold fairly clear religious views, since the problem of a righteous God allowing suffering is one of the most vexatious of all theological issues. But some counsellors at such a point might wish to provide some comforting spiritual words; while others, who perhaps do not have a view of God as personally directing people's lives, might wish to raise doubts about such a client's assumptive beliefs.

It is deceptive to think that only pastoral counselling or counselling with religious clients raises these types of question and the consequent dilemmas surrounding personal views. In fact, there are many counsellors working in other contexts who are also faced with belief systems and philosophical questions, even though they are not necessarily framed in religious terms, and the counsellors may not subscribe to a religious faith. Everyone has some kind of philosophy, and counsellors are no exception. In some cases their philosophy is as well-defined as a religious one, and held to with the same conviction: humanistic therapy and counselling, for example, has a strong belief in human potential; feminist counselling and therapy takes a clear stand on the significance of political and social structures and a conviction of the need to change them; Marxist thinking, radically altered though it has been in recent years, or other political philosophies might also inform counselling and therapy. I concentrate here upon one set of belief-systems, but others raise similar issues.

ETHICAL DILEMMAS

All counsellors, whether or not they take an active interest in religious or political philosophies, face moral issues in the difficulties their clients bring to them. I do not mean here ethical codes of practice, which are accepted as essential for all practitioners in the field of psychotherapy and counselling. Although these codes differ in minor details from organization to organization, they have so many features in common that they are not largely a matter of dispute or difficulty. The greater ethical dilemma for counsellors is what they themselves think about, and how they respond to, the moral issues that their clients present.[3]

Counsellors are probably of a type that ensures a common core of values, most of which present little difficulty in working with the majority of their clients. The expression of physical violence, for example, is not just alien to the way counsellors think about what is appropriate in human relationships: most of their clients will think the same, even if some of them struggle to cope with their violent wishes and acts. The majority of clients, where they show a capacity for violence, wish to prevent it happening. They are as anxious to avoid its physical expression as their counsellor. Very few people hold personal violence to be acceptable, and in these cases a counsellor will want to make their own views and limits of tolerance clear. It is no use working with someone who is convinced, and is determined to remain convinced, that beating a partner or their children is a right.

Some issues are clear-cut. Acting out (particularly of violence) in counselling is generally felt to be wrong. Similarly, most counsellors have no ethical difficulty in working with clients who talk about *phantasies* of violence (although in practice they may find it emotionally and technically hard to handle). They trust that such phantasies will become less powerful, by taking their clients' wishes seriously (which is not the same as condoning them), and by helping them to express the full force of their rage in words, often towards the counsellor as well. There is then less danger of these phantasies being acted out.

What may be more difficult is when clients express the wish, and also the intention, to act in certain ways that are not necessarily clear-cut in their moral implications. I do not presume in such a context to suggest any 'right' answer, but there are *some* counsellors who might appropriately experience their own moral dilemmas about working with some or all of the following clients:

- a political exile who wishes to return to his country of origin to engage in armed struggle against a corrupt regime;
- a woman who wants an abortion;
- a person who expresses fascist sympathies, and believes in the superiority of his or her own ethnic group;
- a woman who tells the counsellor of a minor (but potentially dangerous) crime;
- a man who says that he once sexually abused his daughter;
- a woman who has had an affair with a married man, but has now been rejected by the man and wants to tell his wife about it.

It is not unusual for clients to present with difficult decisions in their own lives, and on occasions clients' views and choices are antipathetic to those of their counsellors. Sometimes counsellors have to look at their own views on these issues, and whether they can work with clients whose values or decisions are diametrically opposite to their own. Counsellors are not alone in this: it is a situation that is unavoidable for doctors, teachers, social workers and clergy who have to engage with everyone whom their contract demands they work with, whatever their views. Counsellors can sometimes be a little too purist about who is suitable for them, although the motivation for change is clearly a factor that distinguishes the decisions that counsellors make about whom they will see. It may be appropriate, as I suggested above, for a counsellor at certain points to make clear her or his own views on some of these crucial areas, so that from their first mention their clients know where they stand. For example:

A male client says, almost in passing, that he periodically gets drunk and is then liable to beat up his wife. But that is not the problem, he says. What he wants to talk about is his compulsion to gamble. As a counsellor, I do not find it acceptable that he should beat up his wife, and I am concerned about his drinking so much, which is damaging him and his relationships. I cannot ignore these aspects. I refuse therefore just to talk about his gambling. I try to bring up the other issues, and if the client refuses to talk about them, I try to work on the barriers he is putting up. I remain clear about issues that I am not prepared to avoid, not just because they are morally wrong, but because such behaviour shows something that is seriously psychologically wrong both in the client and in his relationship with his wife. For myself, I try not to preach at my client about his behaviour, or make moral statements about the right way to act; but I continue in a dogged way to help the client recognize the gravity of his difficulties. I do not give up on him, but neither do I give up on my focus; although if my client cannot take my persistence, it is of course possible that he will give up on me.

Hurding, in a book on Christian counselling, gives an example where a counsellor's biblical conviction that a woman's wish for an extramarital affair is wrong might lead him to challenge a client with the biblical commandment against adultery. He justifies this as representing a cognitive approach to Christian counselling which is aimed at 'replacing wrong thinking and behaviour with right thinking and behaviour'.[4] It is an interesting parallel, because cognitive therapy and counselling in the secular context tends to have its own 'evangelical' flavour, with therapists appearing to tell their clients appropriate ways to think. The danger is that Hurding's example will be taken as a licence to make many other such moral statements in the context of pastoral counselling, although in one way it could be argued that such statements are (in their own way) little different from a counsellor refusing to condone violence.

In fact, Hurding goes on to describe other approaches to Christian counselling, such as one that is more closely modelled on the analytic (or psychodynamic) approach, where the Christian counsellor would be more concerned at opening up the same woman-client's poor self-image, because she feels unloved by her husband. This other model adopts, in Hurding's words, a 'visionary and reflective style' where the counsellor 'must be prepared to be patient and trust God's timing'.[5] The danger of the first approach is that it appears that the Christian counsellor's *first* concern is to prevent 'sin', whereas in the second approach (which is more in line with the underlying philosophy of this book) the counsellor tries to acknowledge her wish for love, even though a Christian counsellor may feel less easy about her wish to go outside the marriage to find it. The reader will wish to judge whether these are similar types of situations and whether counselling in a pastoral context involves more concrete prescription of what the counsellor believes to be right and wrong; and, if so, what makes a personal stance right in one situation but not in the other.

There are other moral issues that clients present where counsellors have their own convictions, but recognize that these are not clear 'open or shut' situations and that the various clients may choose to act differently. There are in such cases no right or wrong answers. Much depends on the circumstances: this was at one time called 'situation ethics'. In such cases a counsellor is concerned that the client makes as clear and as informed a decision as possible, even though it may be different from the counsellor's own, were he or she in the same predicament. For example:

> A young woman comes to see a counsellor because unintentionally she has become pregnant. She does not want the baby, and indeed it could be very difficult for her were she to go full-term with the pregnancy. But the client firmly believes that abortion is wrong. Let us imagine a pastoral counsellor has a much more open mind on the issue of abortion, and on the face of it feels more inclined to support the side of this client that does not want the baby. But the counsellor does not say this, respecting the woman's right and responsibility to make her own choice. The counsellor therefore works with her to help her make her decision, within the limits set by her own convictions, but perhaps gently challenging her in some of her thinking, in order to help the choices open to her to be more real.

There are yet other issues where counsellors may not be at all clear about their own moral values. Although each situation throws up unique concerns, there may be right or wrong ways of handling them. It may help in such circumstances for counsellors to share their confusion with clients, while at the same time expressing the wish to help them make thoughtful and wise choices. For example:

> A male client comes to see a counsellor because he is depressed. The client is a gay priest, living with a partner. Although he is sure about his homosexual orientation, and about the relationship with his partner, he is clearly depressed because his relationship has to be kept secret. If it became public the church authorities would have to ask him to break off the relationship or leave his work. The counsellor feels there is a basic dishonesty about the client's position, at the same time recognizing that it was imposed on the client by dishonesty too in the authorities' position. The counsellor is aware of how difficult this situation is for his client, the partner, and for those in authority as well. Although in other circumstances the counsellor might want to support the client in any decision he might make to come out, in this situation it is impossible to know what is right. What may help is the counsellor offering support to the client by sharing in the tortuous dilemma: 'I don't know what to suggest. I can see how difficult it is to know what to think about this, and how impossibly hard it is to act.'

There are some occasions when what look like ethical questions are better approached by looking at them in terms of the psychological issues they raise. The following example is a case in point:

> Vince was one of my most likeable clients. He was a social worker, deeply caring and kind, but a little too soft-hearted. He told me that he and his wife were having difficulties. His wife was being subjected to a lot of verbal abuse from some loud-mouthed adolescents who lived in their street: every time she went in and out of the front door they would taunt her. As a result she had become very depressed. Vince explained that he found it difficult to tell the boys off. He felt very weak, since he could not protect his wife. He went on to tell me that one of his best friends had come round recently and had witnessed this taunting behaviour. The friend had really lammed into the adolescents and frightened them off. This had filled Vince's wife with admiration.

Some few sessions later Vince returned to this situation. His wife had told him that she had fallen for his friend, and that she wanted to sleep with him. The friend wanted this too. Vince was obviously in a dilemma. Should he let his friend and his wife sleep together? After all, it was what a lot of people were doing these days and, if his wife wanted to, surely it was not up to him to stand in her way? He believed that she had to make her own choices about such matters.

Although it is not my style to talk at such times about the sanctity of marriage, I might have been tempted to question whether this was what was really meant by partners in marriage allowing each other freedom. I could have found myself caught up in the ethical question of open marriage, since that was the way Vince was framing his dilemma. Vince was trying to be generous, and he was sure that a husband cannot run his wife's life as if he owned her.

Had I followed this line, I believe I would have missed the important issue, which was not just an ethical one. What I did was to ask Vince what he himself felt, putting to one side for the time being what his wife and friend felt about the idea. Vince promptly replied that he did not want her sleeping with his friend at all. I put it to him that it seemed difficult to be firm enough to say that to her: 'You have your opinion too. Your wife doesn't have to take notice of it, but I suspect she at least wants to know what it is. You're afraid of telling people what you feel, especially when it comes to setting limits.' I wondered if it was possible that Vince's wife was testing him to see if he was as assertive and as dominant as his friend was.

Vince gradually began to push himself more, at home as well as in outside situations. There was at first a lot of turmoil, as other people in his life tried to adjust to this new situation. His wife adapted to his new image, although on the way he lost the best friend. But it appeared that Vince's marriage in the end became much richer, as a result of finding much more equality in their relationship, and his being able to assert himself more.

Finally, there are occasions when the counsellor can do no more than accept the inevitable. Decisions cannot be challenged when it is clear that no further talking or interpretation is likely either to change them or even add to their validity.

This does not mean that counsellors agree with all the decisions their clients make, although they will rarely say so. The following might be examples of such rare exceptions:

> 'I think you would be unwise to make that decision now, while we are still considering the issues. But if you have to make that choice at this point then obviously you will have to go ahead with it.'

> 'I can't stop you from acting as you are, but if you are determined to go on doing so, you are putting me in an impossible position and I may have to stop seeing you.'

PSYCHOANALYSIS, COUNSELLING AND RELIGION

It is impossible to discuss religious beliefs and practices in relation to the issues that might arise in counselling without reference to Freud. He was not only the founder of a psychotherapeutic approach that has had enormous influence on the development of therapy and counselling, but he is also renowned for his views on religion. This has at times led people to think that psychotherapy and counselling are antipathetic to religion.

Freud certainly held that much religious belief is an expression of a universal neurosis.[6] He suggested that images of God are formed as a result of the projection of people's need for a super-parent to protect them against fears of the immensity of the universe.[7] There is considerable merit in some of this thinking, since there is no better object for transference projections than God, who is (by theological definition too) 'invisible' and 'unknowable'. This makes it difficult, if not impossible, to distinguish the 'reality' from 'transference' in any talk about God.

Freud's anthropological studies, in which he makes his strongest attacks on religion, are highly speculative, if not fanciful.[8] In his more clinical writing, Freud has much to teach us about the structure of personality and about technique, and this can if necessary be separated from what he says about religion. Nevertheless, even in his critique of religion, he has some important points to make. Like other thinkers before him, and like some theologians before and since, Freud criticizes some of the attitudes that seem to accompany religious (and particularly Christian) belief. As Lee writes in *Freud and Christianity*:

> If psychoanalysis helps to clear away the rubbish that clings to Christianity and frees it to grow to its full strength and maturity, it will do it an immeasurable service. If Christianity insists on clinging to neurotic manifestations of the unconscious as true religion for full-grown men and women it dooms itself to be cast aside in man's upward struggle towards the natural goals of freedom, power and love. It will cease to be truly 'Christian'.[9]

At the end of Chapter 8 I listed some of the defensive barriers that draw their effectiveness from a religious perspective, which illustrate some of this neurotic thinking and behaviour.

Other psychoanalysts within a broad Freudian tradition have been less antagonistic towards religious faith. In *Psychoanalysis and Religion* Fromm reminds us that Freud's dictum that religion is a collective neurosis of mankind was accompanied by the parallel dictum that neurosis is a private form of religion.[10] Anyone who fails to achieve maturity and integration (and that presumably means everyone?) develops a neurosis of one kind or another.[11] Fromm draws a valuable distinction between authoritarian and humanistic religion: in the former (which is not confined to religion as such, but is also seen in secular belief systems such as fascism or some forms of communism) the life of the individual becomes insignificant. The worth and strength of human beings is denied. Authoritarian religion is based upon the desire for power, or upon a leader to whom personal conscience is sacrificed (as indeed Freud pointed out using the example of the Church in his study of mass psychology[12]).

Humanistic religion, on the other hand, is centred around human beings and their strengths, promoting the power of individual reason and assisting people to recognize their limitations as well as their capabilities. It encourages principles and norms to guide people in developing their powers of love for themselves and for all living things. Faith is conviction based upon a person's own thought and feeling, and not on obedience to the dictates of others. The mark of humanistic religion is 'joy' while that of authoritarian religion is 'sorrow' and 'guilt'. By humanistic religion Fromm does not mean humanism. 'Inasmuch as humanistic religions are theistic, God is a symbol of *man's own powers* which he tries to realize in his life, and is not a symbol of force and domination, having *power over man*.'[13]

Others have devoted more thought than I have to the theological and psychological implications of psychoanalysis and theology.[14] I have however explored the psychology of belief[15] in a book which might extend the understanding of those involved in pastoral care and counselling where religious issues are included in the content of the work. It is important to stress the positive significance of times of questioning and doubt, as natural phases in the development of thinking and belief. But in the remainder of this chapter I concentrate more upon the actual practice of counselling when religious questions and practices are raised in sessions.

RELIGIOUS PROBLEMS

Because religion can be used defensively, it sometimes gives rise to particular problems for those who are or have been members of churches or other religious groups. Religious convictions may mean having to defend against unacceptable 'sinful' thoughts and feelings. One problem that arises for some Christians (though it is not confined to them) is the relationship between their thoughts, their words and their actions. The Sermon on the Mount seems to suggest that if a person feels anger or expresses it verbally, it is tantamount to murder; and that to have sexual phantasies is as good as (or as bad as!) committing adultery. These words have lodged deep in the consciousness of many religious people; and unfortunately collude with the child's conviction that their phantasies are very powerful, and, even if they are kept secret, can cause dreadful things to happen. Jesus probably intended to convey something different: that those who think they are holy just because they have *done* nothing wrong are no better than others, since their thoughts and words reveal that they have the same basic human emotions. Nevertheless, people continue to

believe that thinking badly about others will hurt them. Counsellors sometimes have to spell out to clients, especially in the
early stages of counselling, that putting negative thoughts into
words does not in itself damage the person they are speaking
about. When these thoughts and feelings can be put into
words, they can then be looked at. Sometimes there are very
good reasons why people feel so hateful. It is not 'their fault'.

Verbalizing dangerous thoughts also often makes them less
threatening and harmful. There is more danger in repressing
or suppressing such thinking than in expressing it in words.
Sometimes it is important to 'rehearse' such feelings with a
counsellor before expressing them assertively, but not violently,
to the actual people who need to be confronted. Too often
people tend to express themselves only when they have bottled
up thoughts and feelings for so long that when they are triggered off they get expressed impulsively and harmfully. This
simply reinforces their fear of 'bad' thoughts, and encourages
them to be suppressed as strongly as before.

The same anxieties and guilt applies to sexual feelings, and
in this case too to the expression of sexuality, although perhaps
less now in religious circles than a generation ago. The Scrip-
tures, the Church or some other religious authority are used
as the justification for suppressing sexual feelings, such as
masturbation, sex outside formal marriage, or even from having
sexual thoughts at all. Despite its affirmation of the body, and
its belated conversion to sexuality, the Church makes many
other statements that show its ambivalence, which is confusing
to those who struggle with their sexuality.

Some religious people use rituals and prayers as a way of
warding off 'sinful' or 'evil' thoughts; or, as I suggested in
considering defences, they feel very guilty if they have not performed their religious practices assiduously. Questions about
religious behaviour and belief are complicated by the difficult
distinction examined in Chapter 8 between displacement and
sublimation. What may be the mature expression of faith for
one person could be defensive for another.

Colin was in his early twenties when he came to see me.
His doctor had referred him, aware of how much of a part
the young man's faith played in his problems. Colin was
obsessed with the meaning of the 'sin against the Holy

Spirit' for which (he told me with utter conviction) Christ had said there was no forgiveness. He had searched avidly through the Bible and biblical commentaries to try and find out whether God really punished sinners. His sin against the Holy Spirit, as he saw it, was that he was a homosexual.

I asked Colin what he meant by saying that he was a homosexual. It soon turned out that he had never had a homosexual relationship, but that what really concerned him was masturbating, which was always accompanied by phantasies that he was being humiliated by another man. Colin described himself as always having been isolated, and when younger he was often bullied. His religious belief had ranged from a brief involvement with Jehovah's Witnesses to a small evangelical group of which he was now a member. This group was clearly very supportive to him, and they had tried, unsuccessfully, to convince him of God's forgiveness. I also began to look for any evidence that in the relationship with me Colin was afraid of being humiliated. This could be the third point of the 'triangle of insight' – being bullied when young, being humiliated in sexual phantasy now, seeing God as another humiliator, and perceiving me as one who would also humiliate him.

Using the idea of the triangle of insight, I thought Colin's two problems were probably linked. His phantasies of humiliation were like experiences of humiliation when younger; and furthermore his picture of God was of one who humiliated sinners. I had to decide at which point to start, whether with Colin's perception of himself, or with his picture of God. I was aware that the latter had not changed, despite the efforts of his evangelical friends to convince him. I decided to focus on trying to relieve some of Colin's shame about masturbation, and to show Colin that *he* found it difficult to accept *himself*. Since the sexual phantasy pointed to a homosexual orientation, I felt that for the time being I could leave that issue on one side. I concentrated instead on pointing out to Colin how his image of God portrayed him as vindictive, rather like the boys who bullied him when he was a young teenager; and also like how he might himself have felt towards his persecutors. I wondered whether it was this that made it difficult for him to allow himself to believe that he was forgiven.

When we met for a second time, Colin was able to tell me more about his sexual phantasies. Sometimes he was able to climax when he thought of himself as a 'pet' being fondled by a sexually experienced woman. I felt that there was now a sign of some confusion in his sexual orientation. I reassured Colin that he did not always have to see himself as isolated, because of his fear of homosexual relationships (especially in relation to his evangelical faith). He might want to move towards relating more fully to women. We agreed to look at both these issues in counselling – his sexuality, and the doubts that he had about God's forgiveness.

This brief example shows how the spiritual and the psychological aspects mingle, with one influencing the other. It also shows how valuable it was in this case to start by focusing on the religious issue, which to some extent prevented Colin from going any further with exploration of his phantasies and his sexuality. Some relief of his guilt in the first session seemed to lead to a fuller description of his phantasies in the second.

Other problems arise in relation to people's views about God (or other religious figures whether in the Christian or other religious traditions). I have already referred to Freud's understanding of descriptions of God as projections that come from the child–parent transference relationship. In fact, some faiths are more cautious about allowing the godhead to be spoken of at all, but those that have permitted representations to be made of God are more open to this criticism. People's ideas about God frequently tell the counsellor more about the thinker than they do about God, just as it was said of the theologians involved in the nineteenth-century quest for the historical Jesus that their portraits said more about them than about Jesus. Some pastoral counsellors have better theological knowledge than most of their clients, but they have no more objective knowledge of God than anyone has. It is important therefore to listen carefully to what clients say about their God, and in particular to see if there are any parallels or contrasts between such descriptions and clients' experience of other significant persons. Such links, when they can be tied in with other difficulties, can sometimes be used to suggest that a client's perceptions need testing, whether they are of other people, or even of some aspects of their religious faith. This can be a delicate matter, since for some people their faith is not open to rational criticism; although it has to be said that other clients may be relieved that someone has at last given them permission to reconsider their views.

The following is a clear example of this. It demonstrates at the same time how different the role of a minister is, when he or she functions as a pastoral counsellor, from that of the minister as a representative of a particular faith. The case also illustrates the place of religious defences and transference as described in earlier chapters. Religious and psychodynamic ideas are interwoven in such a way as to make it unlikely that the course of counselling would have been the same had the counsellor been working in a secular setting:

A thirty-two-year-old married man came for pastoral counselling because he was often depressed, and because he had recurring phantasies involving young boys and girls. He was frightened of these phantasies, though he had no history of actually molesting children. He was a capable man in his profession, but he had turned down an opportunity for promotion because he felt unable to handle the extra responsibility. At home, at least on the surface, he appeared to be a model husband and father. In fact, he was very passive when it came to handling family finances, the discipline of his children, and the initiation of sexual intercourse with his wife.

His family history was elicited in the first session. His father had been an alcoholic, who had died when the son was eighteen. Yet his father had had a good job and had only drunk at home in the evenings and at the weekends, until he fell asleep; this meant his relationship with his son was always distant. His mother was involved in the church, which the son had attended with her twice a Sunday. Every night mother and son had knelt at his bedside, and she had prayed. Her prayers consisted mainly of instructions to God, as to how she wanted her son to behave and not turn out like his father. His mother had handled the father's pay cheque and made many of the decisions. She was the capable one in the marriage, and she had resented men being intrusive. His father was passive and dependent. This seemed to tie in with the complaints of the client's wife about his own passivity in sex and in the discipline of the children.

At the end of the first session the man asked the minister to pray for him. The minister replied, 'It doesn't seem appropriate for me to pray for you right now. Let's forgo prayer for a while until we understand more clearly just what's wrong.' His client reacted with surprise and silence, and then angrily. He said the counsellor was not a real minister, otherwise he would not have refused a request to pray for him. He agreed to return for another session, on the understanding that prayer would be discussed.

The following sessions were very difficult. They centred around the counsellor's refusal to offer prayer for his client. It emerged that the client was not a man who prayed himself. He had switched off when prayers were offered in church. It took over a year for the client to get insight into his expectation that his counsellor would take his mother's place, and pray for him in order to solve his problems. The client was able to tolerate his anger which arose when his passive dependent needs were not met. He began to see how his wish to be taken care of through prayer was a feature of other aspects of his life – wanting his wife to take responsibility for sex and the children; and at work refusing promotion because he wanted to avoid having to shoulder responsibility and possible blame.

With this insight he began to pray himself, and to reflect upon the content of his prayers. He saw a conflict between wanting his problems to go away or be solved by someone else, and a desire to discover how to solve his own difficulties. Thus he was able to see a relationship between his attitude to prayer and the transference of his relationship with his mother on to his counsellor. As he desired to pray for himself the transference also changed.

After a few weeks of being on top of the world and learning to pray on his own, his new-found freedom began to crumble. His desire to pray was swiftly followed by a refusal to do so, because God did not listen anyway. He even wondered if God existed at all. The pastoral counsellor now suggested that there was possibly a link between these difficulties and his feelings towards his passive and distant alcoholic father.

His father had not listened to his son's need for help in
growing up, because he was lost in his alcoholic sleep. As
this relationship was discussed the anger towards the father
emerged. The client refused to pray, or even discuss prayer
in the counselling.

As he accepted and mastered his anger, he became aware
of great sadness too, remembering a few times when his
father talked to him about his own childhood. He had felt
close to his father then, feeling how kind and gentle he
could be. As the sadness came through, he began to pray
again, feeling the sadness in his prayers, and feeling that he
really understood the cry from the cross, 'My God, my God,
why hast thou forsaken me?' He felt God was with him in
his sadness, and he began to listen to the prayers in church.
His phantasies about children subsided, and he showed
greater fatherly concern for the activities and welfare of his
own children. His continued membership of the church
provided him with a way to grow further as a maturing
'man of faith' long after the counselling had finished.[16]

By working through the two transference distortions that
emerged in the counselling, this man's religious life became
a way of finding real strength and maturity, rather than continuing, as it had done in the past, to perpetuate the struggle
with parental figures inside himself (later projected on to the
counsellor and on to God). This example illustrates that over a
period of time pastoral counselling was able to lead beyond the
presenting conflicts to a faith and a life that was both realistic
and mature.

PARTICULAR ISSUES IN THE PASTORAL SETTING

Some clients approach a pastoral counsellor, or a lay or ordained
pastor, because they want someone who will not only accept
(and not challenge) their religious views, but someone who
will also incorporate religious practices into the counselling.
They may want to be 'taught' more about the faith, especially
if they are blaming their lack of faith for things going wrong;
they may wish, as in the example above, for the counsellor to
pray with them or to lay hands on them, since they believe

such rituals have a special power. This is sometimes a religious person's parallel to a patient's request to the doctor for a prescription. The helper feels obliged to 'do something'. There is clearly in pastoral care an overlap between spiritual direction, the healing ministry and counselling, which merits greater attention than I can give it here. But while spiritual direction and the healing ministry now take greater cognizance of the value of counselling skills, these remain more directive and active ways of helping, and counselling itself, even in a pastoral setting, needs to remain distinct from both these approaches. I do not mean by this that counsellors are not interested in what clients want to talk about in relation to what they call their 'spiritual life', as well as the 'symptoms' that they wish to be healed. Indeed it is important that nothing gets split off as if body, mind and spirit were solely separate provinces of different specialities.

Sometimes potential clients ask for the name of 'a Christian counsellor', or ask the counsellor to whom they have been referred whether they are Christian. I suggest below how the latter might be answered. In the case of recommendations of counsellors, my own convictions about the nature of counselling lead me to suggest that such enquirers ask for a 'good' counsellor rather than a 'Christian' counsellor, just as they would want a good surgeon rather than a Christian surgeon if they had to go into hospital. I do not think that it is appropriate for a counsellor to offer prayer (I have considerable doubts about prayer as a personal spiritual shopping list), although I take the request for prayer very seriously: clearly the client who asks, desperately wants support.

I work in a secular setting, and one of my clients who had stated her agnostic views, and indeed her bitter criticism of religion, once asked me at the end of a session whether I was a priest. I said that she was right. She had in the session expressed great anxiety about having to go into hospital for a minor operation that week, fearing she would die under the anaesthetic. After her question to me, she got up to go, and as she moved towards the door she asked if I would pray for her. To my own mind this felt like panic measures, when she normally did not even believe in prayer. I simply replied, although with a sincerity that I hope eased her anxiety, 'I'll be here next week and I will see you then.'

Some counsellors, particularly when they work in a religious context, find it appropriate to suggest to a client who asks for prayer that the client expresses her or his own. The client may even say a prayer in the session. Their words (like extempore prayers in church and at house meetings) may provide the counsellor with some clues as to the way the client thinks and what the client wants. There is a considerable difference of attitude between phrases such as:

'God, make me well'
'God, help my counsellor to make me well'
'God, help me to help myself'
'God, help me to accept whatever happens to me'

As long as counselling is distinguished from the more active, focused and corporate approach of the healing ministry, some pastoral counsellors, like some of their secular counterparts, may feel that touch can be positively supportive. What counsellors need to avoid is any notion of magical ceremonies, such as is sometimes experienced in religious rituals in the laying on of hands. The religious setting is one where physical touch tends to be legitimized as a ritualized action, but this does not excuse a pastoral counsellor from serious consideration questions of the value and danger of touch within the intimacy of the counselling session (this was raised in Chapter 6).

Sometimes clients ask about a counsellor's religious faith. This can happen as much in a secular setting as in a pastoral one, just as others can ask about a counsellor's political views or counselling philosophy. I see no reason not to disclose such information, as long as it is quite clear that counsellors do not seek to impose their views and beliefs upon their clients. It is also important to check out how a client reacts to such disclosure by the counsellor. What I cannot see is valuable is *unsolicited* disclosure, particularly about personal faith, whether it is a committed Christian telling a client about his religious views, or a committed sceptic telling a religious client about her agnosticism. The only circumstances in which this might be necessary is when a counsellor holds a particular belief or ethical view that is completely at variance with the client's. If the counsellor feels this dissonance could in time threaten their working relationship, he or she might feel it wise to declare their interest:

> 'You've said that you feel very antagonistic towards religion. You might want to know that I am a Christian minister, but I shall certainly not force my views upon you. Neither will your views offend me. But you may want to consider whether that makes me the right counsellor for you if you are worried about the position.'

Or, from an agnostic humanist counsellor:

> 'I don't hold your particular religious faith. In my work I don't need to agree or disagree with your views, but you may not think I'm the best person to help you.'

Such honesty may actually make a change of counsellor unnecessary, and obviate the risk of the client being taken by surprise and feeling let down later on.

Those who work as pastoral counsellors, or who use counselling skills in their pastoral work, have also to consider the opposite reaction to them of some of their clients. It may be assumed, because the counsellor works in a pastoral setting, that his or her faith is completely orthodox. Yet pastoral counsellors may not believe everything that the setting itself might suggest they do. Pastoral counsellors can therefore become identified with a church or a religious group of which they are in fact very critical. Whether they stay with this identification or reject it early on is a question that can only be resolved in each context and with each client. Premature disclosure can sometimes forestall a client's strength of feeling about a religious question, which would be better expressed *before* the counsellor corrects the client's misapprehension.

If some clients want to be given the support, teaching and rituals of their faith, other clients fear that it may be thrust upon them. If some see religious counsellors as not challenging their faith, other clients fear that the counsellor is going to pronounce upon matters of doctrine and morals, a possibility that is not surprising given the way the Church, with which they may be identified, is often perceived as doing this. They may fear that pastoral counsellors are trying to root out and expose 'sin', and will condemn them if they say too much of what they really feel, or what they have really done. Although some of these perceptions of pastoral counsellors are projections or transference reactions, there is sufficient reality in the historic stance of the Church and the traditional response of many religious people for them to be taken seriously. These anxieties will not disappear in one session, nor simply through the reassuring self-disclosure of the counsellor's own position on such matters.

These worries can also be experienced by clients who are active in the Church. I once saw a lay reader in the secular setting in which I worked, without him knowing my own background. We worked well together, until by chance he was told by someone else that I was ordained. Although he took this relatively well, he said that he was disappointed, because he now saw me 'as one of the goodies' when he had wanted to be able to work with a 'baddie'! I suspect that had he known that before we had built up a trusting relationship he would not have been able to be so open.

Counsellors have an important role, in whatever setting they work, of acting as 'devil's advocate': able when necessary to put the other side, trying to help clients to explore alternative dimensions and opposite positions. Playing devil's advocate is not so straightforward when a counsellor is apparently aligned to a particular faith or philosophy. Feminist counsellors, for example, have similar difficulties challenging the views of some of their feminist clients. Nevertheless, done well, such a function can be very freeing for a client, who is able to look at alternatives without feeling so guilty. This is especially valuable when an authority figure, such as a counsellor who is part of a traditionally 'guilt-tripping' institution, can suggest and model thinking differently. In pastoral counselling such a role might be more accurately identified with the prophetic function, critical of the establishment, and scathing about false religion. Like the prophets of the Old Testament, or Jesus in the New, counsellors are concerned not just with outward behaviour, but with underlying motivation as well:

> One of my clients started attending church and talking about her belief in the Christian gospel, despite her saying only a few weeks before that she was a lifelong agnostic. I

had a feeling that this new-found conviction might not be genuine: that what she wanted to do was to identify with me (she knew I had been ordained), and to curry favour with me. Although this could have been a positive step forward for her, particularly giving her some ideals and objectives to live for which were more healthy than her previous idealizations, it was important to take a closer look at the reason for her change of heart.

One of the difficulties for counsellors in pastoral settings is that the result of this type of helping work may mean gaining a client but ultimately losing a member of a church. Successful pastoral counselling, as it is sometimes with student counselling or marital counselling, can involve helping people to give up and let go. Counsellors clearly are in theory practised in letting people make their own choices, although it may be hard on occasions for some of those engaged in dual roles (as counsellor and minister) to see some of their clients as mature on the one hand, and yet on the other hand (and as a result of their growth), to see them leave the institution. It is perhaps even harder than other endings in counselling, which, as the next chapter suggests, also involve many different feelings.

One of the greatest difficulties in considering these questions of faith and belief (and indeed any subject that consists of more than hard, dull facts) is to be objective. One of the greatest problems in assessing moral and religious situations is knowing what belongs to us, what belongs to other people, and what belongs elsewhere. One of the greatest issues in understanding is distinguishing reality from illusion (which can be helpful), and illusion from delusion (which is not likely to be helpful). Freud put squarely on the contemporary map of knowledge the fact that human beings have an infinite capacity to deceive themselves. The majority of counsellors, whether they work in a pastoral or any other setting, subscribe to the ethic that beliefs and choices should not be forced upon clients, whether by giving authoritative or authoritarian advice, by teaching, or even by seducing and manipulating them. Yet Freud's warning suggests that it is impossible to avoid totally more subtle ways of influencing people: for example, in the way counsellors and therapists tend to support and encourage what they believe to be positive moves and right thinking, and yet question or explore behaviour that they feel to be less mature. We all give such signals to our clients, with a style that, from one perspective at least, looks quite close to the rewards and punishments of Pavlovian behaviourism. Clients soon get to know what their counsellors approve of, and what they think might need to be looked at and changed.

We all have belief systems, whether or not they are dressed up in religious beliefs and language. But then so too do our clients. Regardless of whether counsellors work in pastoral settings or elsewhere, or helpers use counselling skills in pastoral care or in the context of other caring work, they need to be aware that world-views, philosophies and faiths of many sorts and of every variety are implicit in what their clients say and do, as well as in the counselling itself. These belief systems are based upon upbringing and experience, as well as upon cultural tradition. They are attempts to make sense of the past, to live with the present, and to anticipate the future. They underpin, sometimes obviously but more often less consciously, every aspect of a person's life.

NOTES

1. For the standard work on defining pastoral care (and by implication pastoral counselling), see W. Clebsch and C. Jaekle, *Pastoral Care in Historical Perspective*. New York: Harper Torchbooks 1967.
2. E. van Deurzen-Smith, *Existential Counselling in Practice*. Sage Publications 1987.
3. For a study of the stages of moral development, see L. Kohlberg, *The Philosophy of Moral Development*. Harper & Row 1981; and the feminist critique of Kohlberg by his colleague C. Gilligan, *In a Different Voice: Psychological Theory and Women's Development*. Harvard University Press 1982.
4. R. Hurding, *The Bible and Counselling*. Hodder & Stoughton 1992, p. 157.
5. ibid., p. 158.
6. S. Freud, *Obsessive Actions and Religious Practices*. Penguin Freud Library, volume 13.
7. S. Freud, 'The Question of a *Weltanschauung*', in *New Introductory Lectures on Psychoanalysis*. Penguin Freud Library, volume 2, ch. 33.
8. For example, H. Philp, *Freud and Religious Belief*. Rockcliff 1956.
9. R. S. Lee, *Freud and Christianity*. Penguin Books 1967.

10. E. Fromm, *Psychoanalysis and Religion*. Yale University Press 1967, p. 27. For other interesting reflections on psychoanalysis and religion, see E. Fromm, *The Dogma of Christ*. Routledge & Kegan Paul 1963; M. Eigen, *The Psychoanalytic Mystic*. Free Association Books 1998.

11. Fromm, *Psychoanalysis and Religion*, p. 28.

12. S. Freud, *Group Psychology and the Analysis of the Ego*. Penguin Freud Library, volume 12.

13. Fromm, *Psychoanalysis and Religion*, p. 37 (Fromm's italics).

14. See, for example, H. Faber, *Psychology of Religion*. SCM Press 1976; P. Homans, ed., *The Dialogue Between Theology and Psychology*. University of Chicago Press 1968; P. Homans, *Theology After Freud*. Indianapolis: Bobbs-Merrill 1970; M. Jacobs, *Faith or Fear: A Reader in Pastoral Care and Counselling*. Darton, Longman & Todd 1987; F. Lake, *Tight Corners in Pastoral Counselling*. Darton, Longman & Todd 1981; H. Williams, *The True Wilderness*. Fontana 1967.

15. M. Jacobs, *Illusion: a Psychodynamic Interpretation of Thinking and Belief*. Whurr Publishers 2000.

16. This example is abbreviated from a much fuller account in J. O'Laughrun, 'Transference and religious practices', *Journal of Pastoral Care* (USA) (1978), pp. 185–9.

CHAPTER ELEVEN

Endings

Death and the end of the world is a constant preoccupation for humankind, and therefore not surprisingly a central concern of Christian and other religious thinking. Modern existentialist thinking finds support in many of the stories that Jesus and other religious figures have taught that the finality of death acts as a spur to present faith and activity. The certainty of death – the only certainty in life – places an end to personal life (whatever a person's attitude to life after death) that has been recognized as philosophically and psychologically significant in the writing of many thinkers. Macquarrie writes:

> Death becomes the eschaton [the last thing], and as such it brings into existence a responsibility and seriousness that it could scarcely have otherwise. Death, in one sense destructive, is in another sense creative of unified, responsible selfhood, the concerns of which become ordered in the face of the end.[1]

Macquarrie recognizes that this does not necessarily prevent people from denying death and the fact that they are themselves finite, nor jumping from one immediate concern to the next in a quest for illusory security.

There is also a considerable interest in death and dying, and in grief and bereavement counselling, perhaps reflecting personal concerns as much as the wish to care for others. But to concentrate simply on the end that must come, or upon death as a natural development from life, is to forget the significance of a whole series of 'deaths', some major and some minor, that take place throughout life. Bereavement counselling training rightly includes these in its study of the experience of loss. Growing through childhood and living as an adult involves

frequent changes, separations, new beginnings and (by implication) many endings. Facing ultimate death is perhaps less
daunting to the person who has come to terms with the many
little deaths that precede it. Erikson even suggests that
'healthy children will not fear life if their elders have integrity
enough not to fear death'.[2]

Counsellors, and those engaged in pastoral or other caring
work, are constantly presented with opportunities to help
people who are going through times of change, experiencing
loss, adjusting to separations, and facing endings. Other
books in this series look at particular times in life when pastors are involved in the emotional and spiritual consequences
of change. But let me briefly illustrate the pervasiveness of
change, loss and endings throughout life, since this is such a
central theme in counselling.

Many of the losses and separations of life are universal; some
happen to many people; a few only occur for the minority.
First there is separation from mother at birth, a literal cutting
off from the sheltered life of the womb to face the harsh
realities of the external world.[3] Good mothering smooths this
transition, but cannot make everything perfect. Babies have to
make their demands felt, they have to wait to be fed, and no
sooner do they get used to having mother available on most
occasions (but not all) than they have to adjust to the further
separation that takes place from breast or bottle in weaning.
A series of rapid changes occurs as a baby begins to move –
partly driven by natural muscular development, partly by
curiosity – away from the all-enveloping parental care towards
coping with her or his own bodily needs and functions. The
wish for greater freedom and autonomy encourages children
to move away from their parents for short periods and short
distances. We see them walk away, and at first run back again,
still uncertain about putting too many yards between them
and Mother or Father. Some of the separations of these early
years are outside a child's control. At any point from a year
old younger siblings may arrive on the scene and take away
Mother's undivided attention. Whether there are other children
or not, it dawns on the baby that others, including older siblings and the other parent, also have claims on their carer's
time and attention. Mother may have to go into hospital when
another baby is born, or because she is ill. Even with better

sharing of child care by both parents, these events might be traumatic. Perhaps a baby or child has to spend some time in hospital. At any time the child may have to face more permanent separation should one of the parents die, or leave the home if a marriage or partnership breaks up.

Even if the family remains intact during infancy and adolescence other changes take place. Each one requires adjustment, and in some children can give rise to considerable distress. A child may go from home to child-minder, or to nursery group, from playgroup to school, with moves from school to school. All of this happens more rapidly in a society where there is greater mobility, where a parent's change of job or relationships often means a new home, a new school and having to make new friends. Some of these changes are relatively easy when children can stay with a group of friends, but there are inevitably adjustments to be made, even for the most adaptable child. As a child becomes a teenager, adolescence brings a whole new set of issues and changes.[4] A young person's body can grow so fast that he or she is not sure of their identity, and changes occur in relation to the outside world that are important ones, normal though they are. There are the moves from school to work (or sometimes to no work which may be even worse); from the observation of parental rules towards the development of their own standards; from friendship groups to closer pairings; from friendships to sexual relationships. Some young people leave home at this time, and a few have already voluntarily or otherwise moved into institutional life – boarding schools and residential care.

These changes are just as evident in adult life, as friendships change, as adults move house, change jobs, or go to another geographical location, or as others move away from them. If it has not already happened by this time, young adults begin to know their own losses through death, as grandparents and elderly relatives die. Some adolescents even have to adjust to the death of a parent, or one of their peers. The point when death is first experienced as a reality, and as a personal loss, can be a difficult one.

With their own partnerships, marriage (and possibly endings of marriages) and children the life cycle begins again, although this time round it is experienced as a parent and a partner. Separation is to some extent inevitable when a new baby intrudes upon the intimacy of husband and wife; and as children grow this series of changes is experienced from another perspective: as 'the older generation'. Redundancy and retirement also give rise to stress, and the older people become, the more their own ageing processes, as well as the death of others, remind them of their own end. Old age no doubt brings many rewards, but it also brings significant losses – possibly of physical strength, of independence, of partner, and of health before the ultimate loss of death itself.

There are many valuable books on bereavement and loss, and on bereavement counselling,[5] so I am not going to dwell here on these many losses and death. In this concluding chapter I want to relate such endings to the actual practice of handling breaks and endings in the counselling relationship itself. Since the work of a counsellor includes integrating the past with the present, within and outside counselling, the process of counselling and therapy involves drawing upon clients' life experiences, and looking at how these significant separations, 'deaths' and endings (literal and metaphorical) affect them. Counselling itself also involves separations and endings in various forms. It therefore provides in itself – in addition to any current problems clients may have with separation and endings – concrete opportunities to work on present feelings, some of which may be reactivated from painful losses in the past. By observing clients' reactions to the present, including those in the counselling relationship itself, counsellors can sometimes throw light upon past experiences.

Because separations and endings in counselling itself are so important, counsellors take care to make their necessity and imminence as clear as possible. It is helpful to signal when coming to the end of a session. It is vital to plan ahead for the breaks that have to take place in counselling because of the counsellor's and client's holidays and other commitments, as well as to have in mind the final break when the counselling contract comes to an end. Counsellors make these dates clear not just because it is efficient practice, and shows respect for the client, but because they recognize that clients sometimes need time to adjust to such breaks (and certainly to the end of counselling); and that putting breaks and endings openly on the agenda enables feelings evoked by them and associations with them to be discussed.

In short-term counselling, or in the more limited contact where counselling skills are used in general pastoral care, clients tend not to become too used to the opportunity to talk, and they probably do not experience too great a distress when contact has to end, as long as their initial concerns have been eased. Where problems are relatively straightforward and can be resolved, ceasing to have a counselling session each week feels like a natural outcome. Unfortunately not all personal difficulties are resolved so neatly, and some people may have to stop counselling prematurely, with unfinished business that they would like to have been able to pursue. Some of them, however brief the contact, react with feelings of being let down to being given such a short time. Endings are much more difficult for them, as indeed they may also be for those who have seen their counsellor for a long time. Even if people have grown much stronger, and learned to find their own feet, ending a long and significant relationship inevitably brings with it feelings of loss. Counsellors become very important to many of their clients, and the more central their role in a person's life, the greater the feelings will be in the separation from it.

Some of the reactions that clients have to endings are perfectly normal: they are the expressions that people naturally feel at ending relationships that they have valued. Counsellors are not afraid of allowing such feelings to be expressed, but they also help clients to express reactions to endings that are apparently inappropriate and exaggerated. In other words, counsellors try to help clients express feelings that are 'real' feelings, to be expected of any significant relationship, as well as 'transference' feelings, that are in a sense more appropriate to earlier separations. Just like any other feelings, the client's experience of the ending is not dismissed. Indeed it is even more important when there is little time left, and therefore no chance of picking up lost opportunities as one might otherwise in later sessions, that even the most painful and upsetting of a client's feelings are given the opening to be voiced as fully as possible. Far from making endings more difficult, this ultimately makes them much better, because it allows counsellor and client to work upon the feelings carried over from the past, as well as a chance to make feelings about the present ending more acceptable than they were allowed to be in previous situations. Counsellors do not want to repeat the trauma of the past by suppressing feelings about loss.

Although counsellors themselves become attached to many of their long-term clients, they are also involved with many people in the course of their work and they can forget how important they become even to those whom they see too briefly to get to know them well. When a counsellor stops seeing a client there is always another to take his or her place. The client, however, particularly when the help given has been effective and valuable, does not so easily forget the person who offered that help. It is no exaggeration to say that for some clients their counsellor becomes one of the most important people in their lives, certainly at that stage of their development. Counsellors occupy, and may even continue to occupy, a unique position. Yet counsellors often have blind spots about endings: they do not realize or they deny to themselves how important their clients are to them, as well as how significant they are to their clients. This may result in counsellors handling endings badly in one of two ways.

The first is to be too matter-of-fact about endings. The counsellor forgets to arrange or announce when breaks are due to take place, does not remind the client for the three sessions before a break; does not plan for a final ending; accepts the client's wish to end immediately; finishes counselling prematurely because of outside pressures; or does not tap into any of the feelings that the client has about stopping counselling. The counsellor may even find it inconceivable that it could be relevant to look at how the client feels about losing the counsellor.

The other error is being unable to let people go. Here the counsellor may be afraid that clients will not cope on their own, especially when they tell him or her this in order to avoid the ending. The counsellor feels the need to protect the client from any future pain and mistakes, and sometimes wishes to protect himself or herself from the client's anger about ending. Such counsellors sometimes fail to recognize their own need to be liked and valued and they may be tempted to hang on to their clients in other ways, giving too much time after the end of a session, or extending counselling sessions beyond the point where they might still be felt to be essential.

A balanced approach to breaks and endings is for the counsellor to ensure that they keep to times, and have regular breaks to encourage clients to use such times to cope without counselling. Therapists usually have at least two-week breaks at Christmas and Easter, and longer breaks in the summer. Counsellors could do well to adopt a similar pattern, even if in the longer breaks they are not themselves always on holiday. Planned breaks need to be announced a number of weeks before they are due to take place, and endings need to be negotiated with the client (if they were not agreed in the initial contract). Where counselling has been taking place over a long period of time, the period for ending needs to be proportionately longer – perhaps as much as a fifth or sixth of the length of counselling to date. In short-term counselling, unless a date was fixed initially that counsellor and client work towards, endings should not normally take place without two or three sessions to review counselling and look at the client's feelings about stopping.

Sometimes breaks in the series of sessions are not planned, but forced upon the counsellor by illness or other circumstances in their own or their client's life. Since there has been no time for preparation, these breaks and interruptions (especially when they are the counsellor's fault) evoke even stronger feelings than those that can be discussed beforehand. In fact, they are all valuable opportunities for using the client's reactions both for the expression of feeling and the understanding of transference implications.

In all these circumstances, whether they are planned or unplanned, whether it is short- or long-term work, whether the reactions are transferred from earlier separations or the natural expression of the end of a good relationship, and whether the counselling has been largely successful or not, there are a number of recognizable feelings about endings and breaks. Counsellors both encourage these to be expressed, and also try to spot them where they are less apparent to the client, so that conscious and unconscious grief processes can be integrated in the counselling relationship.

REACTIONS TO ENDINGS

DENIAL

Although I have stressed that clients tend to have reactions to ending counselling that come from the value they have received from their work with the counsellor, some clients find it difficult to acknowledge that the ending means a lot to them. This may be more so of short-term counselling work than it is of a longer series of sessions, and in these circumstances counsellors need to be careful not to press too hard for reactions. Denial might be more significant when it occurs in the context of longer-term counselling and therapy. The counsellor feels that there should be some response to a break or to an ending, and suggests a feeling that the client might have about it, only to be met with surprise and incredulity. I do not believe that denial is necessarily defensive, although in the following example subsequent events proved it was:

When I first began to teach the practice of counselling, I used to give as an example of denial the reaction of a client of mine who by all accounts should have shown some reaction to the breaks in the counselling. Wendy showed considerable distress when talking to me about past separations, and even her present distance from her family, but she constantly denied any feelings about the breaks that occurred in our counselling time. At the end of each term, over the last three meetings, I would take up all her references to the separations from home and from other people, which she always talked about. I would link them to the impending vacation, and her not coming to see me. On one occasion, after several such ends-of-term which had yielded nothing about her reactions to the break, Wendy snapped at me: 'I don't know why you keep going on about that – it's not at all relevant.' Her retort put me firmly in my place. I gave up trying to make those links in subsequent terms.

Having then used this example (appropriately disguised) in my teaching about denial of endings, in Wendy's penultimate term she told me she had just been to her last choir practice and had suddenly realized that she was not going to be at university for much longer. She felt very sad at the thought. I reminded her that leaving would also mean leaving me. To my surprise she agreed that this would be difficult too. It had taken a major break to help her acknowledge that she did indeed have strong feelings about ending with me. The ending was more significant than any of the breaks had been.

RELIEF

It is rare in the literature about endings in therapy to see any reference to the client's feeling that the end of counselling is in some respects welcome. If the uncovering of self has been painful and uncomfortable, despite the counsellor's efforts to be gentle and to ease the client's self-criticism; or if a client is frightened of becoming too dependent; or where a client has come under pressure from others – relief at ending is an understandable response. Counsellors none the less need to be aware of this aspect, and not to be taken by surprise as I was the first time it happened. I said at the end of a session that had been very distressing for the client: 'I'm sorry. That's a difficult point at which to have to finish today.' The client visibly brightened and replied: 'That's all right . . . I'm quite relieved that I don't have to go further into that at the moment.' Since then I have been aware of how relevant this remark can also be to the end of counselling itself.

SADNESS AND DISAPPOINTMENT

Sadness is one of those natural feelings that clients and counsellors alike experience when they have met together for a long time. If it is transference at all, it can only be called an expression of the positive transference. I prefer to see it as part of the real relationship. Counsellor and client have grown used to each other, they like each other, and they feel sorry that they will no longer meet. In short-term work clients may similarly feel milder sadness, in their disappointment that they cannot take it any further. There is in neither case intense anger or intense grief, although when either have been expressed and worked through, sadness might still be expected at the end. I doubt whether there is ever a right time to finish, but when ending comes at roughly the right point, sadness is accompanied by hope for the future. I once read a description of a client who left the last session with tears in his eyes but a smile on his face,[6] and since then I have seen the same reaction in some of my clients (and indeed experienced the same feeling myself).

ANGER

It is more difficult for clients who are both appreciative and sad when counselling has to end to acknowledge in themselves, and to express to their counsellor that they might also be feeling angry about having to end. Of course others, with more feeling of justification about being let down or disappointed, may find it easier to experience such anger, although sometimes they are less sure about telling the counsellor. It is hard when parting to appear ungracious – indeed, some of a client's past losses may have been made all the more difficult because accompanying angry feelings could not be expressed at the time.

The strength of these feelings will range from irritation to raging fury, and may be expressed either openly or obliquely. The strength of the anger may be justified by the circumstances, but also by the degree of transference from past frustrations:

> A woman client who was seen for assessment could only see a counsellor in the evenings. The counsellor who assessed her was unable to offer any free times after 5 p.m. The client demanded to be seen, claiming that all sorts of other people did shift work, so the counsellor should too. The counsellor persisted in saying it was impossible, and offering her the names of counsellors and therapists who might be able to offer a better time. The strength of this woman's feelings were partly that she was frustrated – she may have been misled in thinking that the counsellor would have a slot at the right time for her. But the anger also seemed out of proportion to the real difficulty both parties were facing in finding a mutually agreeable hour.

Some people are angry that they have to finish just as they feel they are getting somewhere. Some feel that the counsellor does not care because his or her limits are seen as a refusal and a rejection. Others are frustrated because in leaving they feel they have got nowhere at all. Some clients even express their anger, when they feel they are being let down by ending, by suggesting that in any case the help they have been given has been no good: 'You haven't been much use, anyway.' They run down the value of their counselling, perhaps because they will then not miss something that is 'no good'; and their denigration of the work can be quite hurtful to the counsellor. Such negative evaluations should not always be taken at face value.

There is a close link between the feelings described here and above. Anger and sadness in counselling are two sides of the same coin. Sometimes the anger is expressed in tears, or sadness is expressed by being fractious and hostile. Since both feelings are part of the grieving process, a counsellor who is presented solely with one emotion might look for opportunities to draw out the other.

APPRECIATION AND REVIEW

Where counselling has helped, and in most cases it does, clients need a chance to express their thanks. It is important to accept their appreciation, because it is one gift that the client can give to the counsellor. Clients often feel they have received much but given little, not understanding just how much they have also given to the counsellor in the course of the relationship. There is no reason why a counsellor should not make his or her own appreciation of the client clear, and share any genuine feelings about working with the client – as long as in such self-disclosure the counsellor does not seek to hold on to the client. Sometimes clients like to give their counsellor a small gift, or a card which expresses thanks. Counsellors and therapists do not generally like to accept gifts (other than any fees they may charge as a matter of course) during their work with a client – at this point gifts may be a way of trying to 'buy' the counsellor or of making reparation. At the end of counselling, especially if the gift is small, counsellors acknowledge that this may be the only way a client can think of that will express a more permanent 'thank you'. The gift may have all kinds of hidden meanings, but then is not the time to interpret it.

A useful part of the process of concluding counselling is the opportunity to assess progress: How far has the client come? What have they achieved? What has changed for them? What still remains an issue for them to be worked upon? Might they want to seek further help at a later date, perhaps with another therapist? Clients sometimes make their own evaluation without prompting, but if this kind of assessment is not volunteered, a counsellor might wish to introduce it at the penultimate or at the last meeting, asking what has been helpful and what has not. In doing this a counsellor provides an opening for the expression of positive and negative feelings that may not yet have been voiced. If counselling has to end prematurely, the counsellor may suggest areas upon which the client may wish to continue to reflect, at the same time making it obvious what progress the counsellor has recognized in the client.

DEFERRING ENDINGS

Some endings involve more than the opportunity to express feelings. I have alluded in Chapter 8 to one form of resistance to ending, which is the 'gain from illness' and the possible return of the original problems, or the bringing of new difficulties. Counsellors may wonder at such points whether they were right to arrange the ending for that time. There are no hard and fast rules for such situations, although when a contract has been made (as is quite usual in formal counselling), and where prior to the approach of the end a client is making considerable progress, the re-emergence of difficulties may well be an unconscious reaction, a way of saying 'Don't leave me now'. By drawing out the client's disappointment and anger a counsellor often finds that the return of old problems is only a temporary phenomenon. It is less easy in informal pastoral contacts, and in other situations where counselling skills are used, to be quite as clear about holding to boundaries, although tapping the feelings described here may similarly help to bring the caring relationship to a satisfactory conclusion.

On occasions a client may ask for more sessions. Counsellors who work to a contract in most instances gently turn down such a request, at the same time paying especial attention to the client's feelings about stopping. On the other hand, there are other clients who suggest stopping sooner than the agreed time. Because endings provide opportunities to work on the significance of loss, and because it is important to give space for feelings about ending to be expressed, it is good practice to suggest to clients who wish to terminate prematurely that they come for two or three more sessions, so that the ending can be worked through and explored. This has the virtue of providing a breathing space, in which a client's decision to leave might be reviewed and reversed, if it was the wrong one. The wish to stop prematurely might be a reaction to some aspect of the counselling, a sign of some resistance, a flight into health (as considered in Chapter 8). The further meetings give time for second thoughts and more considered action.

Other clients make excuses, which means they miss the last appointment or even the penultimate one. While there may be an element of 'tit for tat' and acting out in this (letting the counsellor down just as the client feels let down), I suspect that such clients prefer not to experience the final sadness or disappointment of moments of separation, and therefore take steps to avoid them.

ENDINGS PAST AND PRESENT

At deeper levels of intervention, such as have been described in other chapters, it is possible to use responses to endings to understand and (even in the last few weeks) to work upon the past and present relationships of clients. In this section I conclude with case examples of the way in which endings can be handled in formal counselling.

In all these cases I had followed the practice described earlier of reminding the client of the impending break (whether it was over a holiday or the actual end). I do this for at least three weeks before the break if it is a brief one, or for many more weeks beforehand if it is the end of the contract. This gives the client a chance to respond immediately to the coming break, and it sows the idea so that I can then listen for any indirect reference to breaks or separations that might be relevant. When working to link past and present, as well as outside experiences and those within the counselling relationship, references of all kinds to breaks and endings might be related to the different points of the 'triangle of insight':

> Yvonne, a woman client in her twenties, was leaving her job and was about to move to another part of the country to find work. This meant that she would no longer be able to go on seeing me. About six weeks before she was due to leave she talked about her dependence on her parents when she was a teenager. She would miss them when she moved, even though she was much less dependent upon them now. Indeed she was often irritated by the way they fussed over her. Although she had not normally responded to the links I had tried to make to feelings she might have about me, I suggested that she might also be concerned at the prospect of not seeing me any more. Yvonne thought for a while,

and replied: 'That's funny – as I was coming here today I was thinking about that. It's true. I will miss you, but there is a difference between you and my parents. You don't make demands on me like they do, and you don't force your ideas on me. It will be more natural to say goodbye to you.'

Ahmed was a research chemist, also in his late twenties. He was seeing me because he was depressed. This was particularly acute in relation to his work where he was highly self-critical. As we approached a summer break, when both he and I were due to take our holidays, Ahmed angrily described how he was being pressed by his father about business matters, and yet he was getting no help from him. His father was not prepared to listen when he tried to talk about money. He felt he was always having to cope with arrangements for other people, who just made him get on with it. His boss too had turned a deaf ear to his request for help with his latest project. He also expected Ahmed to get on with it and did not give him any advice. This accumulated list of complaints gave me justification for observing that Ahmed probably felt that he did not get all the help he wished from me either, and that with the summer break coming up he was angry with me at being left to cope with these various decisions on his own. Ahmed agreed, and said that when he did not have me to talk to, he worried that his decisions would go wrong, and this made him even more depressed.

My last example is more detailed, in order to illustrate more fully the context in which endings can be used in counselling. It shows how significant drawing attention to separations can be. In this case it allowed new and important material to emerge, from which fresh insights could be followed through, even at a late stage in the counselling. It illustrates how what is sometimes disparagingly thought of as 'purely technique' is never an end in itself, whether it is used in connection with endings or with other aspects of the counselling relationship. It serves a deeper purpose, which is the enrichment of the counselling process. Used well, and with the sensitivity and accuracy of judgement that I have constantly stressed, handling these issues leads to greater self-awareness.

Jackie was a writer of short stories that appeared in monthly magazines. Her first husband had paid little attention to her and her marriage had been short-lived. She now had a new partner and they were considering getting married. The main problem she came to me with was a meeting with her father which was soon due to take place. She was feeling very anxious about it, since she had not seen her father for many years. After the assessment interview I suggested that we meet for twenty sessions in all, the ten weeks that would lead up to the crucial meeting, and ten weeks afterwards.

Jackie's family history emerged quite quickly in the first two sessions, which were packed with information because she talked very fully and quickly. Her parents had divorced when she was eleven years old, and she had not seen her father since. She had been told by her mother that one of the reasons for the divorce was that her father had been very mean with money and done little to support the family. (After she had met her father, she found out that this was not true.) Jackie's words tumbled out in such a rush that I thought she must be very anxious. I asked her in the third session if she felt disappointed when I said it was time to finish, since she appeared to have so much to say. Jackie replied that she was not disappointed: indeed, she said how grateful she was to have a time limit, and also a fixed number of sessions. She was concerned that otherwise she might come to see me one week with nothing to say and that I would then suggest stopping early. She obviously valued the opportunity she had to talk. None the less, I still felt that leaving was an issue for her (as we might expect knowing her father had left when he did). I wondered if endings were linked to feelings of rejection for not being co-operative. As it turned out, Jackie feared rejection for almost the opposite reasons.

The sessions proceeded very well. Jackie was a thoughtful client to work with: she had a lot of insight and she worked very hard. Nothing of particular note to this example occurred until the third session before the last, when Jackie started by suggesting that she thought it was only necessary to meet once more. She would not mind missing the last two weeks. I responded by saying that I thought she wanted to avoid the feelings associated with stopping, and with this slight pressure from me she agreed to stick with the original arrangement.

At the penultimate session Jackie began to talk about her parents' marriage in a way that she had not done before. She told me at this point that although she was eleven when she had last seen her father, her parents had in fact separated when she was five. She remembered, even at that age, wondering why. She had been a very high-spirited and excitable little girl, and she thought that it was her exuberant enthusiasm that had made her father go away. When she lived with her mother on her own, Jackie became subdued and introverted. She played on her own; she lived in a make-believe world, in which she made up adventures about Robin Hood and Maid Marion. Typically, given the speed with which she had worked throughout our meetings, she said she was very anxious to have everything sorted out before her sessions with me ended, because she did not want to have unanswered questions in her mind – as when her parents had separated.

The final session was different again. Jackie arrived dressed completely in black – a colour that she did not normally wear. She announced that she had given up her writing, and she had decided to leave her partner, of whom she had previously always spoken warmly. She explained that she was not getting enough love from him, and that she did not feel a real woman with him. She was angry also that her father had not taken more trouble to see her after her parents' separation. I felt that Jackie was reacting very strongly to the ending with me, and that giving up her work and her boyfriend was a sign of her acting this out. I intervened at several points in the session, aware that this time it was I who was having to work very quickly. I pointed out that she was dressed in black as if for a funeral. I said that she seemed to feel rejected by me from the excitement and enjoyment of talking to me. I imagined that the artificial end of counselling was like the abrupt end of her parents' marriage. I thought she was seeing me as deserting her and rejecting her as a woman, and this was like the feeling Jackie had had when she was five, when she felt that her father rejected her because (as she had thought then) she was too high-spirited and excitable. I guessed that by giving up writing

she was taking out on herself the anger she felt with her
father and with me, and that she was also taking it out on her
partner by projecting her feelings about us on to him. I tried
to link her impulsive responses to the feelings of rejection
that she was experiencing with me, which were underneath
her more obvious sadness at our separation.

I did not say all these things at one time, but gradually; and
as the session went on Jackie's mood began to change. She
described the positive changes that had taken place in her
over the last few months. She expressed her appreciation to
me for allowing her to vent her anger, which she had indeed
felt very strongly. A week later she wrote to me, saying:

> I thought I would drop you a line to let you know that you
> were right yet again. I think at our last meeting I was feel-
> ing terribly neglected, though up until that time I don't
> think I ever really appreciated how much my sense of self
> and sexuality was tied up with sharing my emotions and
> thoughts. One of the most important things I have learned
> about myself through our conversations is how much I
> try to curb my emotional and intellectual enthusiasms;
> and yet it is from them that I receive greatest fulfilment.

She concluded by saying that she was working well again,
and was ready to begin facing the implications of her relationships with her partner and other people.

CONCLUSION

My final example shows how the ending of a therapeutic relationship might hold as much significance as the whole of the
rest of counselling. Where endings can be handled fully, this
makes the process of letting go slightly easier for both the
client and the counsellor. In letting go of this book (as it turns
out for the second time) there is a strange parallel with the
work I did with Jackie. In concluding the first edition of this
book I yielded to the temptation of ending with an example
of how effective counselling can be, especially when working
with a well-motivated and enthusiastic client. It was (and still
is) understandable that most of my examples illustrate the

successful application of counselling technique within the context of a caring therapeutic relationship. If there are fewer examples that demonstrate my inappropriate handling of difficult situations, it is because – as one of my own training supervisors put it – 'We teach by our successes: we learn from our mistakes.'

As it turned out, some time after the first edition of this book was published, Jackie returned to see me and entered a new counselling contract that lasted somewhat longer. A few years later I heard from a colleague that she had for the third time asked for help, and was indeed seeing another counsellor. None of these subsequent events invalidate the original work we did, and which is recorded above, although time showed that the limited contract may have had drawbacks as well as advantages. What these later occasions illustrate is the impossibility of ever knowing just how effective counselling has been when new situations arise, which test the changes and insight that have come from it. Freud, in what was perhaps significantly one of his last papers, written at the end of his long life, wrote about 'Analysis Terminable and Interminable'.[7] Counselling and therapy is not about miracles. It achieves much, but not everything. It often helps settle the past and smooth the present, but it is no guarantee for the future. In the words of one classic account of therapy, 'I never promised you a rose garden'.[8] Such a realistic outlook is relevant and important in questions of loss, death and endings.

Counselling starts or supports an ongoing process. Training for counselling is similar. Books on counselling and therapy can only take the reader so far. Each new client adds to our experience and learning, especially when our counselling work can be shared in supervision: such confidential discussion with colleagues enables us to learn more from our practice.[9] Through the careful use of our own thoughts and feelings, through listening to the 'still small voice' within us and within other people, the work of a counsellor, and the use of counselling in pastoral ministry, helps to contribute to emotional, intellectual and spiritual fulfilment.

These chapters, the examples in them, the concluding story of Jackie and its sequel, show just what great complexity there is in human emotions and relationships. Much religious sentimentality and popular piety fails to recognize this, although the major figures in different religions have not been afraid to grasp and live through the intense dilemmas of human existence. Peace of mind is rarely attained without first enduring pain and distress. While most religious hymns and much popular religious verse have little to say to those who suffer, the words of one popular hymn are an apposite way of summing up the faith and hope of pastoral counsellors, in phrases that may in some measure also speak to those whose counselling takes place in other contexts:

> Drop thy still dews of quietness,
> Till all our strivings cease:
> Take from our souls the strain and stress,
> And let our ordered lives confess
> The beauty of thy peace.
>
> Breathe through the heats of our desire
> Thy coolness and thy balm;
> Let sense be dumb, let flesh retire:
> Speak through the earthquake, wind, and fire,
> O still small voice of calm!

NOTES

1. J. Macquarrie, *The Principles of Christian Theology*. SCM Press 1966, p. 69.
2. E. Erikson, *Childhood and Society*. Penguin Books 1965, p. 161.
3. For a lively account of infancy and childhood, see S. Fraiberg, *The Magic Years*. Methuen 1959.
4. M. Laufer, *Adolescent Disturbance and Breakdown*. Penguin Books 1974.
5. e.g. C. Murray Parkes, *Bereavement*. Penguin Books 1972; E. Kübler-Ross, *On Death and Dying*. Tavistock Publications 1970; S. Lendrum and G. Syme, *The Gift of Tears*. Routledge 1992.
6. I have never been able to trace this reference. Nor, judging from lack of response to my appeal in the first edition, does anyone else recognize it. Perhaps I dreamed it?
7. S. Freud, *Analysis Terminable and Interminable*. Standard Edition, volume XXIII. Hogarth Press 1951.
8. H. Green, *I Never Promised You a Rose Garden*. Pan Books 1967.
9. *Supervision – A Professional Necessity*, a new filming of the video

featuring the author supervising a counsellor, available for purchase from The Publications Officer, BACP, 1 Regent Place, Rugby, Warks CV21 2PJ. Other videos made or directed by the author, demonstrating various aspects of counselling practice, are available for hire and on sale from Audio-Visual Services, University of Leicester, Medical Sciences Building, University Road, Leicester.

Bibliography

The vast range of publications on counselling and psychotherapy presents the interested person with limitless opportunities to extend their reading. This Bibliography only lists references cited in the main text and notes, although in itself it contains many suggestions for further reading on topics that interest the reader. Inevitably, some of the books listed below are now out of print.

A Conversation with Peter Lomas (1990), video available from Audio-Visual Services, University of Leicester, Medical Sciences Building, University Road, Leicester.

Adler, A., *The Practice and Theory of Individual Psychology*. Routledge & Kegan Paul 1929.

Alexander, F., and French, T. M., *Psychoanalytic Therapy: Principles and Application*. New York: Ronald Press 1946.

Becker, E., *The Birth and Death of Meaning*. Penguin Books 1972.

Berne, E., *Games People Play*. Penguin Books 1964.

Bettelheim, B., *Freud and Man's Soul*. Penguin Books 1989.

Bowlby, J., *Child Care and the Growth of Love*. Penguin Books 1972.

Brown, D., and Pedder, J., *Introduction to Psychotherapy*. Tavistock Publications 1979.

Clarkson, P., *Gestalt Counselling in Action*. Sage Publications 1989.

Clarkson, P., 'A multiplicity of therapeutic relationships', *British Journal of Psychotherapy* (1991), 7, 2, pp. 148-63.

Clarkson, P., *The Therapeutic Relationship*. Whurr Publishers 1995.

Clebsch, W., and Jaekle, C., *Pastoral Care in Historical Perspective*. New York: Harper Torchbooks 1967.

Counselling - a Definition. British Association for Counselling 1979.

Cumming, S., File, R., and Worthington, M., *I Didn't Seem to Say Very Much.* Vaughan College, St Nicholas Circle, Leicester LE1 4LB.

Dryden, W., 'Some uses of audio-tape procedures in counselling: a personal view', *Counselling* (April 1981), 36.

Dryden, W., *Rational-Emotive Counselling in Action.* Sage Publications 1989.

Dryden, W., ed., *Hard-Earned Lessons from Counselling in Action.* Sage Publications 1992.

Dryden, W., ed., *Questions and Answers on Counselling in Action.* Sage Publications 1993.

Eadie, H., 'The psychological health of clergymen', *Contact - Interdisciplinary Journal of Pastoral Studies* (1972), 41.

Eadie, H., 'The helping personality', *Contact - Interdisciplinary Journal of Pastoral Studies* (1975), 49.

Eigen, M., *The Psychoanalytic Mystic.* Free Association Books 1998.

Erikson, E., *Childhood and Society.* Penguin Books 1965.

Faber, H., *Psychology of Religion.* SCM Press 1976.

Fiedler, F. E., 'A comparison of therapeutic relationships, in psychoanalytic, non-directive and Adlerian therapy', *Journal of Consulting Psychology* (1950), 14, pp. 436–45.

Fordham, F., *An Introduction to Jung's Psychology.* Penguin Books 1953.

Foskett, J., and Lyall, D., *Helping the Helpers: Supervision and Pastoral Care.* SPCK 1988.

Fraiberg, S., *The Magic Years.* Methuen 1959.

Francis, L., 'Personality theory and male Anglican clergy: the EPP', *Contact - Interdisciplinary Journal of Pastoral Studies* (2000), 133, pp. 27–36.

Freud, A., *Normality and Pathology in Childhood.* Penguin Books 1973.

Freud, S., *Analysis Terminable and Interminable.* Standard Edition, volume XXIII. Hogarth Press 1951.

Freud, S., *Constructions in Analysis.* Standard Edition, volume XXIII. Hogarth Press 1951.

Freud, S., *Formulations on the Two Principles of Mental Functioning.* Penguin Freud Library, volume 11.

Freud, S., *Group Psychology and the Analysis of the Ego.* Penguin Freud Library, volume 12.

Freud, S., *New Introductory Lectures on Psychoanalysis*. Penguin Freud Library, volume 2.

Freud, S., *Obsessive Actions and Religious Practices*. Penguin Freud Library, volume 13.

Freud, S., *An Outline of Psychoanalysis*. Penguin Freud Library, volume 15.

Freud, S., 'The question of a *Weltanschauung*', in *New Introductory Lectures on Psychoanalysis*. Penguin Freud Library, volume 2.

Freud, S., *Recommendations to Physicians Practising Psychoanalysis*. Standard Edition, volume XII. Hogarth Press 1951.

Freud, S., *Repression*. Penguin Freud Library, volume 11.

Freud, S., and Breuer, J., *Studies on Hysteria*. Penguin Freud Library, volume 3.

Fromm, E., *The Dogma of Christ*. Routledge & Kegan Paul 1963.

Fromm, E., *Psychoanalysis and Religion*. Yale University Press 1967.

Gilligan, C., *In a Different Voice: Psychological Theory and Women's Development*. Harvard University Press 1982.

Glasser, W., *Reality Therapy*. New York: Harper & Row 1965.

Green, H., *I Never Promised You a Rose Garden*. Pan Books 1967.

Greenberg, I. A., *Psychodrama: Theory and Therapy*. New York: Behavioral Publications 1974.

Greenson, R. R., *The Technique and Practice of Psychoanalysis*, *Vol. 1*. Hogarth Press 1967.

Guggenbuhl-Craig, A., *Power in the Helping Professions*. Dallas: Spring 1971.

Guntrip, H., *Personality Structure and Human Interaction*. Hogarth Press 1961.

Guntrip, H., *Healing the Sick Mind*. Unwin Books 1964.

Halmos, P., *The Faith of the Counsellors*. Constable 1978 (2nd rev. edn).

Hawkins, P., and Shohet, R., *Supervision in the Helping Professions*. Open University Press 1989.

Homans, P., ed., *The Dialogue Between Theology and Psychology*. University of Chicago Press 1968.

Homans, P., *Theology After Freud*. Indianapolis: Bobbs-Merrill 1970.

Horney, K., *New Ways in Psychoanalysis*. Routledge & Kegan Paul 1947.

Horney, K., *The Barefoot Psychoanalyst*. Karen Horney Institute.

Hurding, R., *The Bible and Counselling*. Hodder & Stoughton 1992.

Jacobs, M., 'Naming and labelling', *Contact - Interdisciplinary Journal of Pastoral Studies* (1976), 54.

Jacobs, M., 'Setting the record straight', *Counselling* (April 1981), 36.

Jacobs, M., *Still Small Voice*. SPCK 1982 (1st edn).

Jacobs, M., *Swift to Hear*. SPCK 2000 (2nd edn).

Jacobs, M., *The Presenting Past*. Open University Press 1998 (2nd edn).

Jacobs, M., *Faith or Fear: A Reader in Pastoral Care and Counselling*. Darton, Longman & Todd 1987.

Jacobs, M., *Psychodynamic Counselling in Action*. Sage Publications 1999 (2nd edn).

Jacobs, M., 'A maturing professional approach', *Contact - Interdisciplinary Journal of Pastoral Studies* (1990), 101.

Jacobs, M., 'The therapist's revenge: the law of talion as a motive for caring', *Contact - Interdisciplinary Journal of Pastoral Studies* (1991), 2, 105.

Jacobs, M., *Sigmund Freud*. Sage Publications 1992.

Jacobs, M., *D. W. Winnicott*. Sage Publications 1995.

Jacobs, M., *Illusion: a Psychodynamic Interpretation of Thinking and Belief*. Whurr Publishers 2000.

Jacobs, M., and Mobbs, B., 'Therapy, counselling and pastoral care', *Contact - Interdisciplinary Journal of Pastoral Studies* (1965), 85.

Janov, A., *The Primal Scream*. New York: Putnams 1970.

Jones, E., *The Life and Work of Sigmund Freud*. Penguin Books 1964.

Jung, C. G., *Memories, Dreams and Reflections*. Fontana 1967.

Kaplan, H., *The New Sex Therapy*. Penguin Books 1978.

Kennedy, E., *On Becoming a Counsellor*. Dublin: Gill & Macmillan 1977 (1st edn).

Kennedy, E., and Charles, S., *On Becoming a Counsellor*. Dublin: Gill & Macmillan 1989 (2nd edn).

Kohlberg, L., *The Philosophy of Moral Development*. Harper & Row 1981.

Kübler-Ross, E., *On Death and Dying*. Tavistock Publications 1970.

Lake, F., *Tight Corners in Pastoral Counselling*. Darton, Longman & Todd 1981.

Laufer, M., *Adolescent Disturbance and Breakdown*. Penguin Books 1974.

Lee, R. S., *Freud and Christianity*. Penguin Books 1967.

Lendrum, S., and Syme, G., *The Gift of Tears*. Routledge 1992.

Lomas, P., *True and False Experience*. Allen Lane 1973.

Lomas, P., *The Case for a Personal Psychotherapy*. Oxford University Press 1981.

Lomas, P., *The Limits of Interpretation: What's Wrong with Psychoanalysis?* Penguin Books 1987.

Lowen, A., *Bio-energetics*. Coventure 1977.

McLeod, J., *An Introduction to Counselling*. Open University Press 1998 (2nd edn).

Macquarrie, J., *The Principles of Christian Theology*. SCM Press 1966.

Malan, D. H., *A Study of Brief Psychotherapy*. Tavistock Publications 1963.

Malan, D. H., *The Frontier of Brief Psychotherapy*. Plenum Medical Books 1976.

Malan, D. H., *Individual Psychotherapy and the Science of Psychodynamics*. Butterworth 1979.

Mearns, D., and Thorne, B., *Person-Centred Counselling in Action*. Sage Publications 1999 (2nd edn).

Murray Parkes, C., *Bereavement*. Penguin Books 1972.

O'Laughrun, J., 'Transference and religious practices', *Journal of Pastoral Care* (USA) (1978), pp. 185–9.

Philp, H., *Freud and Religious Belief*. Rockcliff 1956.

Racker, H., *Transference and Counter-transference*. Hogarth Press 1968.

Rayner, E., *Human Development*. Allen & Unwin 1986 (3rd edn).

Rieff, P., *The Triumph of the Therapeutic*. Penguin Books 1973.

Roazen, P., *Freud and His Followers*. Penguin Books 1979.

Rycroft, C., ed., *Psychoanalysis Observed*. Penguin Books 1968.

Ryle, A., *Cognitive-Analytic Therapy: Active Participation in Change*. John Wiley 1990.

Searles, H., 'Oedipal love in the counter-transference', in H. Searles, *Collected Papers on Schizophrenia and Related Subjects*. Hogarth Press 1965.

Searles, H., 'The patient as therapist to his analyst', in H. Searles, *Countertransference and Related Subjects*. New York: International Universities Press 1979.

Segal, J., *Melanie Klein*. Sage Publications 1992.

Stewart, I., *Transactional Analysis Counselling in Action*. Sage Publications 1989.

Stewart, I., *Eric Berne*. Sage Publications 1992.

Stiles, W. B., Shapiro, D. A., and Elliott, R., 'Are all psychotherapies equivalent?', *American Psychologist* (1986), 41, 2, pp. 165–80.

Supervision – A Professional Necessity (video). Audio-Visual Services, University of Leicester, Medical Sciences Building, University Road, Leicester.

Thorne, B., *Carl Rogers*. Sage Publications 1992.

Trower, P., Casey, A., and Dryden, W., *Cognitive-Behavioural Counselling in Action*. Sage Publications 1988.

Truax, C. B., and Carkhuff, R. R., *Towards Effective Counseling and Psychotherapy Training and Practice*. Chicago: Aldine Press 1967.

van Deurzen-Smith, E., *Existential Counselling in Practice*. Sage Publications 1987.

Wachtel, P., *Psychoanalysis and Behavior Therapy*. New York: Basic Books 1977.

Whitmore, D., *Psychosynthesis Counselling in Action*. Sage Publications 1991.

Williams, H., *The True Wilderness*. Fontana 1967.

Winnicott, D. W., *The Maturational Processes and the Facilitating Environment*. Hogarth Press 1965.

Wolberg, L. R., *The Technique of Psychotherapy*. Heinemann 1967.

Index

abusive practice 29, 56, 59–60, 71, 73, 124, 175, 224

acting out 116–17, 158, 208, 245

Adler, Alfred 25

advice and guidance 6, 83–4, 87, 106, 181, 187, 227

aggression 60–1, 64, 74, 166–7, 170–1, 186, 208–9, 216–17, 238–40, 246

aim-inhibited love 74

Alexander, Franz 20

altering arrangements 109–10, 116, 158, 182, 233, 235–6

altruism 79

ambivalence 160–2, 217

anger see aggression

appreciation of counsellor 240–1, 246

artificiality 45, 100–5

asceticism 168

assessment 21, 82, 95–6, 146–7, 149

Association for Pastoral and Spiritual Care and Counselling 33–4

Association of Christian Counsellors 34–5

atmosphere, therapeutic 50, 51, 130

bass (base)-line listening 47–8

Becker, E. 174

behaviour therapy 16–17, 18, 23, 29–31, 147, 169, 210, 228

belief systems 205–7, 216

bereavement 12, 36, 109, 166, 169, 185–6, 230, 233, 236

Berne, Eric 28

Bettelheim, Bruno 15

blank screen 127

blind spots 197, 235

body therapies 29

boundaries 106–29, 201, 241

Bowlby, J. 26

British Association for Counselling and Psychotherapy 8, 31

British Psychological Society 31

Brown, D. 137–8, 152

burn-out 62

challenging see confrontation

Charles, S. 104, 172

Clarkson, P. 201–2

cognitive therapy see behaviour therapy

cognitive-analytic therapy 20

communication with others 97–8

concordant counter-transference 197–8

confession see reconciliation, sacrament of

confidentiality 97–8, 129, 147–8

confrontation 133–7, 142–7

conscience 142, 152

contract 19, 21, 37, 112–13, 120, 122, 141, 158, 209, 233–4, 241–2, 244–5, 247

conversion 10, 77-8
core conditions 28, 67, 102, 130-1, 179
counselling relationship *see* relationship, the counselling
counselling skills 6-7, 8, 10, 28, 36, 43-54, 58, 102, 107, 122-4, 129, 162, 203, 223, 225, 241
counter-transference 74, 180, 183-4, 186, 196-200
criticism by counsellor 46, 51, 53-4, 138, 154, 201, 225-6
cycle of deprivation 71

death 230-3, 247
defences 9, 21, 24, 36, 93, 142, 145-6, 150-76, 183, 196, 215, 217, 220, 237
definitions 8, 14-20
demanding clients 63-4, 108, 111, 113, 120-3, 146
denial of feelings 62, 155-6, 157, 163-5, 168, 236-7
dependency on counsellor 110-11, 113, 168, 195, 197, 220-1, 238
depression 167, 206
displacement 158, 170-2, 217
door handle remarks 117

Eadie, H. 58, 65, 72-3
eating disorders 169
eclecticism 26, 29, 31
ego 142, 152-3
emergencies 112-13
empathy 49, 182, 185, 199
endings: deferring 241-2; sessions 112, 114-15, 117-19; with clients 63-4, 158-9, 227, 230-48
Erikson, Erik 25, 170, 231
erotic transference 192
ethical dilemmas 207-14
existentialist counselling 33, 206, 230
exploratory work 132-8, 146, 181
external reality 8

Fairbairn, W. R. D. 26

faith 10, 13, 25, 33-6, 78, 174-7, 178, 205-28, 230, 248; development 215
fantasy *see* phantasy
feminist counselling 226
first sessions 82-7
fixation 170
flexibility 141-2, 146
flight into health 159, 241
focus of counselling 20, 66
forgiveness 127, 218-19; *see also* reconciliation, sacrament of
frequency of meeting 4, 19-21, 108-11, 113, 141-2
Freud, Anna 25
Freud, Sigmund 8, 11, 15, 17, 20, 22-3, 24-5, 28, 37, 51, 67, 73-4, 142, 152-3, 164, 171, 192, 214-15, 219, 227, 247
Fromm, Erich 25, 215-16

gain from illness 158-9, 241
gender pairings 126, 131, 201
Gestalt therapy 18, 27, 67
gifts from clients 240
Greenson, R. 181-2, 184
grief *see* bereavement
group therapy 16, 24, 95, 161
guilt 65-6, 216-19, 226
Guntrip, H. 72

Halmos, Paul 11
helplessness, feeling of 87-90
history-taking 95-6, 117-18, 136, 141, 220
Horney, Karen 25, 181
humanistic religion 215-16
humanistic therapies 18, 23, 27-9, 33, 225
Hurding, R. 210
hypnotherapy 29, 51

id 142, 152
idealization 126, 147, 168, 189
identification 166, 183, 197-8
insight 21, 22, 141, 151, 155, 179, 193, 203

intellectualization 163, 184
internalization 183
interpretations 23, 133–4,
    137–8, 143, 170, 181, 186,
    193–5
intervention, levels of 130–50,
    178–9, 241
introjection 165–7, 183
isolation 163–5

Jesus Christ 8, 34, 219, 226, 230
Jewish community 33, 206
Jung, Carl 17, 25, 69

Kennedy, E. 104, 145, 172
Klein, Melanie 17, 25, 26

lateness 115–17, 119
Lee, R. S. xi, 215
life crises 11–12, 231–3
listening 7, 9, 11, 27, 47–50, 93,
    106, 181, 193
loaded remarks 53–4
Lomas, Peter 102–3, 184
long-term therapy 20–1, 140,
    235, 238

Macquarrie, J. 230
magical expectations 85–6, 146,
    224, 247
Malan, D. H. 20
management of client 140–2
masochism 70–1, 166
mastering anxieties 61
meaning 13, 90–3, 206–7
mistakes 121, 247
Mobbs, B. 37
motives for counselling: in
    counsellor 56–79, 81; in client
    67, 97, 146–7, 209, 246
multiple personality 153

negative feelings in counsellor
    61–3, 196–7
Neo-Freudians 25–6
non-directive counselling 27,
    103–4, 130–2

non-possessive love 28, 61, 74
note-keeping 50

object relations theory 26
obsessional behaviour 165, 168,
    174

paraphrasing 52, 93
parts of personality 7, 25–7, 142,
    152, 154, 214
past, importance of the 22, 138,
    143, 190–4, 196, 233, 242–6
pastoral care 32, 36–8, 107–10,
    174–6, 241
pastoral counselling 3–4, 6, 9–10,
    12–13, 15, 31–8, 174–6, 205–28,
    248
Paul, the apostle 152
Pavlov, I. 29, 228
Pedder, J. 137–8, 152
Perls, Fritz 28
person-centred counselling 18,
    24, 67–8, 74, 76, 103, 130, 201;
    see also Rogers, Carl
personality structure 18, 142, 152
phantasy 22, 72–3, 75, 186, 195,
    208, 216, 218–20, 222, 245
phobia 40
power of counsellor 29, 61,
    74–6, 113–14, 181–2
prayer, use of in counselling 33,
    221–4
primal therapy 29
projection 157, 166–8, 175, 214,
    219, 226
psyche see spirit
psychiatry 16, 37, 141, 147–9,
    180
psychoanalysis 15, 17–18, 24–5,
    28–9, 157, 164, 214–16; in
    Britain 26
psychodynamic counselling
    18–19, 21–7, 30, 67, 74, 103,
    143, 153, 171–2, 179, 184, 200,
    210, 220
psychologist, clinical 17, 147,
    169, 187

psychosomatic symptoms 159, 165
psychotherapy 14-15, 17-31

questions 8, 52, 96, 132, 136-7

Racker, H. 197
rational-emotive therapy 30
rationalization 169, 175
Rayner, E. 61, 170
reaction formation 168-9, 196
real relationship 100-3, 180, 184-8, 202, 238
reassurance 142
reconciliation, sacrament of 6, 127, 175-6
referral 140-1, 147-9, 172-4, 223, 239
regression 113, 138, 142-3, 170
rejection, feelings of 147-8, 245-6
Relate (Marriage Guidance) 10, 31
relationship, the counselling 24, 71-4, 99-104, 122, 143, 146, 170, 178-203, 234
reliability 108, 109-10
relief at ending 238
religion 11, 25, 136, 171, 174-6, 205-28; counselling as 11-12
reluctant client 172-4
remembering 46, 49-50, 128, 138
reparation 68-71
reparative relationship 180, 188, 200-3
repetition of the past 24-5, 138, 165, 190-4, 200, 234-5, 242-7
repression 22, 165, 192, 197-8
resistance 24, 144, 151-76, 193, 241-2
resources for referral 147, 223
responding 5, 7, 9, 11, 28, 51-4, 131-6
revenge 68-71, 166, 242
review of counselling 240-1
Rieff, Philip 11
ritual 30, 174-5, 217, 223-5
Rogers, Carl 27-8, 30, 130, 179

roles, mixed 19, 123-4, 126-9, 220
Rycroft, C. 200-1

sacramental ministry 127-8
sadism 70-1, 166
sadness 185, 198, 238, 246
Scripture 3, 34, 175-6, 216
Searles, H. 73
self-disclosure 48, 101-3, 224-5
self-knowledge 56-79
sex therapy 30, 136
sexual abuse 124-5, 136, 202-3, 209
sexuality 61, 71-4, 186, 216-18, 246
shadow, the 69
shame 154
short-term counselling 19, 66, 128, 179, 183, 234, 236, 237, 238
silence, use of 52, 93-5, 131, 134-5
Skinner, B. 29
slips of the tongue 165
social skills 30, 147
soul *see* spirit
spirit, spiritual 7, 13, 15, 24, 33
splitting 160-3
starting sessions 82-7, 115-16, 134
sublimation 170-2, 175, 217
super-ego 142, 152
supervision 9, 34, 50, 59, 99-100, 157, 187, 196, 247
supportive counselling 20, 132-42, 145, 146, 147, 159, 179, 181
sympathy 185

talion, law of 71
tape recording 50
Tavistock Clinic 20
themes 112
therapeutic relationship *see* relationship, the counselling
therapy *see* psychotherapy; psychodynamic counselling

third parties 96-9, 172-3
time boundaries 107-22
touch, use of 122-6, 224
training 5, 10-11, 20, 43-4, 56, 59, 129, 161, 178, 247
transactional analysis 18
transference 21-3, 36, 101, 127, 138, 180, 183-6, 188-96, 200, 202-3, 214, 219-22, 226, 234, 236, 239
transpersonal psychology 23-4, 27
triangle of insight 22, 193-5, 218, 242

turning against the self 167

unconscious, the 7, 22-4, 138, 143, 152-3, 158, 236
undoing 168
United Kingdom Council for Psychotherapy 18
unsuitable clients 140-1

Watson, J. 29
Winnicott, D. W. 26, 51, 103, 201
working alliance/relationship 132, 178-84, 188
working through 138